The Struggle for Control of Public Education

The Struggle for Control of Public Education

Market Ideology vs. Democratic Values

Michael Engel

Temple University Press
PHILADELPHIA

Temple University Press, Philadelphia 19122

Published 2000
Printed in the United States of America

♾ The paper used in this publication meets the requirements of American National Standard for Information Sciences—Permanence of Paper for Printed Library Materials, ANSI Z39.48-1984

Library of Congress Cataloging-in-Publication Data

Engel, Michael.
The struggle for control of public education : market ideology vs. democratic values / Michael Engel.
p. cm.
Includes bibliographical references and index.
ISBN 1-56639-740-5 (cloth : alk. paper)—ISBN 1-56639-741-3 (pbk. : alk. paper)
1. Public schools—United States. 2. Politics and education—United States. 3. Education—Economic aspects—United States. 4. School choice—United States. 5. Charter schools—United States. I. Title.
LA217.2.E533 2000
371.01'0973—dc21 99-34615

For Jackie, Sara, and Emily

Contents

	Preface	ix
	Acknowledgments	xi
1	Introduction	1
2	Market Ideology	18
3	Democratic Education	44
4	School Choice	68
5	Educational Technology	93
6	School Restructuring	120
7	Curriculum	148
8	Civic Education	176
9	Conclusion	211
	Index	221

Preface

This book is a product of theory and practice. The theory part comes from my personal and professional concern with the politics of education. The practice part comes from my participation in community and campus organizing, union activism, and, perhaps most important, service as a school board member in the small town of Easthampton, Massachusetts.

As a student at the City College of New York in the 1960s, I was well aware of its almost unique tradition as a tuition-free public institution. And as an instructor in the City University system during the following decade, I learned how vulnerable that tradition could be if powerful economic and political interests were determined to destroy it. The state college system in Massachusetts, where I have taught for over twenty years, has always been the educational stepchild among the state's prestigious private institutions, which possess overwhelming political influence. And the assault on public elementary and secondary education has been a major feature of national politics over the same period. A concern with protecting public education thus became a personal matter, which I made my specialty as a political scientist.

But the real education came when, after holding other elective offices, I won a seat on my local school committee (the New England term for school board). What immediately struck me was the recurrence of certain themes that seemed to receive unqualified acceptance from everyone involved with the school system: cooperation with the business community, the prime importance of computer technology, corporate models of school governance, an emphasis on collaboration among various "stakeholders" in the system, the economic rationality of school choice, and rigid state standards and assessments in the name of reform. With the exception of choice, these concerns were unfamiliar to me. As a student of the politics of education, I knew a great deal about finance, racial and ethnic issues, and conflicts over curriculum, but the matters central to the school committee's focus were new to me. The more familiar issues did come up, but the others set the tone for most of the board's work. It became clear to me that these themes were not just local idiosyncrasies but also reflections of national trends backed by a strong consensus in the educational system. I came to witness the power of a set of ideas in directing a highly complex and decentralized system along a single path. In other words, the issues of concern established the framework for the daily operations of a small-town New England school system, run by a board of average citizens who never questioned it and who brought it into line with the actions of thousands of other boards just like it. After further theoretical inquiries, it became apparent that the common bond behind these seemingly disparate trends was the ideology of market economics. The dominant position of this ideology explained both the unquestioning acceptance that these trends were given and the somewhat puzzled responses that I received when I questioned them.

What also became clear was that despite the sincere concern for students held by almost everyone connected with the school system, the market-oriented policies we were pursuing were motivated by anything but that concern. In addition, I became aware of the difficulties involved in making that contradiction apparent to my colleagues, particularly as an individual member working alone.

Although this book started to take shape before my tenure on the board, it was that experience that made me understand the real issues of the politics of U.S. education at the end of the twentieth century. The purpose of this work, therefore, is to call attention to those issues, which are often obscured by more well-publicized controversies, and to offer a point of view about how they are tied to one another. In the words of a well-known nineteenth-century social and economic analyst, however, the point must be not only to interpret the world but to change it. Thus, the purpose of this text is also to demonstrate the pedagogical and political possibilities for a well-established alternative to the market model—democratic public education. I hope that those who read this book will find a way to use this understanding to fight for a school system that really cares enough about members of the younger generation to give them the ability to shape their own future, collectively and democratically, whether we approve of their direction or not.

Acknowledgments

Most books of this kind involve a network of scholars and activists who assist the author with advice and criticism and who are given credit for their efforts. It is probably to the detriment of this particular work that such a network did not exist in this case. No one writes a book alone, however. I therefore extend my appreciation to numerous academic colleagues, community and union activists, and education professionals from whom I have learned over the years. My involvement during the 1970s with the United Community Centers in Brooklyn, New York, deepened my concern with and understanding of the politics of education. Discussions with colleagues at Westfield State College; involvement with fellow members of our faculty union; exchanges with scholars at professional conferences; debates arising during my tenure on the school committee in Easthampton, Massachusetts; anonymous reviews from those who read the first drafts—all of these and more are reflected in this book. Above all, the experience of teaching in public colleges has given me an appreciation of the value and importance of public education and some insight into its complexities. My special thanks go to Michael Ames of Temple University Press and to the production staff at P. M. Gordon Associates. It has been a pleasure to work with them.

The Struggle for Control of Public Education

1 Introduction

The most creative, challenging, and inspiring visions of what U.S. public education could be have always been rooted in a democratic value system. Their optimism about human and social development has been linked to optimism about the benefits and potentialities of democracy. Thomas Jefferson saw public education as the means of producing a citizenry capable of defending its right to govern and using that right constructively. Horace Mann sought to build a public education system that would strengthen a democratic value consensus as a basis for social progress. And John Dewey envisioned the public schools as potential microcosms of a democratic society.

Mass movements have advanced similar goals. The Workingmen's parties of the 1820s and 1830s fought for public education as a means of promoting political equality. A century later, progressive educators attempted to put Dewey's ideas into practice. And in the 1960s, women, racial minorities, and other excluded or marginalized social groups successfully organized to extend equal educational opportunity. Of course, they all encountered opposition, and the resulting political struggles shaped the educational system as we know it today: a peculiar amalgam of contradictory ideological and pedagogical directions.

It was the democratic impulse, however, that provided the forward motion. David Tyack and Larry Cuban (1995, 10–11) criticize what they call "pie-in-the-sky utopianism" of "extravagant claims for innovations that flickered and failed" but praise "a different kind of utopianism—a vision of a just democracy—that has marked the best discourse about educational purposes over the past century. That discourse promoted the idea that the schools could enable citizens to take an active and positive role in shaping their society. In this way, the people were to be ends, not means; subjects, not objects; and creators, not machines. They were to be valued in and of themselves, not for what they could do to suit the purposes of others. They were to own U.S. social and political institutions, which they would control for their own benefit rather than having the institutions own and control them. And the purpose of the public education system was to help make all this possible.

Today's educational visionaries express the same sentiments. Maxine Greene chooses a philosophy of education based on "utopian thinking . . . that refuses mere compliance, that looks down roads not yet taken to the shapes of a more fulfilling social order, to more vibrant ways of being in the world" (1995, 5). Eleanor Duckworth calls for schooling that helps children develop their own "wonderful ideas," so that "they will someday happen upon wonderful ideas that no one else has happened on before" (1987, 2). Deborah Meier advances a "vision of education . . . [in which] all children could and should be inventors of their own theories, critics of other people's ideas, analyzers of evidence, and makers of their own personal marks on this most complex world" (1995, 4). Neil Postman (1995) sees the "false gods" of consumership, economic utility, technology, and separatism standing in the way of an educational system that would enable students to see themselves as, among other things, "world makers." The editors of *Rethinking Schools* advocate "creating classrooms for equity and social justice" through educational practices that are grounded in students' lives, anti-racist, participatory, experiential, activist, and "hopeful, joyful, kind, visionary" (1994, 4–5).

These ideas are all expressions of a thoroughly democratic perspective. Indeed, Meier connects her commitment to public education to "her passion for democracy and [her] fears for its future" (1995, 5). A pedagogy that rewards openness, creativity, social awareness, and idealism can flourish only when people are able to take control of their own lives by controlling the direction of their society, including the schools. If social and educational purposes are dictated by forces beyond popular control, the avenues of reinvention and growth are closed off.

This is a particularly critical matter for young people. If they learn that they have no voice, that their life decisions will be made by others, and that intellectual risks are heavily sanctioned, they will become, at best, compliant and complacent cogs in an economic machine or, at worst, potential recruits for antidemocratic social movements. Even if they rebel, that rebellion will take highly individualistic, idiosyncratic, and perhaps violent forms that produce no constructive results, as is the case at the turn of the twenty-first century. The visions advanced by democratic educators and progressive social movements over the past two hundred years have offered the promise of encouraging and energizing young people to take control of their world and make it a better place. We cannot afford to let those visions dim.

In that light, it is nothing short of disastrous that more than ever before, one antidemocratic system of ideas—market ideology—almost exclusively defines the terms of educational politics and charts the path of education reform. Policy alternatives falling outside its boundaries have been increasingly marginalized since the 1950s, when the progressive education movement collapsed and the politics of education began following a conservative course. For all their positive accomplishments, the radical educational movements of the 1960s did not effectively challenge or alter that course—in fact, their individualistic and libertarian orientation reinforced it. As a result, current-day discussions about the future of education are conducted almost entirely in the language of the free market: individual achievement, competition, choice, economic growth, and national security—with only occasional lip service being given to egalitarian and democratic goals. The educational visionaries referred to at the beginning of this chapter are widely read and respected, but their prescriptions are generally ignored. This state of affairs is in sharp contrast to the intense conflicts that customarily raged in the past over the ideas of those who sought to build a system of common schools that would create a democratic citizenry and a more humane and egalitarian society.

In fact, school privatization—the ultimate goal of market ideologues—is poised for a great leap forward. Despite the well-publicized failures of certain education management organizations (EMOs), entrepreneurs are still optimistic about the possibilities of for-profit public education. Educational Alternatives, Inc. (EAI), made the mistake of trying to manage entire school districts—Hartford, Connecticut, and Baltimore, Maryland. According to one analyst, "The new plan . . . is to do business with individual public schools and private schools. That plan may be paying off . . . . In November [1996] EAI struck a deal to manage a French international school in Boston. And in January [1997] EAI showed its ability to rebound from its setbacks when it secured a multi-million dollar contract to run 12 charter schools in Arizona" (Bushweller 1997, 21).

This kind of rebound is possible because EMOs can rely on sources of funding unavailable to public schools: venture capitalists and conservative think tanks. Among the former is EduVentures, an investment banking service for educational entrepreneurs, which publishes the monthly newsletter *Education Industry Report*. According to the January 31, 1996, edition of the *New York Times,* the chief executive officer (CEO) for EduVentures, Michael Sandler, described educational investment opportunities in highly optimistic terms: "When you look at the raw numbers, this is a very big industry with an enormous potential for growth. Education has reached the point where the status quo is no longer acceptable." That same year, both Lehman Brothers and Smith-Barney held sizable conferences to provide information for investors in privately managed public education (Bushweller 1997, 19).

The Pioneer Institute, located in Boston, Massachusetts, has been a major promoter of charter schools, the most suitable vehicle for privatization. "In 1995, Pioneer raised more than $500,000 for charter schools . . . . Pioneer also distributes a how-to manual, *The Massachusetts Charter School Handbook,* and sponsors seminars bringing together entrepreneurs selling curriculum packages, management systems, and assessment and evaluation programs" (Vine 1997, 14). Pioneer has played a major role in creating Advantage Schools, Inc., which was running seventeen charter schools in 1998, using $5 million in seed money from investors. Advantage projected revenues of $42 million by the 1999–2000 fiscal year and the likelihood of a profit. Michael Milken, upon his release after almost two years in federal prison for securities fraud, invested $500 million to establish Knowledge Universe. Three years later, Milken's company was earning annual revenues of $1.2 billion. Among other holdings, it owned Children's Discovery Center, "the nation's sixth-largest preschool company, with 25,000 toddlers in nearly 300 locations across the United States" (Baker 1999). Milken also had a stake in Nobel Education Dynamics, which runs 139 schools in thirteen states. As Russ Baker describes it, "Companies like Milken's are not just competitors with public schools; they are poised to supplement the traditional classroom, viewing public and nonprofit educational institutions—as well as for-profit forms—as both potential customers and avenues to a vast consumer base" (1999, 12). With the number of charter schools reaching one thousand in 1999, and with President Bill Clinton's blessings for the creation of at least two thousand more, school privatization appears to have reached the takeoff stage and may well be headed for a bright future.

Effective political organizing by conservative forces in all areas of social life, including education, has brought us to this point. In particular, they have been able to control the agenda of education reform since about 1960, even though liberals have shared responsibility for its implementation. That control is already continuing into the twenty-first century. This success, however, is due, at least in part, to ideological confusion among many of those who might chart a different path. To a considerable extent, they have accepted the language and criteria of market ideology themselves or, even worse, rejected the entire concept of ideological frameworks as fraudulent or obsolete in a postmodern era. Therefore, by default, conflicts over the direction of the public schools are played out within the political rules of the game defined by market ideology.

To some observers, this may constitute a realistic recognition of the schools as an "imperfect panacea" with a limited capability for changing society (Perkinson, 1968). If we abandon utopian goals, it is claimed, we can focus on more rational and achievable objectives for the school system. Mainstream policy analysts in particular argue that consensus is healthier than constant conflict and that a stable educational system that develops out of negotiation, bargaining, and compromise among a plurality of interests is far more beneficial for the nation. With the addition of what is assumed by these analysts to be a conservative shift in U.S. political values, it stands to reason that educational policy would follow suit.

This argument is examined and challenged in Chapter 2, but even if we assume that limited goals are all we can achieve, the narrow ideological terrain of contemporary educational debate is not a normal or healthy phenomenon. Three hundred years of conflict over educational ideas and values shows that there is no logical basis for assuming that market ideology is the only possible framework for the consideration of policy alternatives for the schools. Most important, however, is the fact that market ideology's virtually unchallenged dominance threatens the very existence of public education as a social institution, because its logic ultimately eliminates any justification for collective and democratic control of the schools. Market ideology and democratic values in education are mutually exclusive. This may be true on a broader social level as well; Robert Kuttner claims that "the celebration of the market has become an insidious form of contempt for political democracy" (1997, 337).

Confirmation of this claim can be found in the arguments of some of the most prominent supporters of market ideology in education. John Chubb and Terry Moe explicitly reject democracy as a means of organizing schools. They call for a school choice system based on the "guiding principle" that "public authority must be put to use in creating a system that is almost entirely beyond the reach of public authority" (1990, 218) and propose the creation of what is essentially a network of publicly funded state-chartered private schools. They argue that student academic achievement—their sole criterion for evaluating public education—depends on the institutional environment of the schools. Democratic control, given the nature of public authority, "is essentially coercive" (28) and inevitably leads to bureaucracy. The combined effect of both is destructive of academic achievement. In their words, "choice is a panacea" that can liberate the schools (217). Citing the observation of Ludwig von Mises that the votes of the losing minority are wasted in a majority-rule system, Joseph L. Bast and Herbert J. Walberg (1996, 154–155) support this point of view and assert that parents are no match for organized interest groups of teachers and administrators. They argue that "privatization rescues parents from this uneven competition by moving the consumer-producer relationship outside the political arena." The free market "is far more effective than the clumsy once-a-year voting for or against elected officials who may or may not represent our specific views or do what they promise once elected." Democracy in the school system is thus seen as a destructive force vastly inferior to the impersonal operations of the market. Although it has been fashionable, since the downfall of communism, to assert that a market economy and democracy are synonymous, advocates of market models for education make no such claim.

Democratic values are a necessary, even if not sufficient, condition for defending the existence of a system of public education. Only from a democratic perspective can one claim that the schools have an impact on and responsibility to the whole society and that as a result they are a matter of collective community concern and legitimate objects of democratic decision making. From Jefferson to Mann to Dewey, and especially during the heyday of progressive education, such ideas were at the center of educational politics. In their absence, there is no longer any convincing rationale to keep the schools public and social in terms of their governance, finance, and pedagogy. The battleground over their future is thus yielded to those who argue that the market can and should make such determinations. This ultimately supports a system of privatized schools in an educational free market, linked to a curricular agenda defined by the needs of a capitalist economy and the national-security state associated with it.

In short, we cannot defend public education, mobilize a constituency behind it, or achieve the visions of democratic educators without a clear and convincing democratic ideological framework that provides a rationale for maintaining a socially owned, controlled, and financed school system. If the market prevails as a model for organizing U.S. education, the possibilities for strengthening a democratic society and developing a democratic citizenry are ended.

Arguments of this kind are, to say the least, not widely accepted among policy analysts, because most discount the significance of ideas and values as formative influences on public policy. But ideologies—comprehensive systems of political ideas and values—serve as the context of political struggle. They affect the political behavior of their adherents, intensify and give form to political conflict, and constitute a powerful force in shaping public policy. Of course, ideologies do not by themselves determine our political choices. But most of us frame our political choices in terms of some kind of value system, however clear or consistent it may be, and that system tends to have a life of its own. Ideology may indeed be frequently used as a facade to mask "real" interests, but it is reasonable to claim that the two coincide more often than not or at least that we try to make them do so. For better or worse, millions of people have sacrificed their property, security, and lives for political ideologies; not many have done so in the name of economic rationality or incremental change.

Educational historian David B. Tyack argues that ideology is important in understanding educational change. He notes that even at the beginning, public schools "were remarkably similar in institutional character and . . . taught similar lessons." Tyack explains this in terms of "the invisible hand of ideology": "The crusaders who spread public education generally shared a set of beliefs: that public education's purpose was to train upright citizens by inculcating a common denominator of nonsectarian morality and nonpartisan civic instruction, and that the common school should be free, open to all children, and public in support and control" (1993, 7–8). Noting the "persistent importance of ideology in school reform," he complains that

> the belief systems underlying much of current American educational reform seem impoverished and incomplete in comparison with earlier ideologies . . . . [They] have moved away from the tradition of a broad-based conception of democratic citizenship, revealed in action. They substitute the aim of economic competitiveness, to be certified by higher test scores. Such a narrowing of purpose omits much that is of value from the discussion of educational policy and constricts the historical vision of the common school. (25–26)

Ideology is nonetheless often overlooked or at best misapplied by mainstream social scientists as a factor in politics. This is due in part to the dominance of quantitative methodologies in political science, which leads to the trivialization of the concept into conveniently measurable but irrelevant labels. And ideology fits rather uncomfortably into structural-functional social theories, which are based on assumptions of value consensus. The study of the politics of education also generally ignores ideology. Most contemporary analysts appear to assume that policy is made on the basis of a commonly accepted definition of education and on the basis of agreement on the criteria we use to evaluate it and that the real battles are over implementation of specific reforms. This seems inconsistent with the complex and contentious history of U.S. educational politics, which has been rife with fundamental disagreements over just such issues since colonial times. Even if those struggles appear to have abated and a consensus seems to exist among policymakers, it deserves some analysis and explanation in relation to that history. Yet today there is not much conscious awareness or discussion of the role of ideology in the politics of education.

Market ideology has triumphed over democratic values not because of its superiority as a theory of society but in part because in a capitalist system it has an inherent advantage. Ironically, market ideology does not really have to compete fairly in a free market of ideas. It therefore dominates economic and political thinking by default in the absence of any serious challenges; in U.S. politics, this is reflected in the rightward drift of both major parties and the decline of liberalism as a political movement. In the area of education, the progressive movement was the last of those challenges. Therefore, for those who wish to prevent the privatization of schools and the corporate control of their direction and purpose, and in particular for those who further wish to reconstruct the system along more democratic lines, it is critical to reject market ideology totally and explicitly as a basis for education reform. In short, the artificial ideological consensus that began in the mid-1900s must be disrupted if there is to be a successful movement for democratic educational change. The first step in that struggle is on the level of ideas, and, fortunately, the last years of the twentieth century brought some promising efforts in that direction. But often, because a form of historical and philosophical amnesia has set in, such efforts end up reinventing the wheel, especially in relation to the more radically democratic aspects of the U.S. tradition. They are also often expressed at a level of theoretical abstraction that lacks a comprehensive elaboration and grounding in the real world of educational politics; this is especially true of postmodernist thinking. This book therefore sets out to further those efforts by dealing with these problems.

Conflicts over educational policy are, of course, played out in the real world of political struggle, not just on the level of ideas.

The specific form those policies take is therefore the outcome of many variables: the nature of the particular issue, the relative strength of contending interest groups, the climate of public opinion, and the response of government officials, among other factors. U.S. public schools, although in many ways strikingly similar in organization and pedagogical style, thus also embody diverse and even contradictory educational principles as well. The curriculum that resulted from years of political conflict is a case in point, says Herbert M. Kliebard: "It serves to liberate the human spirit and also to confine it; it is attuned to the well-being of children and youth and also contributes to their disaffection and alienation from the mainstream of social life; and it represents a vehicle for social and political reform as well as a force for perpetuating existing class structures and for the reproduction of social inequality" (1987, 270).

This kind of pluralism in educational politics may be coming to an end. It thrives only in an environment of competing ideas and values. If the school system is truly to reflect a legitimate community consensus on educational goals and purposes, there needs to be an extensive menu of alternatives from which to choose. If the debate over the future of the schools is conducted entirely within the limits of one theoretical or ideological framework, the quality of that debate degenerates. It loses sight of ends and discusses only means. Educational policy may still be the outcome of negotiation, bargaining, and compromise, but the context and terms of those deliberations unacceptably limit the options. David Plank and William L. Boyd describe this as an "antipolitics" of education, "in which disagreements about educational policy and practice are increasingly likely to be addressed in conflict over the institutions of educational governance rather than in open debate on the merits of alternative goals and strategies" (1994, 264). If only one point of view on the goals and purposes of education predominates, democratic political decision making ends.

The progressive education movement, for all its flaws and inconsistencies, once provided the menu of alternatives. Its demise created an intellectual and political vacuum that has not been filled since. The final chapter of Lawrence Cremin's *The Transformation of the School* chronicles the rapid decline of the progressive education movement after World War II. Faction ridden, lacking any connection to the grass roots of educational politics, and mired in its own "conventional wisdom," it could not survive in the conservative political climate of the 1950s. This did not mean its ideas were obsolete or irrelevant. Cremin states that "the authentic progressive vision remained strangely pertinent to the problems of mid-century America. Perhaps it only awaited the reformulation and resuscitation that would ultimately derive from a larger resurgence of reform in American life and thought" (1964, 353). His 1960s prophecy proved wrong during the resurgence that followed shortly thereafter, and at the end of the twentieth century, progressive educational theories, which seem curiously anachronistic, were not included in any realistic agenda for educational reform. In fact, across all shades of the ideological spectrum, the tendency of reformers has been to ignore or at least push to the background the broad issues of educational philosophy that progressives constantly raised. As Joseph Kahne describes it, "Educational policy makers tend to focus on the technical issues surrounding educational practice. That is, policy analysts and evaluators tend to explore varied means of efficiently and equitably pursuing an array of educational goals. They less frequently debate the desirability of these goals or the way different educational goals and processes shape individuals and society" (1996, 2).

The most prominent thinkers among progressive educators—John Dewey, Boyd Henry Bode, William Heard Kilpatrick, Harold Rugg, Theodore Brameld, and George S. Counts, to name a few—who were committed to building a new, more democratic and egalitarian society, for the most part advanced their educational programs within that context. Even if they did not succeed in remaking the school system, their efforts had two important results. First of all, they precipitated an intense political and ideological debate over the purpose and direction of education in relation to the socioeconomic system. This was especially true during the 1930s, when the progressive educators known as social reconstructionists challenged the legitimacy of a capitalist socioeconomic system by explicitly advocating the use of the schools as instruments of transformation to a democratic socialist society. Second, their efforts raised the issue of the schools' responsibility as public and social institutions. Community debate over the broad social purposes of education makes sense only if it is assumed that the schools belong to the people as a whole and that decisions about their future ought to be made collectively and democratically. From that perspective, the educational system does not necessarily exist to serve the particular preferences of individuals or interest groups; it exists to serve a more general public purpose that the public itself must decide. But the most significant outcome was that by promoting a political agenda based on concepts of "democracy," progressive educators raised the important question of what that word actually means and thus indirectly, what U.S. society is all about.

A progressive agenda for education in the twenty-first century therefore requires a reopening of the ideological debates over its future. Toward that end, the introduction to this book is followed by a review of the nature of market ideology and a critical analysis of its impact on educational politics in the last half of the twentieth century. Thereafter, taking ideas about human development, popular democracy, and pedagogy developed by Dewey and others, the discussion attempts to elaborate them—in a more contemporary context—into a democratic value system that can apply to the schools of today, and the argument is made for the necessity of a move in that direction.

The remaining chapters present the view that market ideology undercuts the basic values of public education. In particular, it abolishes social and democratic control of the schools, and it eliminates the possibility of using the schools as a means of strengthening a democratic society. The critical focus is on five policy issues that have been in the forefront of education reform in the 1990s: privatization in all its forms, especially charter schools; collaborative and decentralized school system governance and management; the expanded use of computer technology; school-to-work programs; and national and state curriculum standards.

This particular list may seem surprising. The proposals appear to be unrelated and, in the case of national standards and decentralization, even contradictory. Support for any or all of these often crosses conventional conservative-liberal ideological lines, and, with the exception of privatization, none is clearly identified with market ideology. In fact, these are not all inherently market-oriented policies; some, such as decentralized management, have definite democratic potential. But market ideology has shaped their development and implementation, and they have thus become the means of imposing market models on the educational system.

School choice, for example, is not inherently subversive of democratic principles in education. Indeed, Meier argues that "choice is an essential tool for saving public education" (1995, 93). However, her idea of choice is within the context of the public system, supported by adequate public funding and designed for the purposes of promoting educational experimentation and building connections between the local community and its schools. Meier argues, "We do not need to buy into the rhetoric that too often surrounds choice: about the rigors of the marketplace, the virtues of private schooling, and the inherent mediocrity of public places and public spaces" (104).

Meier may be correct, but it is that rhetoric, not her perspective, that provides the rationale for almost all school choice proposals. Thus, school choice in actual practice destroys the community cohesion necessary to build democracy and renders impossible community control of the schools. In the form of vouchers, privatization, charter schools, or competitive interdistrict open enrollment, choice creates separate and unequal school communities that cannot communicate with one another. Thus, it obstructs the interchange and comparison of diverse ideas and experiences that enrich the learning process. School choice develops new educational ideas and approaches only if they are backed with sufficient capital. Investment in the market can be justified only by an adequate financial return or other material benefit to the particular investor; in the school system, as in the economy, this generally precludes any attempt at investment in any program that cannot produce quantifiable results. The product is a school system with no clear direction or coherent national purpose, because just as the market cannot plan for the economy in the long term, it cannot plan for the school system in the long term. The best evidence for this is in charter schools—a reform favored, ironically enough, by many who call themselves progressives—and in the programs of school choice now in effect in several states and localities.

Similarly, the use of computer technology in the schools does not by itself necessarily determine the direction of the curriculum, although it is by no means a neutral force. However, the most prominent arguments for its widespread use come from advocates who employ revolutionary rhetoric—the language of the so-called Third Wave—to describe its impact on education and emphasize its possibilities for liberating students from the bureaucratic and hierarchical barriers that obstruct the learning process. In fact, this rhetoric represents profoundly conservative, individualistic, market-oriented ideas about the goals of education and the purpose of schooling. Insofar as these ideas guide the introduction of computers into the classroom, the result is increased corporate control of the curriculum, isolation of students from one another and from the community, and the destruction of any possibility of public and democratic governance of the educational process.

"Site-based school management" is one of a number of currently fashionable phrases describing what appear to be attempts to democratize school governance. Across the country, there is a concerted effort to develop more decentralized and collaborative methods of educational decision making as a part of restructuring schools. And indeed, such reforms may have democratic potential and could go a long way toward reducing bureaucratic control. Yet in actual practice, they have exactly the opposite effect—not because they are improperly implemented but because they are based on corporate models, which in turn derive from market ideology. Thus, they result in the creation of an artificial consensus on the goals of education, isolating and stifling dissent in the name of teamwork. This strengthens the hand of school administrators, reducing the possibility of challenges to those with the most clout in the educational process or to the conventional—that is, market-oriented—ideas about the direction of education.

Battles over what should be taught in the schools—the curriculum—are highly complex and certainly not reducible to any clear-cut ideological conflict over market values. Classic conservative-liberal disputes over such issues as religion in the schools, the teaching of values, multiculturalism, and cultural literacy, to name just a few, continue unabated. As important as these conflicts are, they are only one dimension of a more fundamental, and perhaps less visible, struggle concerning the overall ends, means, and measurement of curricular change: What and whose criteria do we use do determine the success or failure of the schools? As state governments take increasing control of curriculum standards, the language of the market—competitiveness, efficiency, productivity—pervades the guidelines established by departments of education and imposes a uniformity of purpose on local schools. That language establishes a vocationalized curriculum on a national basis, even without federal action, and effectively precludes any use of the schools as a means of democratic civic education. Although this seems to be in conflict with decentralizing reforms such as site-based management—and indeed many free-market ideologues oppose national standards of any kind—that appearance is deceptive. Power to decide educational goals and control resources is being centralized; the process of executing those decisions within preestablished financial limits is being decentralized. The result is an antidemocratic corporate model of school management that matches the structure of the economic market—the owners determine what will be produced, who will produce it, and how much will be invested in the process; the workers take responsibility only for implementing those decisions. Accompanying this is a movement for productivity measurement through the application of statewide standardized tests, which become the basis for determining the allocation of public funds to the schools.

Alternatives to these policy directions, or at least more democratic variants, are both practical and achievable. With some exceptions, they can be redirected in a way that strengthens democratic public schools. This can occur if market ideology is explicitly rejected as a basis for change and democratic values are applied in its place. This book does not draw a complete blueprint for democratic reform, since no one book can do so. My primary concerns are the preservation of a democratically controlled system of public schools and the strengthening of democratic values in the United States. The focus is therefore on how policies based on market models render these goals unachievable and how alternative policy directions might work toward them.

We obviously do not now have democratic public schools, but a basically democratic administrative and financial framework—elected school boards and a trend toward equalization—still exists for the time being. Far from being utopian, then, democratic public schools are politically realistic, since the concept rests on popular democratic values, which—though now in eclipse—have deep historical roots in U.S. politics and society. Indeed, the political strength of market ideology in educational politics is based on its fraudulent appropriation of the language of equality and democracy. In the educational system of the twenty-first century, a choice between genuine democracy and consumer sovereignty in the market must be made. As it now stands, the market will triumph unless its basic tenets and assertions are directly challenged on the basis of an alternative perspective that preserves the public schools as a social institution subject to democratic control and directs them toward developing a citizenry that can preserve and strengthen a democratic society.

References

Baker, Russ. 1999. "The Education of Mike Milken." *The Nation,* 3 May.

Bast, Joseph L., and Herbert J. Walberg. 1996. "Free Market Choice: Can Education Be Privatized?" In *Radical Education Reforms,* ed. Chester Finn Jr. and Herbert J. Walberg. Berkeley: McCutchan Publishing.

Bushweller, Kevin. 1997. "Education, Ltd." *American School Board Journal,* March.

Chubb, John, and Terry Moe. 1990. *Politics, Markets, and America's Schools.* Washington, D.C.: Brookings

Cremin, Lawrence A. 1964 *The Transformation of the School.* New York: Vintage.

Duckworth, Eleanor. 1987. *The Having of Wonderful Ideas and Other Essays on Teaching and Learning.* New York: Teachers College Press.

Editors, *Rethinking Schools.* 1994. *Rethinking Our Classrooms.* Milwaukee: Rethinking Schools.

Greene, Maxine. 1995. *Releasing the Imagination.* San Francisco: Jossey-Bass.

Kahne, Joseph. 1996. *Reframing Educational Policy.* New York: Teachers College Press.

Kliebard, Herbert M. 1987. *The Struggle for the American Curriculum 1893–1958.* New York: Routledge and Kegan Paul.

Kuttner, Robert. 1997. *Everything for Sale.* New York: Knopf.

Meier, Deborah. 1995. *The Power of Their Ideas.* Boston: Beacon.

Perkinson, Henry J. 1968. *The Imperfect Panacea: 1865–1965.* New York: Random House.

Plank, David, and William L. Boyd. "Antipolitics, Education, and Institutional Choice: The Flight from Democracy." *American Educational Research Journal* 31: 263–281.

Postman, Neil. 1995. *The End of Education.* New York: Knopf.

Tyack, David B. 1993. "School Governance in the United States: Historical Puzzles and Anomalies." In *Decentralization and School Improvement,* ed. Jane Hannaway and Martin Carnoy. San Francisco: Jossey-Bass.

Tyack, David B. and Larry Cuban. 1995. *Tinkering toward Utopia.* Cambridge: Harvard University Press.

Vine, Phyllis. 1997. "To Market, to Market . . . " *The Nation,* 8 September.

2 Market Ideology

> The utopian vision of the marketplace offers . . . an enthralling religion, a self-satisfied belief system that attracts fervent and influential adherents. The wondrous machine of free-running enterprise has fantastic capabilities and people defer to its powers, persuaded it will carry them forward to millennial outcomes. Abstracted from human reality, the market's intricate mechanisms convey an entrancing sense of perfection, logical and self-correcting. Many intelligent people have come to worship these market principles, like a spiritual code that will resolve all the larger questions for us, social and moral and otherwise, so long as no one interferes with its authority. In this modern secular age, many who think of themselves as rational and urbane have put their faith in this idea of the self-regulating market as piously as others put their trust in God.
>
> William Greider, *One World, Ready or Not*

Market ideology is indeed a form of secular religion and, as such, rests on certain ideas about human behavior and the nature of society that are based more on faith than on science. Most of these concepts are what pass for common sense in a capitalist society and are therefore quite familiar. A thorough analysis of all of them is obviously not necessary to understand the impact of market ideology on educational politics and policy, but especially because the ideas seem like common sense, it is important to establish that, as far as education is concerned, they are quite the opposite.

Four particular assumptions are at the root of market ideology: (1) Human nature is a more or less unchangeable assortment of basic character traits; (2) society is best understood as an aggregation of individuals, and the social structure is best understood as the net result of their individual choices; (3) self-interest is the primary motivator of these choices, and personal material reward is the primary goal; and (4) protecting and maximizing the range of individual freedom of choice must be the primary purpose of any form of social organization. If these assumptions are accurate, a market system makes no sense; if they are accurate, no other system can possibly function.

Given these premises, it follows that the way to accomplish tasks in any society is to turn them over to the economic free market: the ongoing and unrestricted exchange of goods and services among producers and consumers in competition with each other. If individuals want a particular good or service, they should be prepared to pay its actual cost. It will be available to the extent that other individuals make a profit in producing it. The providers will compete with one another in the market to attract buyers by offering the best product or service at the lowest price. The result ought to be a continuous process of competition and bargaining that provides goods and services at the equilibrium price: the point at which an exchange becomes equally advantageous to both buyer and seller. If the market is allowed to function this way without any outside interference or coercion, the production and distribution of what people need or want will be arranged as if by an invisible hand. The market itself will regulate supply and demand. There will be no need for any external force to tell an individual what to produce, how to produce it, or what to buy. The society must not limit or control an individual's choices with subsidies paid for by other people. Such subsidies obstruct both the freedom of all concerned to invest their resources as they see fit and an understanding of the true cost of those choices.

The allocation of goods and services will therefore be determined by impersonal, objective, and nonpolitical market forces. People will work to the extent that they want to be able to participate as consumers. What they earn will depend on their individual ability to sell their labor to producers, who will profit depending on their ability to satisfy the market for their products. The major obstacle in this process is government, which arbitrarily and clumsily makes rules and regulations that obstruct the otherwise smooth workings of the market. It seems to follow, then, that the best government is that which governs least.

There are, however, some legitimate functions that government has to perform. The economists Milton and Rose Friedman (1980, 19–25) offer the clearest expression of market ideology in relation to its proper role. They see four duties for government, the first three of which are derived from the philosophy of Adam Smith, whose major work, *The Wealth of Nations,* is the Bible of capitalist economics. The first is the protection of society from threats of coercion, which involves the task of national defense. The second is the protection of individuals within society from coercion by other individuals, which requires the establishment of a criminal justice system. The third is the provision of public goods: goods or services for which a user charge cannot be calculated in the market or that cannot be collected practically. Finally, the government must protect the interests of those—and only those—who are unable to make free choices, a category that Friedman and Friedman limit to "madmen or children" (24). All others are, at least in theory, physically and legally capable of choosing for themselves how they will use whatever resources they have and they are to be given the freedom to do so.

Although there may be differences among the perceptions of free-market advocates as to where to draw the lines of responsibility and what the most appropriate methods of applying market ideology to specific policy issues are, the consensus is that the general principle is sound and universally relevant to all areas of human endeavor in all societies. If one applies it to education, justification for government involvement on any level relies exclusively on one of two criteria: (1) the extent to which education enhances national sovereignty and security (that is, freedom) against external military or economic threat, or (2) the extent to which education can provide specific, tangible, and quantifiable benefits to the smooth functioning of the market economy itself.

Market ideology also provides a logically consistent but somewhat more problematic approach to the specific questions of how much should be spent, who should pay the price, and what kinds of goods and services should be purchased. From the point of view of free-market advocates, the price system is capable of answering those questions. As the Friedmans put it, "Adam Smith's flash of genius was his recognition that the prices that emerged from voluntary transactions between buyers and sellers—for short, in a free market—could coordinate the activity of millions of people, each seeking his own interest, in such a way as to make everyone better off. . . . Economic order can emerge as the unintended consequence of the actions of many people, each seeking his own interest" (1980, 5).

Although education is not a tangible commodity with a measurable physical output, its production consumes resources and imposes costs in much the same way as anything else offered for consumption. Society therefore has to make a determination on the share of resources to be allocated to the production of education. According to market ideology, the price system can resolve this problem. Demand for schooling can be measured by response to higher or lower prices, its quality can be regulated by pursuing educational programs that yield a profit in the market, and people can vote with their dollars to determine the purposes of education.

There are, however, imperfections in this system. A major difficulty arises when one addresses the issue of distribution. The free market itself cannot even function without universal education, at least on the primary level. But, inevitably, some people will be either unwilling or unable to spend money on schools. And since education produces externalities—benefits to people other than those who purchase it—the price system will not send accurate signals about consumer demand. In the language of economics, there is market failure in the form of underinvestment in educational services, which will harm the society. The operations of the market itself cannot correct this.

Moreover, any attempt to calculate the optimum level of social rather than individual investment in education again runs into the externality problem. Education benefits the society as a whole as well as the particular individuals who pay for and consume it. Given the intangible nature of education as a commodity, it is difficult to separate the direct individual material benefit of schooling from its external benefits in order to decide precisely how to allocate shares of financial responsibility. Yet this is a task that must be accomplished if we are to develop an economically rational basis for school funding within the context of free-market ideology.

Market ideology thus dictates that the extent of government intervention in the operations of the market economy to provide educational services must be determined on the basis of the needs of national security and the market economy. It also requires that the extent of public responsibility for financing those services must be calculated in relation to their external benefits. Any other justification lacks economic rationality and runs the risk of disrupting the orderly workings of the market economy.

The internal logic of this perspective is impeccable; indeed, that is part of the reason for its hegemony. The problems arise when it is applied to the real world, especially the educational system. The major programs of education reform since the 1950s have been consistent with the tenets of market ideology, and there is certainly a wealth of literature analyzing and criticizing those reforms from a variety of perspectives. What may not be so obvious or widely discussed, however, is the political impact of the ideological constraints. They have gradually undermined democratic values in the educational system by weakening the rationale for maintaining it as a publicly controlled institution and by pushing civic education for democracy off the pedagogical agenda. Commenting on the reform movement of the 1980s, Barbara Finkelstein states, "It reveals a retreat from democracy. . . . Indeed, contemporary public discourse about education reveals an omnipresent, uncharacteristically single-minded preoccupation with the meaning of educational achievement. . . . Contemporary reformers seem to be recalling public education from its traditional utopian mission—to nurture a critical and committed citizenry that would stimulate the processes of political and cultural transformation and refine and extend the workings of political democracy" (1984, 275, 277, 280).

Plank and Boyd offer a similar description of contemporary educational politics as "a propensity to embark on a flight from democracy in the search for solutions [to educational problems]." They criticize what they see as "the low value placed upon democratic governance by a wide variety of scholars, policy analysts, and activists. Many of those concerned with educational policy have explicitly repudiated democratic control over schools as inimical to the attainment of large public purposes. . . . The costs of this repudiation have seldom been taken into account, however" (1994, 264). Tyack and Cuban state, "In the last generation, discourse about public schooling has become radically narrowed. It has focused on international economic competition, test scores, and individual 'choice' of schools. But it has largely neglected the types of choices most vital to civic welfare: collective choices about a common future, choices made through the democratic process about the values and knowledge that citizens want to pass on to the next generation" (1995, 140).

These are astute, uncommon, but understated observations. It would be even more accurate to argue that the ideological foundations of those reforms are actively hostile to any utopian mission. The tenets of market ideology applied to education reform preclude any consideration of nurturing democracy or democratic governance of the schools by establishing criteria that they cannot meet and priorities that crowd them out. This becomes evident from a review of some of the major policy initiatives taken by the government in the last half of the twentieth century.

In the early 1950s, the weakened and disorganized progressive education movement became the target of choice for those troubled by what they saw as the lack of U.S. educational preparedness in the face of the so-called Soviet threat. A flood of books and articles blamed the movement—more or less unfairly and inaccurately—for promoting curricular innovations that de-emphasized academic subject matter and intellectual skill development. The Cold War, it was argued, required schools that would provide rigorous academic training to produce the brainpower that would put us ahead of the Russians. Thus, the reaction to the October 1957 Soviet launching of the first orbiting space satellite, *Sputnik*, was hardly surprising. As Kliebard describes it, "Within a matter of days, American mass media had settled on a reason for the Soviet technological success. . . . [It was] a victory of the Soviet educational system over the American. . . . While American schoolchildren were learning how to get along with their peers or how to bake a cherry pie, so the explanation went, Soviet children were being steeped in the hard sciences and mathematics needed to win the technological race that had become the centerpiece of the Cold War" (1987, 264–265).

The National Defense Education Act (NDEA) of 1958 was intended as a response to this problem. It explicitly cited national security as the basis for funding curriculum revision projects in science and mathematics, to be conducted by university academic departments and the National Science Foundation. The first principle of market ideology—that the government's responsibility to defend its citizens from external threats to their freedom—was thus the primary rationale for the NDEA. The ultimate beneficiary, of course, was the military establishment. In terms of its political effects, Kliebard argues that the NDEA "dramatically altered the relative strength of various interest groups . . . but did not obliterate the victories that had been achieved over the previous 65 years of curricular reform" (1987, 269). This is probably true, but it set a distinct ideological precedent: The first direct intervention by the federal government in educational policy making was intended to help fight the Cold War.

This direction became even more pronounced when President John F. Kennedy took office in 1961 pledged to a program of military preparedness and economic expansion. At the same time, there was an increase in public awareness of pockets of poverty left behind during the prosperity that followed World War II. Economic growth, accompanied by a modest redistribution of wealth, was seen as the solution, and the educational system was regarded as one of the means. This was not a new role for the schools, but for the first time it was given what appeared to be empirical justification in the form of human capital theory.

Human capital—a concept first developed in rudimentary fashion by Smith—is defined by economists as the stock of knowledge and skills possessed by the labor force that increases its productivity. It is analogous to the concept of physical capital, which is the plant and machinery used in production. Starting in the 1950s, several economists began to explore what they saw as the relationship among education, human capital, and economic growth. With this area of study as the theme of his presidential address to the American Economic Association in 1961, Theodore Schultz promoted and popularized the use of the concept of human capital in relation to the economic effects of education. He asserted that the increase in national income could not be accounted for in terms of land, labor, and physical capital and called for research into how investment in human capital—in particular, education—might explain the discrepancy. This prompted an outpouring of work on the subject, most notably Gary Becker's *Human Capital* (1964), which attempted to develop an approach to the calculation of the income-enhancing effects of such investment. He concluded that there was a highly significant rate of return on individual investments in education as measured by income, exceeding even rates of return on business capital. The most influential work in this area was done by Edward Denison (1963), whose research on the specific contribution of education to economic growth became the most frequently cited in arguments favoring social investment in education. This line of thinking was taken further by Burton Weisbrod, who concluded that "education and health care are not merely consumer-type expenditures, but are investments in human resource productivity; and . . . benefits from these investments do not merely accrue just to the persons in whom they are made, but extend to other persons as well" (1966, 20). Government therefore has a responsibility, he said, to inform people about the benefits of education and provide aid and loans to facilitate individual investment.

This research was immensely attractive and useful to advocates of greater spending on public education. It provided an empirical and quantitative rationale in terms of economic growth, the ultimate goal of a market economy. It justified government action on the basis of arguments consistent with the principles of market ideology. Money for the schools could be regarded not as consumption spending but as an investment in human resources that would pay off in the future. As Walter Heller, President Kennedy's chairman of the Council of Economic Advisors, put it, "It is not, after all, caprice which has led to the substitution of the term 'investment in education' for the term of earlier decades, 'expenditures on education'" (OECD 1962, 33).

These ideas spread rapidly among elite policy-making institutions and education interest groups and provided what appeared to be hard data to support President Lyndon Johnson's Great Society programs in education, most notably the Elementary and Secondary Education Act (ESEA) of 1965. Of course, it was the liberal and reformist political climate of the early and mid 1960s that made ESEA possible. And the administration's decisions on the structure of ESEA, especially its choice to propose categorical rather than universal federal school aid, were based on political calculations to avoid certain controversies (such as aid to religious schools) and guarantee its passage. Still, its overall approach

> followed in the tradition of federal involvement in education that had been evolving since World War II, [which] was manpower planning for the national economy. In the 1950's . . . the emphasis had been on channeling talented youth into higher education. In the early 1960's the emphasis shifted to the proper utilization of the manpower of the poor through equality of opportunity. President Johnson . . . clearly reiterated this theme in his educational message to Congress. . . . He warned, "Nothing matters more to the future of our country; not our military preparedness, for armed might is worthless if we lack the brainpower to build a world of peace; not our productive economy, for we cannot sustain growth without trained manpower." (Spring 1989, 149–150)

This point of view was reiterated the following year in the report of the U.S. Council of Economic Advisors. Education, they claimed, yielded high returns on investment, supported economic growth, and constituted "the most powerful tool we have for raising the productivity and motivation of children of poor families, and for breaking the cycle of poverty and dependency" (1966, 107).

Of course, one can conclude that whatever the justification for the means, the ends were positive. If market ideology can be used to promote a worthwhile social program for education, what is there to complain about? This makes sense, but it is important to recognize the downside to justifying national government involvement in the language of free-market economics and the empirical methodology of mainstream economists. First of all, human-capital theory requires a quantitative assessment of externalities. Education for any noneconomic purpose—such as a democratic citizenry—may well be an externality, but its value in relation to economic growth is minimal, if it can even be calculated. On that basis there is no rationale for including it in the reform agenda.

Second, human-capital theory may have no validity in the real world. It should be noted that there is a large volume of research exposing the limitations of human-capital theory (Berg 1970; Braverman 1974; Machlup 1970; Thurow 1972). The critics' claims include the assertion that the studies affirming human-capital theory are rife with methodological shortcomings, unsupported assumptions, and obvious but usually unstated value biases. The studies did not lead to more detailed research on specific aspects; rather, they petered out during the following decade and left most of the methodological issues unaddressed. This had no effect on the standing of the idea among policy-making elites that somehow increased education promotes increased employment and economic growth in ways that can be tested and measured. The reality, however, is that although the assertion seems intuitively correct, there is no solid evidence for it. It remains more a statement of faith than a statement of social scientific fact.

Finally, and most important of all, there are the consequences of stalled or declining economic growth despite more spending on the schools or, in economists' terms, if the rate of return on investment in education decreases. This concern is expressed by economist Neil W. Chamberlain: "When the analogy of human capital to other forms of capital is pressed too far, not only does it break down on purely logical grounds but it invites conclusions which are both dangerous to social welfare and demeaning to the economics profession. . . . As soon as one talks about investments, he invites a consideration of any one investment with the alternative possibilities. . . . We [therefore] put education in the position of having to defend its value in the form of a rate of pecuniary return" (1971, 3–4).

That was precisely the outcome of the wave of school reform that began in the 1980s. It was prompted by the 1983 report on the National Commission for Excellence in Education, *A Nation at Risk*, which combined the themes of national security and human-capital development. It asserted that "our once unchallenged preeminence in commerce, industry, science, and technological innovation is being overtaken by competitors throughout the world." School systems in other nations were ostensibly "matching and surpassing our educational attainments. . . . If an unfriendly foreign power had attempted to impose on America the mediocre educational performance that exists today, we might well have viewed it as an act of war" (5). The commission's prestige and the urgency of its rhetoric led to wide publicity for its findings, despite their rather weak empirical support. Its specific proposals were strengthening high school graduation requirements in what it called the Five New Basics (English, mathematics, science, social studies, and computer science), more rigorous and measurable standards, a longer school day, improved teacher education, and increased financial support for schools—although not necessarily from the federal government.

The report, backed by the administration of President Ronald Reagan and promoted by a good deal of media attention, reinforced and helped shape ongoing state-level efforts at education reform in the following years. Leadership in these efforts came from governors, state legislatures, and business interests; educational professionals and citizens groups were largely left out of the process. Many of these leaders, such as Governor James Hunt of North Carolina, promoted their efforts in the language of human-capital theory brought up to date with references to the salutary economic effects of high technology: "The U.S. economic system is undergoing fundamental change today. Technology greatly affects how we do our work, and other countries have become major competitors with the U.S. for the world market. . . . We must respond to this shift with a renaissance in education. We must educate our young people for the jobs of tomorrow. . . . We must begin immediately to invest more in our human resources by strengthening the education and training of all our students. To achieve sound economic growth, we must make these investments now" (Hunt 1984, 18).

This has become the conventional wisdom underlying almost all state educational reform programs. Educational excellence has largely come to mean the development of skills needed to improve the U.S. market position in global economic competition. Thus, higher student standards and tougher graduation requirements have been a top priority, and many states have imposed testing programs to create a more uniform curriculum that emphasizes the so-called basics. State, but not federal, appropriations for public schools have been increased in many cases, and higher professional standards have been mandated for teachers. The federal reform program known as Goals 2000 is little more than a set of broad mandates representing the same approaches.

The impact of these approaches on the idea of democracy in school organization and curriculum is illustrated by a review of some of the state reports on education reform issued in the 1980s. The reports are virtually unanimous in excluding any direct participation by the community served by the schools and advocating only the most rudimentary education for citizenship. The Wisconsin Department of Public Instruction report (1985, 16) calls for a "high degree of parent/community involvement," but this is specifically applied only in the proposal that "the school utilize the family relationship to support student achievement. For example, if the school has developed a homework policy, this policy should be made clear to parents." The Pennsylvania Department of Education report (1983, 22) calls for school districts to "expand their efforts to involve parents in the education process" by asking them to "enforce good study habits, encourage their children to take more demanding courses [and] help parents understand what colleges and employers expect of their sons and daughters, so that parents can help insure that their children are prepared for the future." The Arkansas State Board of Education's public-involvement initiatives are even more patronizing: "Each school shall systematically and at least annually explain its policies, programs, and goals to the school community in a public meeting that provides opportunities for parents . . . to ask questions and make suggestions concerning the school program" (1984, 16). Parents and the communities are not to be part of the decision-making process but rather vehicles to transmit established school policies to the students. The recent shift to site-based management is ostensibly rooted in a far more participatory value system, but these comments raise some interesting questions about the depth of this new commitment (see Chapter 5 of this volume).

As far as democratic citizenship in the curriculum is concerned, adjustment, acceptance, and passive participation are the norms. The report of the Ohio Commission on Educational Excellence states that "working and living in a democracy require the ability to work with others in formulating constructive alternatives and to compete within the free enterprise system" (1985, 5). The Governor's Educational Review Commission of Georgia demands student competencies in "demonstrating knowledge" of the nation's geography, economy, and social structure and "the skills necessary for a caretaker of the environment," the "development of government and law," and, again, the "free enterprise system" (1984, appendix A). According to the West Virginia Board of Education, social studies are to "enable the students to solve problems, make responsible decisions, and function effectively within a pluralistic society" (1983, 116).

This wave of education reform appears to have run its course without any appreciable improvement in either the quality of education or our standing in the global economy. What it has accomplished, however, is the institutionalization of market ideology as the unchallenged point of view on the purpose and direction of education, which has turned a retreat from democracy into a rout. The reforms have had at least three effects along those lines, all of which are elaborated in the course of this book, but it will serve the immediate purpose simply to list them here.

First, human-capital theory and the insistence that education improve economic competitiveness has set up a cost-benefit straitjacket for curriculum development. If productivity as measured by corporate profit becomes the yardstick for educational effectiveness, no program of learning oriented primarily toward such noneconomic values as democratic citizenship could possibly measure up. Second—and ironically, given the antibureaucratic orientation of free-market ideology—assessing education on quantifiable outcomes revives what used to be called the social efficiency approach to school management and puts the state in the position of measuring educational productivity according to rigidly quantitative standards (see Chapter 7). This has the effect of weakening local control and undercutting or diluting what is known as site-based management, as well as eliminating educational outcomes that are nonquantifiable. Finally, if the market is making the big decisions about the direction of education, then the community is not. It is one thing to make production and investment decisions in education on the basis of economic development; it is quite another to bring people together to discuss those decisions collectively and make choices based on consensus or majority rule. If we emphasize the former, we move away from the latter and thus preclude any kind of democratic decision making for the schools. Ultimately, the institutionalization of market ideology eliminates democratic alternatives from the ideological competition in the politics of education.

The more we become accustomed to thinking of the schools along the lines of market ideology, the more likely it is that we can be convinced to pursue even more radically market-oriented reforms the next time the education crisis–school reform cycle begins. The history of education reform from the 1950s to the 1980s has established a trajectory that promises to continue well into the twenty-first century, and the reform agenda of the 1990s (discussed later) bears this out.

The more orthodox proponents of market ideology might be the first to object to this characterization of education reform. Their pet project, school vouchers, has not been widely adopted, and many of the reforms have been implemented by those whom they would call liberal advocates of big government. Moreover, during the same period, public education has changed in other ways not related to or perhaps even contradictory to free-market thought, most notably in increasingly egalitarian approaches to women, racial and ethnic minorities, and the physically and mentally disabled. This is reflected especially in the proliferation of various multicultural and compensatory programs and in the requirement of equal treatment toward all groups regardless of the financial or administrative burden. Indeed, some argue, "political correctness" rather than economic rationality has come to dominate public education. To a considerable degree, that is an exaggeration promoted in the media by conservatives in order to advance their own agenda. But even to the extent that any of the argument is true, these objections miss the point.

The major education reforms of the forty years following World War II were, in fact, designed and advanced primarily on the basis of their effects on our ability to maintain economic growth at home and political and economic superiority in the world. The reality that so far free-market conservatives have not achieved everything they wanted and that formerly excluded groups have managed to gain more equal access to educational services does not fundamentally contradict this fact or lessen its political impact. The overall direction of educational change continues toward the goals dictated by the values and principles of market ideology, and this ultimately lays a foundation for the completion of its agenda.

What, then, is wrong with this trend? In Chapter 1, it was noted that incrementalism and practicality might make better sense as guidelines for educational policy development. What is more, given the centrality of market ideology in U.S. society, why should schools proceed in the opposite direction, even if they could? What is wrong with linking education to economic productivity and national military superiority, especially if that is what is required to mobilize public support? Are there not other means of reinforcing democratic values in the society? If the schools can still perform their more conventional educational tasks, and if in fact there is little organized opposition to market models, why should there be any sense of urgency about democracy and education? Can we not continue on a path of gradual improvements and practical adjustments to changing conditions? After all, what can we expect of an imperfect panacea?

In addition, a broad-based ideological challenge to the current trend in educational policy hardly seems politically realistic. The history of educational politics is littered with failed revolutions. Tyack and Cuban are optimistic about improving schools and committed to democratic values, yet they are cautious about overreaching in the direction of reform: "The typical rational and instrumental assumptions of educational reformers fail to give due weight to the resilience of schools as institutions. The institutional structure probably has more influence on the implementation of policy than policy has on institutional practice. . . . To bring about improvement at the heart of education . . . has proven to be the most difficult kind of reform" (1995, 134–135). Therefore, would a pragmatic and incremental approach to change not make more sense?

It is not enough merely to reply that democracy is better. Rather, the answer to these questions must come from a consideration of how educational policies based on market models affect young people in the schools. If, in fact, we are doing serious damage to the next generations with such policies, then radical alternatives to the present course must demand our serious attention. In that regard, there is a need to go beyond the usual discussions of academic achievement to consider, first of all, the ideas and perspectives of young people on the subject of education and, second, their wants and needs as developing human beings.

The first objective is hard to reach, since there is almost nothing in the literature of school reform on how students feel about or what they want from the educational system. This omission reflects in part the typically patronizing adult attitudes toward the opinions of youths. It also reflects the market perspective on people, and perhaps especially young people, which regards them exclusively as consumers and human resources. Other roles become irrelevant, and the social context of individual choices disappears. Young people in the schools thus become nonpersons whose opinions do not count. Even worse, they are often perceived as the problem that the schools have to solve. That is the point of view of Laurence Steinberg, who declares school reform a failure, since it is the attitudes and behavior of students that need to change: "Student achievement is as much a product of the ways in which children and adolescents arrange and structure their lives—the activities they pursue, the priorities they hold, the endeavors they value—as it is a product of the schools they attend. . . . Unless and until students and their parents view success in school as a necessary and worthwhile goal . . . students will not seek it with passion or commitment." The problems are "parental disengagement and a peer culture that is scornful of academic excellence"; the solutions are tougher standards and more parental involvement (1996, 181).

This argument is typical of mainstream education reformers, and it is part and parcel of what Annette Fuentes calls "the new mood of meanness toward children," which has produced "a crackdown on kids." Citing a survey indicating that only 23 percent of adults had positive things to say about children, Fuentes states, "The generation gap is old news, but this sour, almost hateful view of young people is different. Adults aren't merely puzzled by young people, they're terrified of them" (1998, 20–21). Mike A. Males refers to young people today as "the scapegoat generation": "American adults have regarded adolescents with hope and foreboding throughout this century. What is transpiring today is new and ominous. A particular danger attends older generations indulging 'they-deserve-it' myths to justify enriching ourselves at the expense of younger ones. The message Nineties American adults have spent two decades sending to youths is: You are not our kids. We don't care about you" (1996, 43). He documents this view extensively by detailing the hypocrisy, double standards, and lack of concern for youths shown in public policymaking in the areas of poverty, criminal justice, substance abuse, and teen pregnancy.

Mike Rose states, "It is striking . . . to behold the image of our young people that emerges in public discussion about the schools.

Their ignorance is calibrated and broadcasted, they drift across charts, inarticulate. They are a threat to the present and future of the nation. It is as if we have projected onto the next generation all the deficits of our own economic and political imagination" (1995, 332). A particular dark vision of the experience of young people in the United States in the 1990s is offered by journalist William Finnegan. Telling the stories of a number of teenagers "growing up in a harder country," he blames the "fecklessness and self-absorption of [his] generation . . . for the darkening, fearsome world that younger Americans face today. As Christopher Lasch, the late social critic, wrote, 'If young people feel no connection to anything, their dislocation is a measure of our failure, not theirs'" (1998, xvii). If this is "a strange and difficult time to grow up in America," it is because of "the rot in the structure of opportunity," "the negative views of [young people] held by their parents' generation," and a "disastrous lag in policy response" by the government to changing economic conditions that increase the pressures on the U.S. family (343–347). A longitudinal study of seven thousand teenagers by Barbara Schneider and David Stevenson entitled *The Ambitious Generation* concludes that "today's teens are the most ambitious, most upwardly mobile generation yet–but also the most isolated generation" (Taylor 1999, 32).

Francis Ianni's study of adolescent life in ten communities concludes that what is lacking is "a supportive network of social institutions working together to create a common, community-based locus for socialization." This has meant a "loss of the sense of the caring community," which has resulted in "the fragmentation of the adolescent experience, as the various social environments function as independent, sometimes isolated, and at times competitive or even conflicting settings for teenagers. It is this community-level dissonance . . . that exacerbates the conflicts of the adolescent identity crisis into the 'adolescent problems' we hear so much about." What young people seek is "a search for structure, a set of believable and attainable expectations and standards from the community to guide the movement from child to adult status" (1989, 261–262).

If any of this is even partly true—and I would argue that this trend indeed describes the contemporary condition of young people—market models of educational policy are not only unable to satisfy that search, but also profoundly destructive of any attempt to build a coherent value system for young people in the schools. In the name of freedom of choice, they exacerbate social fragmentation and dissonance. Market ideology, in its insistence that we are nothing more than our material self-interest, constructs an educational system that sets adolescents adrift. It reduces them to commodities, rather than developing human beings. Their value is measured in dollars, not in their humanity. It is this kind of social damage that warrants serious consideration of radical change, because our young people are at stake.

In light of all this, it is particularly disappointing to see how feeble the resistance to market ideology in education has been within the academic community. At least in theory, educational professionals might be expected to generate the ideas that could stimulate oppositional thinking. In the 1960s oppositional thinking came primarily from what some have called the romantic critics of conventional education; in the 1990s it came from the postmodernists. Neither of these groups, however, presents a serious political challenge to market ideology; indeed, both fit in rather comfortably with or at least can be structurally accommodated by it.

The political atmosphere of the 1960s encouraged attacks on established social, political, and economic institutions, and the schools were among the major targets. As during the preceding decade, numerous studies were published attacking not only the standard curriculum but also the public schools themselves. This time, however, the target was their bureaucratic and authoritarian structure, which, it was argued, destroyed all possibility of genuine learning by repressing and depersonalizing students. Reform was impossible, since the institution of school itself was oppressive. Its effect on students was to force them to conform to irrational rules and meaningless standards over which they had no control. Thus, the goal was to be the liberation of both teachers and students from the structural constraints that obstructed genuine learning.

Among the typical proposals for change was that of John Holt (1972), who advocated replacing formal schooling with a totally child-centered curriculum. Holt adopted—without explicit acknowledgment—many of Jean-Jacques Rousseau's ideas, including the notion that the discipline of nature itself could be the teacher. Ivan Illich (1970) went even further by advocating deschooling. This meant replacing the schools themselves with voluntary networks of educational opportunities and situations that he called learning webs. These and similar ideas generated tremendous interest among those favoring radical change in the educational system. As a practical matter, however, complete deschooling could not constitute the core of a program for public education. What did arise in the late 1960s was a substantial network of so-called free schools, which attempted to put into practice child-centered and unstructured approaches to education. For a time, these schools and the theory behind them were highly influential in shaping educational dialogue and practices and, hence, educational politics. The implicit political strategy was, unlike the progressive education movement, to take the opposition outside the system and create an external base of operations that would provide a refuge and training grounds for new models of education to prompt changes in the old system.

By and large, however, the free schools were failures. Often they ended up as stereotypical representations of white, middle-class, college-educated teachers' attempts to impose their highly abstract concepts of individual freedom on children from low-income black and Hispanic families, who were not happy to wait until their sons and daughters felt like learning how to read. Even where the educational approach was more sophisticated, financial support was hard to find. It was also difficult to maintain a permanent free-school structure and long-term commitment to students on the basis of a philosophy that rejected all kinds of structure as inherently oppressive. Thus, free-schools pretty much vanished from the scene in the 1970s, and along with them the challenge to conventional methods of education.

For all their radical language and revolutionary posturing, advocates of the free schools were acting squarely in the individualistic tradition of the free market by promoting a new product to compete with the old. The new product thus offered no serious challenge to that tradition, since the old product had a monopoly. Radical politics in the 1960s involved, among other battles, an ongoing struggle between those who wanted to work within the system and those who wanted to destroy or at least weaken it by establishing alternative institutions. Educational radicals during that time primarily chose the latter course of action. Although some positive changes in the schools did in fact result, the overall strategy proved a failure, leaving the structural and ideological foundations of the existing educational system largely intact. What is worse, because of its own individualistic and unstructured approach, the strategy failed to establish any coherent or lasting organized opposition to the dominance of market ideology in the politics of education. The tradition of the 1960s has not faded, however; it is reflected in the interest in charter schools held by many contemporary progressives.

The most recent wave of educational radicalism has come from the so-called postmodernists, who maintain that all the metanarratives of modern society—liberalism, capitalism, Marxism, fascism, and other grand theories and ideologies—no longer make sense in explaining how the world works or how it ought to work. The immense and constantly changing variety of human experiences defies such comprehensive descriptions. Similarly, they argue, rational scientific analysis as a basis for human progress—an intellectual hallmark of the modern era—is not as objective as it appears to be. As a structural mode of thinking, it establishes meanings that sound logical but are in fact essentially arbitrary. The language we use to define historical, political, or economic concepts is never neutral—it is part of a discourse that reflects the distribution of power in a particular society. In short, the standards we have learned to apply in organizing our understanding of the world have no universal, inherent, or lasting validity. They make sense only within the context of a power structure and are used to protect the interests of that particular arrangement: "Postmodernism presents itself as a critique of all forms of representations and meanings that claim transcendental and transhistorical status. It rejects universal reason as a foundation for human affairs, and poses as alternatives forms of knowing that are partial, historical, and social. . . . It rejects the European tradition as the exclusive referent for judging what constitutes historical, cultural, and political truth. There is no tradition or story that can speak with authority and certainty for all humanity" (Aronowitz and Giroux 1991, 116).

Thus, in a nation like the United States, those with wealth and power are able to resist change by establishing their own particular discourse—the language they use to interpret the world—as the only one that is valid. Using their language, argue the postmodernists, forces us into their frame of reference and makes change impossible. The schools help serve that purpose by excluding alternative ways of understanding, especially those that might strengthen the position of people who lack significant wealth or power.

As a perspective on education, postmodernism has a number of vocal exponents but not much substantive influence outside certain sectors of higher education. In contrast to the radical educational movements of the 1960s, and the progressive movement of the 1930s, it has had very little impact on pedagogical practices in the public schools. However, since a considerable portion of the critical literature on U.S. schools has come from that quarter, postmodernism deserves some attention.

The postmodern perspective leads to conclusions about ideology and educational policy that appear to be not unlike those advanced in this chapter. Henry Giroux correctly points out that

> educational reform has become synonymous with turning schools into "company stores" and defining school life primarily in terms that measure their utility against their contribution to economic growth and cultural uniformity. [It] points to a definition of schooling that is so restricted that it almost completely strips public education of a democratic vision. . . . At the heart of this ideological shift is an attempt to reformulate the purpose of public education around a set of interests and social relations that define academic success in terms of the worst features of the dominant ideology. (1988, 18)

Giroux's alternative, and that of most other radical postmodernists, is a school system that leads to a more democratic and egalitarian society. Since, according to their perspective, no comprehensive program of political action has any universal application, however, the curriculum cannot be aimed toward a particular social goal. Radical postmodernists argue instead that a curriculum based on a critical pedagogy can empower people with the conceptual tools and self-confidence to challenge the existing oppressive social order. What remains is only the possibility of challenging the dominant discourse—the language of those in power—by deconstructing it and developing alternative discourses based on the experience and culture of the particular groups that are excluded and exploited by the system.

A postmodern curriculum based on "critical practice," says Cleo Cherryholmes, "must attend to how power influences, shapes, produces, and is produced by theoretical and practical discourses-practices. . . . Descriptions and explanations should be offered about the way subjectivities are conditioned and constrained by existing social structures [and] alternative accounts of what is going on should be explored, regardless of their source" (1988, 93). Once the dominant discourses have been deconstructed, the schools can create new learning by building upon the knowledge derived from the cultural resources that students already possess. This means a student-centered learning regime emphasizing popular culture, most of which today is electronically mediated. Postmodern educational theory has therefore spawned a great deal of academic work in what is called cultural studies, which involves the analysis and deconstruction of themes in movies, television, and popular music.

In a postmodern high school, "students and teachers have final authority. . . . [They] negotiate which courses, if any, are to be required." The teacher should "attempt to integrate [traditional disciplines] within a series of projects chosen jointly with students. The project may be a study of rap music, sports, the Civil War, neighborhoods, youth in society, race relations, sexuality, or almost anything else." The lecture format is eliminated, and the classroom becomes open, with students involved in a wide variety of academic endeavors, individually or in groups, inside the classroom or in the field (Aronowitz and Giroux 1991, 21). In this respect, postmodern education resembles the vision of the romantics of the 1960s. But where the romantics took as their starting point the liberation of the individual from the constraints of the social order, the postmodernists seek to change the social order by empowering the individual. And rather than instructing teachers to stand back and leave the students to learn on their own, postmodernists want teachers to assume the role of transformative intellectuals who have the historical and philosophical understanding to help students empower and emancipate themselves.

The vision of radical postmodern educators is not the restructuring of the school system based on an alternative metanarrative but rather the conduct within the schools of an endless, ongoing conversation between teachers and students that gradually transforms how young people see themselves and their world. It is hoped that this will lead to a more democratic and egalitarian community, or perhaps, more likely and more modestly, "the unreflective reproduction of what we find around us, including some of its injustices, might be tamed and changed a bit" (Aronowitz and Giroux 1991, 186).

Most of the criticism of this perspective has come from politically conservative defenders of the academic canon rather than from other radicals. Thus it retains a curious and somewhat ironic status as the "canon" of those opposing mainstream educational thinking, especially former Marxists looking for another theory. The problem is that it provides no real direction for change. What postmodernism lacks by its very nature is a political goal—a metanarrative of its own. Although it is critical of market ideology, it is similarly critical of all ideologies. All that postmodernism provides is a game plan for unending intellectual guerrilla warfare in the schools, which it cannot win. It therefore may have the capability of deconstructing free-market conservatism, but it offers nothing as a replacement. In the real world of politics, this is not an effective strategy for any kind of transformation of the educational system.

The clearest criticism of postmodernism along these lines is offered by Landon Beyer and Daniel Liston. Noting Jonathan Kozol's (1991) descriptions of the appalling conditions of underfunded schools in *Savage Inequalities,* Beyer and Liston argue that any struggle to change this must come out of an "outrage" that "must be rooted in a moral condemnation of injustice and inequality." Postmodern premises, however, "foster an insularity and narcissism of discourse . . . and a lack of substantial moral imagination. This leaves us stranded, without a clear direction to pursue in the alleviation of the inequalities Kozol describes. . . . No substantive changes will take place through exclusively individual initiatives and isolated events." Moreover, political action requires a "community that endorses solidarity and collaborative moral action" that the postmodern emphasis on "particularity, the local, and the specific" renders impossible (1996, 154). If postmodern education is all that radicals have to offer, conservatives need not worry.

Half a century of educational policy development in line with the tenets of market ideology have brought us to a point where alternative perspectives are unthinkable and where the only education reforms considered practical and realistic are those consistent with its world view. This has happened for a number of reasons. The environment of Cold War politics was inhospitable, to say the least, to any educational policy tainted by the term "progressive." In that context, building a political constituency supportive of increased aid to education, especially from the federal government, required policymakers to employ the language of national security and economic growth. The growing strength of the conservative movement after the 1970s elicited only a defensive response from liberals. And finally, progressive educators demonstrated a lack of resolve and imagination in responding to market ideology assaults on their ideas and programs.

The result, as later chapters show, is the predominance of educational policies that literally devalue young people, or more precisely, see their value only in terms of a return on investment. This trend is occurring at a time when children face unprecedented social and economic pressures in the course of growing up. It ought to be the schools that give them the personal and intellectual resources to cope with these challenges, but the market ideology fixation on economic growth and national security has made that impossible. It therefore becomes critical to develop an alternative perspective on educational policy based on democratic values.

References

Arkansas State Board of Education. 1984. *Standards for Accreditation*. Little Rock.

Archie, Stanley, and Henry Giroux. 1991. *Postmodern Education*. Minneapolis: University of Minnesota Press.

Becker, Gary. 1964. *Human Capital*. New York: Columbia University Press.

Berg, Ivar. 1970. *The Great Training Robbery*. New York: Praeger.

Beyer, Landon, and Daniel Liston. 1996. *Curriculum in Conflict*. New York: Teachers College Press.

Braverman, Harry. 1974. *Labor and Monopoly Capital*. New York: Monthly Review Press.

Chamberlain, Neil W. 1971. "Some Second Thoughts on the Concept of Human Capital." In *Human Capital Formation and Manpower Development*, ed. Ronald A. Wykstra. New York: Free Press.

Cherryholmes, Cleo. 1988. *Power and Criticism: Poststructural Investigations in Education*. New York: Teachers College Press.

Denison, Edward. 1963. "Measuring the Contribution of Education to Economic Growth." In *The Residual Factor and Economic Growth*, ed. Study Group in the Economics of Education. Paris: Organization for Economic Cooperation and Development.

Finkelstein, Barbara. 1984. "Education and the Retreat from Democracy in the United States, 1979–198?" *Teachers College Record* 86: 275–281.

Finnegan, William. 1998. *Cold New World*. New York: Random House.

Friedman, Milton, and Rose Friedman. 1980. *Free to Choose*. New York: Harcourt, Brace, Jovanovich.

Fuentes, Annette. 1998. "The Crackdown on Kids." *The Nation*, 15 June.

Giroux, Henry. 1988. *Schooling and the Struggle for Public Life*. Minneapolis: University of Minnesota Press.

Governor's Educational Review Commission [Georgia]. 1984. *Priority for a Quality Basic Education*. Atlanta.

Greider, William. 1997. *One World, Ready or Not*. New York: Simon and Schuster.

Holt, John. 1972. *Freedom and Beyond*. New York: Dutton.

Hunt, James B. Jr. 1984. "Education for Economic Growth: A Critical Investment." *Phi Delta Kappan*, April.

Ianni, Francis. 1989. *The Search for Structure*. New York: Free Press.

Illich, Ivan. 1970. *Deschooling Society*. New York: Harper and Row.

Kliebard, Herbert M. 1987. *The Struggle for the American Curriculum 1893–1958*. New York: Routledge and Kegan Paul.

Kozol, Jonathan. 1991. *Savage Inequalities*. New York: Crown.

Machlup, Fritz. 1970. *Education and Economic Growth*. Lincoln: University of Nebraska Press.

Males, Mike A. 1996. *The Scapegoat Generation*. Monroe, Me.: Common Courage Press.

Ohio Commission on Educational Excellence. 1985. *Responsible Reform: Focussing on the Future*. Columbus.

Organization for Economic Cooperation and Development (OECD). 1962. *Policy Conference on Economic Growth and Investment in Education*. Washington, D.C.: OECD.

Pennsylvania Department of Education. 1983. *Turning the Tide: An Agenda for Excellence in Pennsylvania Schools*. Harrisburg.

Plank, David, and William L. Boyd. 1994. "Antipolitics, Education, and Institutional Choice: The Flight from Democracy." *American Educational Research Journal* 31: 263–281.

Rose, Mike. 1995. *Possible Lives*. Boston: Houghton Mifflin.

Schultz, Theodore. 1961. "Rise in the Capital Stock Represented by Education in the United States, 1900–1957." *American Economic Review* 51 (March): 1–17.

Spring, Joel. 1989. *The Sorting Machine Revisited*. New York: Longman.

Steinberg, Laurence. 1996. *Beyond the Classroom*. New York: Simon and Schuster.

Taylor, Ihsan K. 1999. "Books: New in Print." *Education Week*, 2 June.

Thurow, Lester. 1972. "Education and Economic Equality." *Public Interest*, Summer.

Tyack, David B, and Larry Cuban. 1995. *Tinkering toward Utopia*. Cambridge: Harvard University Press.

U.S. Council of Economic Advisors. 1966. *Annual Report*. Washington, D.C.: U.S. Government Printing Office.

U.S. National Commission for Excellence in Education. 1983. *A Nation at Risk*. Washington, D.C.: U.S. Government Printing Office.

Weisbrod, Burton. 1966. "Investing in Human Capital." *Journal of Human Resources* 1: 5–21.

West Virginia Board of Education. 1983. *A Master Plan for Education*. Charleston.

Wisconsin Department of Public Instruction. 1985. *A Plan for Excellence 1985–1987*. Madison.

3 Democratic Education

An effective challenge to the educational policy directions in place since the 1950s requires a challenge to market ideology. This process involves not only describing a democratic alternative in theory but also explaining its pedagogical advantages in practice. Developing a democratic value system for education does not require the invention of new ideas about human behavior, social structure, and learning theory; it requires, instead, a more thorough exploration of existing ideas and how they relate in the context of contemporary issues in educational policy. This investigation should result in a position from which progressive educators can reject market ideology and set alternative directions for public education.

Using democracy as a standpoint for such a challenge also requires a political justification. Given the international situation in the 1930s, the future of democracy was understandably a critical issue for progressive educators. But today there is a widely held belief that, after the fall of communism, democracy—far from being endangered—has in fact triumphed. This conviction is based on the notion that market economy and democracy are not only mutually reinforcing but in some respects identical. From that point of view, it makes little sense to argue that educating for democracy is somehow antithetical to market ideology—unless the concept of democracy is understood differently. Robert B. Westbrook, Dewey's most prominent biographer, raises just this issue:

> In some respects, to be sure, there need be no conflict between preparing children for a more active citizenship and girding them for competition in the "global marketplace." Education for public life and education for work are not inherently at cross purposes. . . . It is much more difficult—some would say impossible—to make the case for wage labor as a reinforcing influence on democratic citizenship. . . . Whether American employers would appreciate employees armed not only with technical skills and [good work] habits but also with the capacity and desire to de-

> liberate on the ends of the enterprise and the economy is another question. . . . Dewey, at least, argued that schooling for democracy would only be fully functional when democracy had been extended to the workplace. (1995, 140–141)

In fact, the democracy that has ostensibly triumphed over communism is not the democracy that was the object of concern for progressive educators. If we use the term's latter meaning, democracy is most certainly under threat, even if not from the same sources as during the 1930s. Many social analysts see a deterioration of democracy no matter how it is defined. Political participation in the United States, even of the most passive kind, is at an all-time low, and political cynicism among citizens is at an all-time high. Added to the tensions resulting from increasing economic inequality, ineffective and corrupt political leadership, and Americans' pervasive doubts about the future, this combination is potentially explosive. As a result, across the ideological spectrum, intense concern has been expressed about the stability of whatever democracy we now have.

Beyond these generalizations, the precise status of democratic civic values among the U.S. people is hard to determine. In recent years, however, social analysts studying the question from a variety of perspectives have taken an increasingly negative view. Jean Bethke Elshtain, writing from the standpoint of seeking to stabilize the existing political system, sees a breakdown. She blames the U.S. emphasis on individual autonomy, "the translation of wants into rights," excessive reliance on the state to solve social problems, and "democracy by plebiscite," and she calls for a "new social covenant" to show citizens "that they are all in it together." "Democratic citizens," she adds, must "remember that being a citizen is a civic identity, not primarily a private sinecure"(1995, 30).

Christopher Lasch, who calls himself a "populist," sees damage to democracy arising from, among other things, the decline of self-governing communities, racial separatism, and the deterioration of public debate. He does not blame the loss on average citizens; rather, he says, "it is the elites—those who control the international flow of money and information, preside over philanthropic foundations and institutions of higher learning, manage the instruments of cultural production and thus set the terms of public debate—that have lost faith in the values, or what remains of them, of the West" (1995, 25–26). Those who, in the past, have had the greatest responsibility for acting in line with democratic norms have abandoned that role in unlimited pursuit of their own economic self-interest.

William Greider aims more directly at the effects of the corporate domination of U.S. politics. In his widely read book *Who Will Tell the People?* he asserts that "American democracy is in much deeper trouble than most people wish to acknowledge. Behind the reassuring facade, the regular election contests and so forth, the substantive meaning of self-government has been hollowed out. What exists behind the formal shell is a systemic breakdown of the shared civic values we call democracy." This has resulted from, among other causes, "mutual contempt" between voters and politicians, the decline of the political parties, a socially irresponsible mass media, and the impact of corporate "fixers" in diluting and circumventing the laws. The United States may thus be facing a serious political crisis: "America won't work as a society if the civic faith is lost. Unlike most other nations, the United States has always overcome the vast differences among its people . . . through the overarching bond of its democratic understandings. If these connections between the governed and the government are destroyed, if citizens can no longer believe in the mutuality of the American experience, the country may descend into a new kind of social chaos and political unraveling, unlike anything we have experienced before" (1992, 11, 16).

William Hudson, in his appropriately titled book *American Democracy in Peril,* describes four models of democracy. Two of them, which he names "protective" and "pluralist," involve a relatively passive role for citizens in a system that does little more than protect diversity, liberty, and property. This tends to be the version favored by most contemporary mainstream social scientists in the United States. "Developmental" and "participatory" categories involve a greater degree of active citizen participation, social and economic equality, and "civic virtue." All of the forms, he argues, are subject to serious challenges in contemporary society, among them radical individualism, trivialized elections, the privileged position of business, and increasing inequality. He proposes a stronger network of social institutions that would reverse the erosion of the "habits of the heart that tie democratic citizens to one another and promote civic virtue" (1995, 102).

Tom DeLuca's examination of political apathy is consistent with these analyses. He argues that apathy may not be a free choice but rather a form of what he calls "complex depoliticization." This "second face of apathy" involves, among other factors, a form of political alienation that he describes as "the indefinite suspension of the ability to achieve and sustain political intentions due to the tightly spun web of depoliticizing ideology, language, social psychology, and technological and economic hegemony, which together form a mutually constituting and reinforcing system that for all practical purposes is closed" (1995, 193–194).

For the most part, these concerns are related to the preservation of liberal pluralist democracy, in which the primary role of average citizens is to choose their leaders in free, competitive elections and to organize interest groups to promote their particular demands. There are, however, theorists who advance a notion of democracy based on a considerably larger role, involving more direct participation in decision making based on a high degree of civic responsibility and political equality. This is what Hudson calls "participatory" democracy and what Benjamin Barber calls "strong democracy":

> [It] is a distinctively modern form of participatory democracy. It rests on the idea of a self-governing community of citizens who are united less by homogeneous interests than by civic education and who are made capable of common purpose and mutual action by virtue of their civic attitudes and participatory institutions rather than their altruism or their good nature. . . . It challenges the politics of elites and masses that masquerades as democracy in the West. . . . It incorporates a Madisonian wariness about actual human nature into a more hopeful, Jeffersonian outlook on human potentialities. (Barber 1984, 117–118)

Frances Moore Lappe and Paul Martin DuBois use the term "living democracy":

> To work, democracy . . . has to be a way of life—a way of life that involves the values and practices people engage in daily in all aspects of their public lives. . . . Democracy requires a lot more of us than being intelligent voters. It requires that we learn to solve problems with others—that we learn to listen, to negotiate, and to evaluate. To think and speak

> effectively. To go beyond simple protest in order to wield power, becoming partners in problem solving. This isn't about so-called good work; it's about our vital interests. And it isn't about simply running our government; it's about running our lives. (1994, 15)

However named—here we will use the term "popular democracy"—these concepts of democracy imply a need for radical reconceptualization of many of the basic concepts associated with governance. If power is simply dominance, if consent always rests on the application of coercion, and if conflict is a zero-sum game among adversaries, popular democracy is utopian. Feminist theorists in particular have underscored this point and have developed new perspectives. Jane Mansbridge argues that conventional democratic theory is based on what she calls the "Anglo-American" concept of "free and unencumbered individuals who associate to promote their own interests," which is the starting place of market ideology. She proposes instead that democratic theory "draw inspiration from or use metaphors derived from the experiences of empathetic interdependence, compassion, and personal vulnerability that the culture usually codes as 'female.'" "Democratic theory and practice as it has evolved in the United States in the last half century has a particular need for these feminist correctives based on 'connection.' . . . But the twentieth-century theory of adversary democracy, and all practices based implicitly on that theory, postulate a radical separation of citizens grounded in their conflicting interests. . . . By contrast, feminist premises of connectedness remind us of the possibility of 'unitary democracy,' where mutual persuasion helps realize shared goals and interests" (1995, 122–123).

Similarly, popular democracy demands a redefinition of authority. Kathleen B. Jones argues that authority based on "norms of impartiality that treats others as 'just like us' masks a bias that is masculinized in its perspective and colonizing in its effects. . . . Subjects who are not like us, not like the judges, must either be domesticated or extradited." In feminist theory, "judgment requires moral reciprocity—taking the standpoint of the other or putting oneself imaginatively in the place of the other," which can lead to a "compassionate authority" more consistent with models of popular democracy (1996, 85–86).

Although little is said by any of these writers about the relationship of popular democracy to market ideology, they implicitly raise a profound and perhaps revolutionary challenge to its individualistic and competitive (feminists would say, "masculine") values and its concepts of human nature. If we need to learn new ways of relating to one another in political life, we must also be capable of learning them. This process implies a significant role for the educational system. Although a new system of education could not by itself create the society envisioned by the advocates of popular democracy, it obviously could not happen without one. Thus, the role and responsibility of the educational system is a critical issue in any discussion of the strengthening of democratic values. Whether we merely want to maintain the democratic processes we already have or radically expand them, educating for democracy must be on the political agenda and any program of education reform must take educating for democracy into consideration.

Of course, this is not a new idea. The educational philosophies of Jefferson and Mann all looked toward the schools as a means of protecting democracy and developing democratic citizens. Jefferson's proposals for a public education system in Virginia were explicitly founded on his belief that a common base of knowledge was necessary to give citizens the ability to utilize and protect their democratic rights. Mann went even further in seeking to build "a common value system which might undergird American republicanism and within which a healthy diversity might thrive. His quest was for a public philosophy, a sense of community which might be shared by Americans of every variety and persuasion. . . . And his tool was the common school" (Cremin 1957, 8).

The most radical formulation of such ideas came during the 1820s and 1830s, when proposals for the establishment of public schools were based on the ideas of Jacksonian liberal democracy: the schools were to make possible a society of limited government and complete equality of opportunity by the explicit teaching of democratic and egalitarian values. In this formulation, democracy and the market could indeed coexist, which may have made sense in the context of the economy at that time. As Rush Welter describes it:

> In these terms, public education had a twofold purpose. On the one hand, it would bring about urgent social reforms by alerting the victims of inequality to the machinations of the aristocracy and the misrepre-

> sentations of the politicians. On the other hand, it would also protect established democratic principles against political and social evils that had not yet materialized. It seemed, that is, a political engine of extra-ordinary promise, which would serve both radical and conservative democratic purposes, immediately and in the distant future. (1962, 48)

These popular democratic sentiments, originating to a great extent with the Workingmen's movements of the time, became quite prevalent in certain factions of the Democratic Party, most notably the so-called Locofocos, and were reflected in the educational policies of such governors as William Marcy of New York and Marcus Morton of Massachusetts. In the 1840s, such founders of the public school as Mann modified these ideas to accommodate a conservative constituency. By the end of the century, however, the concepts had been discarded almost entirely. As Welter puts it, "The idea of universal democratic education shaping our social and political institutions has been fragmented into separate and sometimes contradictory parts" (1962, 326). David K. Cohen refers to it as a "dissenting tradition" in school politics, emphasizing "power and dignity for teachers, equal treatment for students, and some role for schools in extending political democracy to economic affairs". "This tradition," says Cohen, "never fully developed. It still needs work" (1984, 260).

Even the progressive educators did not achieve that goal. As Westbrook notes, "Dewey himself, alas, had relatively little to say about the particulars of civic education, though most of what he had to say about 'democracy and education' is at least indirectly relevant" (1995, 138). Nonetheless, it was the progressive educators who made civic education an issue at the beginning of the twentieth century. Obviously, it would be insufficient simply to revive their ideas, but an understanding of their historic contribution and a reformulation of their views in contemporary terms is necessary. As one researcher put it after reviewing some of the old, obscure works of progressive educators, perhaps we must begin looking back to look forward (O'Connor 1995). As Kathe Jervis and Carol Montag point out, "The progressive education movement has remained largely ignorant of its real history. . . . Not knowing this history, we are unable to build realistically on the strengths and weaknesses of the past. This is part of the reason why it's hard for us to develop a tradition we can build on in a cumulative way, why we keep resurrecting progressive education from the grave instead of getting on with the vital work" (1991, ix). That work is increasingly being done and is referred to throughout this book. But there is a continued need to develop a pedagogy based on the principle that the maintenance and expansion of democratic citizen participation is a critical goal for the schools. I argue here that the dominance of market ideology in educational policy and politics is a major impediment to this goal and that a challenge to that dominance requires a different way of looking at the purposes of education.

Popular democracy, and an educational system consistent with it, is antithetical to market ideology. Market ideology's views on human nature and on the relation between individuals and society and its focus on economic rationality as the ultimate criterion for a desirable social system all lead away from popular democracy. What might be called a more holistic view of human behavior, on the other hand, provides a basis for considering democracy as a way of life. Indeed, if the assumptions of popular democracy make sense, no other system is more functional or desirable. This perspective begins with the assertion that men and women become fully developed as human beings only within the context of their relationships to others. Contrary to the assumptions of market ideology, there is no such thing as the "individual" considered separately from his or her social environment. There is also no definable "human nature" and no "inner" man or woman, so we cannot neatly distinguish between what is hereditary and what is environmental and we cannot designate certain types of behavior, such as self-interest or competitiveness, as inherent or instinctive. The character of individuals can neither be evaluated in isolation from the world around it nor considered by itself as an independent variable in shaping that world.

This perspective rejects a passive or reactive role for human beings in relation to their social systems. In other words, it is not a sufficient or ultimately satisfying role either to devote oneself exclusively to making consumer choices on a utilitarian basis within a market society or simply to criticize, deconstruct, or withdraw from an unjust social order. This view assumes that we are most fully human when we are consciously and collectively participating in directing the evolution of the social order and re-creating ourselves as we re-create our social environment.

A holistic perspective rejects both the dualism and the ideological limits of market ideology. There is no clear dividing line between human beings and the social order. Each is the product of interactions with the other; therefore, one cannot readily sort out what is individual and what is social. The process of social and individual growth and development is open-ended and interconnected. Thus, human behavior and the social order are not fixed, permanent entities. Although societies may strive toward certain goals on the basis of certain values, there can be no such thing as a final destination. There is only the process itself—and if that process involves universal access to participation on an equal basis, if it considers all points of view, and if its path is determined by free and open deliberation among all people, it can be called democracy, which is the most desirable form of human organization. From this perspective, the educational system needs to be organized to reinforce the modes of behavior and methods of thinking necessary to make constructive decisions as part of a community in a democratic society.

Dewey is, of course, the most prominent exponent of this point of view in relation to education. This statement must be made with some caution, however, since—as with most great thinkers—quotes from Dewey's "gospel" have been used and misused to defend all kinds of ideas. Moreover, although Dewey is considered a philosopher, the immense, theoretically complex body of work that he produced crossed all conventional disciplinary boundaries; therefore, any attempt to summarize his ideas runs the risk of oversimplification. Finally, Dewey fell considerably short in the actual application of his concepts as part of a political program to change the schools. Nonetheless, his writings provides the most comprehensive articulation of a holistic and democratic perspective and its connection to learning.

Dewey rejects individualism, asserting that human development occurs only in a social context. "My Pedagogic Creed," which he wrote in 1897, asserts that "all education proceeds by the participation of the individual in the social consciousness of the race" (1959, 19). That process has psychological and sociological aspects that cannot be isolated from each other. "The individual who is to be educated," says Dewey, "is a social individual and . . . society is an organic union of individuals. If we eliminate the social factor from the child, we are left only with an abstraction; if we eliminate the individual factor from society, we are left only with an inert and lifeless mass" (1959, 22).

Rejection of dualistic either-or thinking is also a dominant theme in Dewey's understanding of social life: "To talk about the priority of 'society' to the individual is to indulge in nonsensical metaphysics. . . . There is no problem in all history so artificial as that of how 'individuals' manage to form 'society'" (1957, 59). The concept of the individual in a state of nature is therefore a useless abstraction. We are human to the extent that we are involved and interact with one another:

> The very process of living together educates. It enlarges and enlightens experience; it stimulates and enriches imagination; it creates responsibility for accuracy and vividness of statement and thought. A man really living alone (alone mentally as well as physically) would have little or no occasion to reflect upon his past experience to extract its net meaning. . . . Social environment forms the mental and emotional disposition of behavior in individuals by engaging them in activities that arouse and strengthen certain impulses, that have certain purposes and entail certain consequences. (Dewey 1966, 6, 16)

Human behavior is therefore not merely a list of particular fixed character traits, and this presents a marked contrast to the theories of other educational philosophers. It is, for example, an ever-changing configuration of attitudes and habits far more complex than Plato's static concept of a human soul divided into three appetites. Dewey argues that even if Plato's three appetites existed, they "were not in truth projected from the breast of the natural individual into society, but they were cultivated in classes of individuals by force of social custom and expectation" (1957, 134). Plato "had no perception of the uniqueness of individuals. . . . There could be no recognition of the infinite diversity of active tendencies and combinations of tendencies of which an individual is capable" (1966, 90).

Also critical of Jacques Rousseau's naturalistic version of human development, Dewey rejects Rousseau's idea of nature as the ultimate teacher. Dewey agrees with him that "evil institutions and customs work almost automatically to give a wrong education . . . but the conclusion is not to provide an education apart from the [social] environment, but to provide an environment in which native powers will be put to better uses" (1966, 111–118).

If we cannot separate humans from society, neither can we separate humans from themselves. Dewey argues against all philosophical theories that conceive of mind and body as distinct entities, and he challenges educational theories that divide thought from action. "It would be impossible," according to Dewey, "to state adequately the evil results which have flowed from this dualism of mind and body, much less to exaggerate them" (1966, 141). Separating "action and soul," for example, has conservative and elitist political implications, because "the dualism enables [some] to do the thinking and planning, while others remain the docile, even if awkward, instruments of execution" (1957, 72). The separation of theory from method is also "connected with the notion of the isolation of mind and self from the world of things" and has a negative effect in that it "makes instruction and learning formal, mechanical, constrained" (1966, 179). Dewey takes the position that thinking and doing are interrelated and inseparable. Their ongoing mutual interaction is what constitutes learning. We apply our intelligence to our actions, change our ideas as a result of experience, and use what we have learned to improve our lives. If there is such a thing as human nature, it is an orientation toward change: "Conscious life," says Dewey, "is a continual beginning afresh" (1966, 360).

Dewey claims that people are creatures of habit, meaning that they have a socially conditioned predisposition to respond in a certain way to particular stimuli. Habits have their origins in the culture, not spontaneously within the individual. Thus, they are changeable by using "impulses"—random, individual behavioral acts—as "agencies of deviation, for giving new directions to old habits and changing their quality" (1957, 67). Therefore, education can guide habits in a more rational, constructive direction. Dewey applies the same kind of thinking to the way we organize our social institutions. If they are flawed, it is not because, as conservatives argue, "such institutions are rooted in an unalterable human nature. A truer psychology locates the difficulty elsewhere. It shows that the trouble lies in the inertness of established habit" (1957, 125). It is therefore desirable to eliminate that inertia through education, which can serve as a means of taking control of our destinies: "There is an alternative between anchoring a boat in the harbor till it becomes a rotting hulk and letting it loose to be the sport of every contrary gust. To discover and define this alternative is the business of mind, of observant, remembering, contriving disposition" (1957, 170).

The meaning of education is thus "an intelligent direction of native activities in the light of the possibilities and necessities of the social situation," so that "a future new society of changed purposes and desires may be created by a deliberate humane treatment of the impulses of youth" (Dewey 1957, 96). Beyond this, there can be no specific goals for education, since there are no universal truths or ultimate ends. Dewey is critical of what he calls "the philosophical fallacy," which is "the supposition that whatever is found true under certain conditions may forthwith be asserted universally without limits and conditions" (1957, 175).

This is not to say that values are either unimportant or all equally valid—quite the contrary, since Dewey believes in democracy. Rather, our moral standards evolve in relation to the way we live in society. "Morals," says Dewey, "is as much a matter of interaction of a person with his social environment as walking is an interaction of legs with a physical environment" (1957, 318). Moral values have no meaning as independent and objective standards outside the context of our experience. This idea also applies to any attempt to organize individual or social life around the accomplishment of a single, fixed goal. Sensible goals require constant reformulation in light of what happens to us as we try to achieve them. "Ends are, in fact, literally endless, forever coming into existence as new activities occasion new consequences" (1957, 232). The value of democracy is that it facilitates this process. All of the elements of this concept have consequences for how we think about methods and purposes of education. If Deweyan holistic assumptions about human consciousness and behavior make sense, then certain approaches to learning necessarily follow and only schools based on democratic values can practice them.

Dewey has much to say about learning theory, but Boyd Henry Bode, an all-but-forgotten figure in the history of educational philosophy, puts it much more clearly. Overshadowed by Dewey, his mentor and colleague, Bode's modest personal style and self-effacing professional demeanor caused him to be pushed into the background. Yet he was more than a mere disciple of Dewey's; he was an independent and original thinker and one of the most prominent leaders of the progressive education movement. Whereas Dewey's prose is often impenetrable and confusing, the development and expression of Bode's ideas is clearly organized in concise and accessible language. His insights into the connection between theory and practice, published in *Modern Educational Theories* (1927) and *How We Learn* (1940), are especially valuable examples. In particular, *How We Learn* is an excellent critique of specific educational approaches based on mind-substance theory, the opposite of the holistic perspective.

Bode shares Dewey's hostility toward dualism. The "assumption of the contrast between mind and matter," argues Bode, leads to "the doctrine that education is a process of inner development or self-development. As to the nature of this process there are conflicting views. Rousseauism, the classical tradition [humanism], and formal discipline [exercising mental skills] disagree widely among themselves, but they all stem from a common stock" (1940, 107). Behaviorism, he says, rejects "mind" and thus "rids us of dualism, but it does so at a price," by eliminating terms like "purpose," "aim," "ideal," and "insight," which he, as a progressive educator, considers indispensable (196). Moreover, "as a tool for scientific discovery, [behaviorism] has been invaluable. But as a transcript of 'cosmic reality,' it has proved to be thoroughly unreliable" (215).

Bode proposes, instead, a "pragmatic theory of mind." Citing Dewey's statement that mind is "the power to understand things in terms of the use made of them," he argues that

> the term "mind" is a name, not for a substance or a mental state, but for a function of the environment. . . . The term "experience" is a name for situations in which this function called mind is in some sense operative. The function of pointing or leading is nature's way of introducing foresight, purpose, intention into behavior. Materialism tries to explain behavior without reference to purpose. Dualism tries to explain behavior

> by importing purpose from some other realm and then trying to hitch it onto the body. Men have struggled for centuries to solve the problems that are thus created. The source of all the trouble lies in the basic assumptions. (1940, 225)

The rejection of dualism has definite consequences for learning. In the words of Bode, it is "neither a matter of developing faculties nor of forming apperceptive masses according to a fixed procedure. If we keep our eye on the fact that learning is a reconstruction of experience, which is a distinctive thing in the case of each individual experience, which is a distinctive thing in the case of each individual pupil, we avoid the danger of mechanizing the learning process. Learning as reconstruction combines thinking, skill, information, and appreciation in a single unitary process" (1940, 249). This view is remarkably prescient of the currently fashionable constructivist approach to education.

Bode's thinking leads to the idea of democracy as an educational goal, bringing us back to Dewey, who described education as "a process of renewal of the meanings of experience through a process of transmission." This concept is based on "the ideal of a continuous reconstruction or reorganizing of experience, of such a nature as to increase its recognized meaning or social content, and as to increase the capacity of individuals to act as directive guardians of this reorganization" (1966, 321–322).

What, then, is education for? "Since growth is the characteristic of life," says Dewey, "education is all one with growing; it has no end beyond itself. The criterion of the value of school education is the extent in which it creates a desire for continued growth and supplies means for making the desire effective in fact" (1966, 53). Perhaps no other statement by Dewey has been subject to more misinterpretation and misunderstanding. By separating the comment from its context, some of his disciples saw the purpose of education as growth of any kind and from any source. Dewey, on the contrary, makes it clear that he is talking about a certain kind of growth: a development of the intellectual skills and personal attitudes needed to build a democratic society. Humans must build an awareness of their connections to each other through "the free and equitable intercourse which springs from a variety of shared interests" (85). This should result in "change in social habit—its continuous readjustment through meeting the new situations produced by varied intercourse" (99). In effect, that is Dewey's definition of democracy:

> An undesirable society . . . is one which internally and externally sets up barriers to free intercourse and communication of experience. A society which makes provision for participation in its good of all its members on equal terms and which secures flexible readjustment of its institutions through interaction of the different forms of associated life is in so far democratic. Such a society must have a type of education which gives individuals a personal interest in social relationships and control, and the habits of mind which secure social changes without introducing disorder. (1966, 99)

This vision of a society as embarked on a path of endless change charted through deliberation among all its citizens is profoundly revolutionary in its implicit threat to all forms of established power. The process of education is therefore inextricably bound up with the expansion of democracy. In *Democracy as a Way of Life,* Bode puts this quite gracefully: "The idea of democracy . . . cannot be disposed of by dealing with it in a separate course and at some fixed point in the curriculum. . . . The meaning of democracy as a way of life must be developed progressively and inwoven with everything else, but without sacrifice of clarity. The school is, par excellence, the institution to which a democratic society is entitled to look for clarification of the meaning of democracy. In other words, the school is peculiarly the institution in which democracy becomes conscious of itself" (1937, 94–95).

In educational policy this approach leads us in the opposite direction from the one prescribed by market ideology. Market ideology dictates that the extent of government intervention to provide educational services must be determined on the basis of the needs of national security and the efficient operation of the market itself. The extent of public responsibility for financing public education must be based on economic rationality, which requires its calculation in relation to externalities. This concept has several significant implications for pedagogy. First of all, a proper curriculum is a utilitarian curriculum; it must be designed to serve certain practical and quantifiable ends, most especially economic productivity. Second, learning is primarily training; that is, the school is a place where young people are taught particular skills that will serve them in the future. Finally, efficiency becomes the primary criterion for educational management. All of these are directly challenged by a holistic-democratic perspective.

"To set up any end outside of education, as furnishing its goal and standard," says Dewey, "is to deprive the educational process of much of its meaning" (1959, 27). Education should not be for the purpose of getting ready for something else. Advocates of social efficiency in the schools provide an example of that kind of thinking. As Kliebard describes these people, they promoted "programs of study that prepared individuals specifically and directly for the role they would play as adult members of the social order. . . . Social utility became the supreme criterion against which the value of school studies was measured" (1987, 90). Beyond his philosophical objections, Dewey was highly critical of the inherent conservatism in the tradition of social efficiency: "There is . . . grave danger that in insisting upon this end, existing economic conditions and standards will be accepted as final. A democratic criterion requires us to develop capacity to the point of competency to choose and make its own career" (1966, 119).

According to Dewey, education should not become an "unfolding of latent powers toward a definite goal." It cannot and should not train students in the formal discipline of using particular mental faculties. Along those lines, he criticizes John Locke's theory of education for "its separation of activities and capacities from subject matter" (65). Similarly, utilitarian approaches to schooling are "tainted by the narrowness of its fundamental premise . . . that every individual acts only from regard for his own pleasures and pains" (300).

Dewey did not want schools to be "a place set apart in which to learn lessons" but a "genuine form of active community life . . . a miniature community, an embryonic society"(1943, 14, 18). This does not mean that schools should be either a replica of the existing social order or a utopia. It means they should be a place where "the experience gained by the child in a familiar, commonplace way is carried over and made use of . . . and what the child learns in the school is carried back and applied in everyday life, making the school an organic whole, instead of a composite of isolated parts.

The isolation of studies as well as of parts of the school system disappears" (1943, 91).

Dewey specifically rejects the customary reliance on a curriculum "where the chief influences in selecting subject matter of instruction are utilitarian ends narrowly conceived for the masses, and, for the higher education of the few, the traditions of a specialized cultivated class." Emphasis on the three R's, he said, "is based upon ignorance of the essentials needed for realization of democratic ideals" (1966, 192). This view does not advocate a return to nature as a teacher or a syllabus of courses in popular culture. Rather, it promotes a curriculum that inspires students to analyze, evaluate, and ultimately improve their social experience. The classroom becomes a place where students can connect their own immediate environment to the world at large, within the framework of conventional academic disciplines:

> Experience has its geographical aspect, its artistic and its literary, its scientific and its historical sides. All studies arise from aspects of the one earth and the one life lived upon it. We do not have a series of stratified earths, one of which is mathematical, another physical, another historical, and so on. We should not be able to live very long in any one taken by itself. We live in a world where all sides are bound together. All studies grow out of relations in the one great common world. . . . Relate the school to life, and all studies are of necessity correlated. (Dewey 1943, 91)

The point is to develop the possibilities for communication, cooperation, and deliberation on how to improve the social order. In that regard, the school should provide a model for democracy, and the experience of the students should serve as the organizing principle for the curriculum. Many identify these views with the radical education movement of the 1960s, and—based on a misinterpretation of his ideas—give Dewey the credit or blame for "free schools." Despite their best intentions, many teachers had a difficult time understanding and applying the concepts. A large contingent of educators affiliated with the Progressive Education Association, of which Dewey was honorary president, gave the ideas a child-centered interpretation, along the lines of Dewey's colleague and ally William Heard Kilpatrick.

Kilpatrick's views promote what he calls the project method of education. Learning, he argues, develops from a child's involvement in "wholehearted purposeful activity." Just as agriculture students were learning from home projects in planting and cultivating crops, the curriculum should be based on the child's choice of what would today be called hands-on experience. The school "must be a place where pupils are active, where pupil enterprises form the typical unit of learning procedure . . . a place of actual experiencing" (1927, 112–113). A new curriculum that used problem-solving projects as a basis would recast teachers as helpers and guides rather than instructors: "As teachers we must make ourselves progressively unnecessary" (123). The old system of education was obsolete, according to Kilpatrick. "Such words as learn, teach, study, subject-matter, curriculum, promotion, textbook, objectives, norms . . . generally imply the static outlook and so prejudice in advance any discussion in which they occur" (135).

This perspective gave an individualistic spin to Dewey's complex ideas about experience and education, which made them far more familiar and vulnerable to oversimplification. Thus, by the 1930s, many progressive schools had become individualistic parodies of Dewey's model, more akin to the ideas of Rousseau. "Experience" came to mean almost anything the child was interested in at any particular moment. "Growth" was interpreted as the outcome of unrestricted individual self-expression. Dewey's emphasis on impulse as a basis for changing behavior led many of his disciples to discard the traditional curriculum entirely, in favor of restricting the teacher's authority while the child followed his or her impulses. The project method, stripped of its intellectual context, became the daily routine. There was increasing accuracy to the stereotype of the progressive school as a haven for spoiled upper-middle-class children who were given free rein to learn or not as they chose.

Written in 1938, Dewey's *Experience and Education*, restates his educational ideas more carefully and concisely in an attempt to eliminate the confusion. Progressive education, he says, is more than just a rejection of traditional models; indeed, "it is more difficult to carry on than was ever the traditional system." (1963, 40). Not all experiences are equally educative. Growth needs to proceed in a fruitful direction. Unlimited freedom is no freedom at all. The guiding principle of democratic values provides the philosophical context for developing a curriculum based on community life. Experiences have to be continuous with one another in developing the social attitudes and skills that children need to participate in a democratic community. This is a purpose that requires the teacher to take an active role: "It is then the business of the educator to see in what direction an experience is heading. . . . The mature person, to put it in moral terms, has no right to withhold from the young on given occasions whatever capacity for sympathetic understanding his own experience has given him" (38). It is doubtful that either this thoughtful critique or a similar essay, Bode's *Progressive Education at the Crossroads,* first published in 1938, had much effect. By that time, the progressive education movement had already begun its decline. Thus, the ideas of the radical educators of the 1960s did have their roots in progressive education—but in the writings of Kilpatrick, not those of Dewey or Bode.

By the same token, Dewey's ideas about reconstructing experience and a rejection of ultimate goals have led such postmodernists as Richard Rorty to count Dewey among them, but the resemblance between Dewey's philosophy and that of the postmodernists is merely superficial (Westbrook 1991, 542). Dewey neither rejects comprehensive social theorizing nor accepts the idealist framework that characterizes postmodernism. He adheres strongly to participatory democratic values as a guide to the construction of a humane social order and as a way of life. He rejects fixed goals, unchanging moral standards, and rigid conceptions of the limits of human nature, not because they are metanarratives, which disguise power relationships, but because they are unnecessary obstacles to the achievement of democracy.

A democratic perspective on education asserts that the social nature of human beings demands that the full development of their intellect and abilities consist of a social process. That process involves an ongoing and unceasing exchange of ideas and experiences that is open-ended, accessible to all on an equal basis, and free of arbitrary restrictions. The schools are not the only possible arena for this kind of collective community effort, but certainly they are the most important—in Bode's words, they constitute the institution in which democracy becomes conscious of itself.

What does this look like in practice? And what difference does it make for young people? Even in a time of market model predominance, democratic classrooms and schools exist, however few and far between they may be. They cannot be described, however, in terms of how they apply a particular theory of learning or a specific set of teaching methods. Indeed, they do not follow an enumerated set of precepts, guidelines, or curriculum frameworks, as is the case with the application of most other educational doctrines. Rather, they are distinguished by adherence to an implicit set of social and personal values. A democratic perspective on the meaning of learning and the value of young people guides the daily operations of these schools and shapes the relationships within them.

Mike Rose, a progressive educator, writes about his nationwide visits to classrooms that embody what he sees as democratic educational principles: "What I began to see—and it took the accumulation of diverse classrooms to help me see it—was that these classrooms, in addition to whatever else we may understand about them, represented a dynamic, at times compromised and contested, strain in American educational history: a faith in the capacity of a people, a drive toward equality and opportunity, a belief in the intimate link between mass education and a free society" (1995, 412–413).

Rose describes the "experience of democracy" in these classrooms: "safety from insult and diminishment," respect for diversity, "multiple sources" for a teacher's authority—"knowledge, care, the construction of safe and respectful space, solidarity with students' background—rather than solely from age or role" (1995, 414). Although most of the classrooms were run in a relatively traditional manner, "in various ways, students contributed to the flow of events, shaped the direction of discussion, became authorities on their own experience and on the work they were doing. . . . These classrooms, then, were places of expectation and responsibility. Teachers took students seriously as intellectual and social beings. Young people had to work hard, think things through, come to terms with each other" (414–415). These schoolrooms taught values, not in the sense defined by the religious Right but rather, in the form of "a language that celebrates human worth and decries all that diminishes it" (432). This is not a kind of pedagogy that can be easily summarized in a list of rules.

George H. Wood—a founding member of the Institute for Democracy in Education, located at Ohio University—took a similar tour. He, too, sees democratic classrooms as allowing children "to play a part in creating their own environment, establishing their academic agenda, asking the important questions [to] maintain a sense of connection and compassion for children who often have too little of either" (1993, 38). Creating a sense of community is a major priority for democratic schools: "As long as kids are isolated and alienated, their struggle with the structures and limits of the institution dissipates energy that could have been used for learning and involvement" (117). "Classrooms of conviction and commitment," says Wood, do purposeful work, "designed with a real audience in mind (often one outside the school), and intended to make a difference." They set a goal of "having students make as many choices as possible." Classwork is "active, experiential, hands-on" "a norm of cooperation exists, and competitive, independent work takes the back seat" (153–161). Democratic citizenship is encouraged by schools that "tie learning together, pull in multiple perspectives on issues, [and] show young people how to ask the right questions and how to find out the needed information" (183). Wood continues:

> In these schools we see all students engaged in comprehensive exploration of curricular materials in ways that help them connect what they learn to who they are and to the world around them. They are learning how to use what they learn so that they can understand and make a difference in the world. They see themselves as useful and important people who have learned that they have something to contribute to their communities and families. They know that what they have learned came about through extended effort, in concert with others, on topics that mattered. They have gained, in short, the ability to learn for themselves and for us. (200)

The Highlander Folk School in Tennessee—organized and directed by Myles Horton from the 1930s until his death in 1990—was not a public school but a training center for social and political activists. Yet its philosophy has had a great deal of influence on democratic educators. Again, its core is not a set of commandments but a way of thinking about people:

> A long-range goal to me is a direction that grows out of loving people, and caring for people, and believing in people's capacity to govern themselves. . . . If you have that hope, when you work with people and try to help them learn—and not teach them, because that gets into techniques and gimmicks—and you believe in them, then you inspire them by your belief. You can't help people grow if you don't think they can, because you are going to find ways to help prevent them from growing. I think your belief in people's capabilities is tied in with your belief in a goal that involves people being free and being able to govern themselves. (Horton 1991, 227)

A democratic school is one that, above all, tries to enable people to create their own world collectively rather than fit into one that is created for them. It operates on the basis of a faith that people are capable of doing this—that is, capable of living together democratically. As such, people are valued for who and what they are, not just for what they can produce or return on a financial investment.

It is not possible to offer empirical or quantitative evidence that a democratic school system is somehow superior to one based on market models. Rather, it is a choice of values that leads in one direction or the other—after all, these are competing ideologies. Ultimately, it comes down to a question of what we think about our young people, what we believe are their capabilities and potentials, and what we would like them to be. If we see them as antisocial elements to be reined in and molded into productive members of a consumer society, the purpose of schooling becomes training in behavior and skills appropriate for a system over which they have no control, and one that they will be unable to change because they will not learn how to do so. Market models then make perfect sense. But if we believe that young people need to see themselves as part of something with a constructive and positive direction that requires their full participation, the purpose of schooling becomes learning how to share in making decisions for themselves and society. That is the essence of a democratic value system in education. If we choose the latter course, current policy directions require a sharp reversal. The next four chapters explain why and how.

References

Barber, Benjamin. 1984. *Strong Democracy*. Berkeley: University of California Press.

Bode, Boyd Henry. 1927. *Modern Educational Theories*. New York: Macmillan.

———. 1938. *Democracy as a Way of Life*. New York: Macmillan.

———. 1940. *How We Learn*. Boston: D.C. Heath.

Cohen, David K. 1984. "The American Common School: A Divided Vision." *Education and Urban Society*, 16: 251–261.

Cremin, Lawrence A. 1957. "Horace Mann's Legacy." In *The Republic and the School*, ed. Lawrence A. Cremin. New York: Teachers College Press.

DeLuca, Tom. 1995. *The Two Faces of Political Apathy*. Philadelphia: Temple University Press.

Dewey, John. 1943. *The School and Society*. Chicago: University of Chicago Press.

———. 1957. *Human Nature and Conduct*. New York: Modern Library.

———. 1959. *"My Pedagogic Creed."* In *Dewey on Education*, ed. Martin Dworkin. New York: Teachers College Press

———. 1963. *Experience and Education*. New York: Collier.

———. 1966. *Democracy and Education*. New York: Free Press.

Elshtain, Jean Bethke. 1995. *Democracy on Trial*. New York: Basic Books.

Greider, William. 1992. *Who Will Tell the People?* New York: Simon and Schuster.

Horton, Myles. 1991. *The Long Haul*. New York: Anchor.

Hudson, William. 1995. *American Democracy in Peril*. Chatham N.J.: Chatham House.

Jervis, Kathe, and Carol Montag, eds. 1991. *Progressive Education for the 1990's*. New York: Teachers College Press.

Jones, Kathleen B. 1996. "What Is Authority's Gender?" In *Revisioning the Political*, ed. Nancy J. Hirschmann and Christine DeStefano. Boulder, Colo.: Westview Press.

Kilpatrick, William Heard. 1927. *Education for a Changing Civilization*. New York: Macmillan.

Kliebard, Herbert. 1987. *The Struggle for the American Curriculum 1893–1958*. New York: Routledge and Kegan Paul.

Lappe, Frances Moore, and Paul Martin DuBois. 1994. *The Quickening of America*. San Francisco: Jossey-Bass.

Lasch, Christopher. 1995. *The Revolt of the Elites*. New York: Norton.

Mansbridge, Jane. 1996. "Reconstructing Democracy." In *Revisioning the Political*, ed. Nancy J. Hirschmann and Christine DiStefano. Boulder, Colo.: Westview Press.

O'Connor, Terry. 1995. "Looking Back to Look Forward." *Democracy and Education*, Summer.

Rose, Mike. 1995. *Possible Lives*. Boston: Houghton Mifflin.

Welter, Rush. 1962. *Popular Education and Democratic Thought in America*. New York: Columbia University Press.

Westbrook, Robert. 1991. *John Dewey and American Democracy*. Ithaca, N.Y.: Cornell University Press.

———. 1995. "Public Schooling and American Democracy." In *Democracy, Education, and the Schools*, ed. Roger Soder. San Francisco: Jossey-Bass.

Wood, George H. 1993. *Schools That Work*. New York: Plume.

4 School Choice

School choice is the ultimate application of market ideology to the educational system. Beginning in the 1960s as a pipe dream of such free-market conservatives as Milton Friedman, the program has become the most widely promoted example of education reform and has gained significant support across conventional conservative-liberal ideological lines. There are, of course, forms of school choice that do not necessarily conflict with a democratic educational system. As Jeffrey Henig points out, there are "other intellectual routes to choice that do not depend on the market metaphor" (1994, 14). But the strongest and most commonly articulated arguments for choice are firmly rooted in market ideology. The logic of the free market leads inevitably to school choice and, for the most part, the reverse is true as well.

School choice is a broad term encompassing a wide variety of programs. As John Witte defines it, "The most common programmatic element is that parents have a greater degree of choice in the selection of schools for their children" (1991, 12). The most limited approach to this system, and the one least connected to market ideology, restricts the menu of options to the public sector. Intradistrict choice programs involve only schools within a particular district and may be subject to controls aimed at such goals as racial balance. Innovative or specialized educational programs, given the freedom to develop without conventional bureaucratic constraints, can be offered as options within the jurisdiction of the public school district. Magnet schools are often part of such a system. Choice within the district can thus provide the administrative flexibility that allows for a greater measure of pedagogical creativity.

Market ideology begins to enter the picture with interdistrict programs, which allow open enrollment among all public school districts in a particular area or jurisdiction. To one extent or another, districts may be able to limit their own participation; however, state aid may follow the student to the school of his or her choice, making nonparticipation a risky option. Only Minnesota has a statewide program. But all of these plans share the characteristic of forcing public schools to compete with each other to attract students.

Public-private choice plans are even more consistent with market ideology. They involve direct or indirect use of public funds to finance privately owned and controlled educational services for the purpose of creating a market of educational commodities available to students and their families. Contracting out for a limited number of specialized educational services is the most common and the most modest of such plans. A more market-oriented program is tuition tax credits, such as those recently implemented by the federal government for higher education. School voucher systems that include private schools go much farther in that direction by redirecting educational funding through families rather than school districts and allowing parents to choose the schools their children will attend. Charter schools are public-private hybrids that operate under the provisions of a contract negotiated between their organizers and a state or local public authority. Privatization, the last stop on the way to a free-market educational system, is contracting out writ large. It involves the transfer of control of school instructional services to managers who are neither elected nor on the public payroll and who are paid with public funds under contract with a governmental body.

This chapter argues that market-oriented school choice programs—that is, all but most intradistrict programs restricted to the public sector—are inherently in conflict with a democratic educational system. First of all, they destroy the concept of public education as a community enterprise. However flawed the existing governance structure may be, at the very least it provides a basis for citizens to involve themselves in a common effort to education their children. School choice, on the contrary, pits families and schools against each other in a battle for survival of the fittest.

A second and directly related effect of school choice is erosion of the social cohesion and intergroup communication that sustains democratic values. If citizens do not understand each other's needs, are not aware of each other's perspectives, and cannot communicate or relate across social and economic divisions, the ongoing exchange of ideas and open dialogue that is critical for any kind of democracy is impossible to sustain. In Dewey's words, cited earlier, democracy must remove "barriers to free intercourse and communication of experience." School choice fortifies those barriers.

Finally, school choice throws civic education for democracy off the agenda. It is impossible to develop a democratic citizenry without an educational effort that is system-wide. Democrats cannot be created one at a time, each pursuing his or her own autonomy or self-interest, individually deciding whether or not to bother learning about democratic values. Educational consumers, acting as individuals, will not and cannot choose to organize their schools around common values. Civic education is what some economists might call a public good; school choice provides an example of market failure in its inability to provide it. The public school system has indeed been relatively unsuccessful in fulfilling the democratic dreams of some of its founders, but there is no other institution more capable of doing so. This fact does not imply that a uniform national curriculum is required or that diversity and innovation in school programs is not desirable; it means simply that a free market in education leads away from democratic values.

This point raises serious questions about all kinds of school choice programs, including those exclusively in the public sector and those—such as charter schools—supported by liberals as well as conservatives. Most of the discussion and controversy over choice has focused on school vouchers. This emphasis is somewhat misplaced, in view of the fact that vouchers are the most politically vulnerable of all such programs and the least likely to find a national constituency. The voucher concept is handicapped by its directness in proposing to abolish the public school system, by the complexity involved in its implementation on anything more than a local level, and by a lack of consensus among its advocates as to the involvement of the private sector and the specific allocation of funds. Much more practical and politically popular are what might be called the stealth weapons against a publicly owned, democratically controlled, and collectively financed school system: local means-tested public-private vouchers; interdistrict public school choice; and most important, privatization in the form of charter schools. These programs, which are the specific policy focus of this chapter, provide the examples needed to address the question of compatibility between market ideology and democracy in the schools.

Before exploring these matters, however, it is necessary to point out that most advocates of school choice consider democracy to be a nonissue and that most opponents have not adequately addressed the question of democracy. For the most part, the arguments do not concern such philosophical and pedagogical issues as the purpose of schools in a democratic society. Indeed, the criterion most frequently used by both advocates and opponents of market-oriented reforms is student achievement as measured by testing. The impact on such social goals as equal access to education and racial integration in the schools is often addressed, but few discussions in the literature speak to the effect of choice on the social fabric of democracy.

As indicated in Chapter 1, the most prominent spokespersons for school choice, such as Chubb and Moe (1990), are also the most explicitly antidemocratic. But, among advocates of choice, the most common approach toward the issue of democracy is no discussion of it at all. When supporters do bother to examine it, they either take the contradictory view that value uniformity can be achieved by individual choice in an educational free market or they denounce any attempt at a standardized curriculum as potentially totalitarian.

William Bennett provides an example of the first response. Unlike Chubb and Moe, he is very specific—indeed, adamant—about the need for schools to teach a specific value system. That necessity includes a level of social awareness and responsibility consistent with democratic citizenship:

> Thomas Jefferson listed the requirements for a sound education in the Report of the Commissioners for the University of Virginia. In this landmark statement on American education, Jefferson wrote of the importance of calculation and writing, and of reading, history, and geography. But he also emphasized the need "to instruct the mass of our citizens in these, their rights, interests, and duties, as men and citizens." Jefferson believed education should aim at the improvement of one's "morals" and "faculties." That has been the dominant view of the aims of American education for over two centuries. But a number of changes, most of them unsound, have diverted schools from these great pursuits. (1992, 56)

Bennett goes on to advocate that "our students should . . . know our nation's ideals and aspirations. We believe in liberty and equality, in limited government and the betterment of the human condition. These truths underlie our society, and though they may be self-evident, they are not spontaneously apprehended by the young" (1992, 62). It is the responsibility of the schools to teach these and other values, and Bennett cites approvingly the nineteenth-century common schools, which "weren't so reluctant to teach them" (57). Yet, in almost the same breath, he advocates the "key education reform" of "parental choice—full, unfettered choice over which schools their children will attend," accomplished through a voucher system and tuition tax credits (64). Since Bennett never addresses the question of how a shared set of moral values will be taught in a free-market school system, we are left to assume that he believes it could accomplish the same goals as the old common schools, which were most certainly not schools of choice. One might therefore infer that he believes no rational educational consumer would accept anything but a school that provides instruction in moral and civic values. At the same time, however, his major theme is the necessity of teaching those values, which are not accessible to "spontaneous apprehension." If this line of reasoning demonstrates anything at all, it is that with strong support from right-wing politicians and generous funding from ultraconservative think tanks, self-contradiction is not a serious obstacle to becoming a leading educational spokesperson.

Louis V. Gerstner, Jr., chairman and CEO of IBM, takes a similar position. He advocates the application of market principles to the nation's schools, largely on the basis of what he believes to be their potential for improving academic achievement. He asserts that "there must be some agreement on the basic purposes of education. . . . Most Americans believe that public education should prepare young people for three roles: citizens of a democracy, workers in a complex economy, and participants in the larger society." Thus, "our common curriculum should include the national goals enunciated in 1990 by President [George] Bush and the governors: English, geography, history, mathematics, science, a second language. It should also include the arts, physical education and health, and community service" (1995, 184). Unfortunately for that argument, Gerstner also takes the position that "goal-setting cannot be accomplished from the top down. While it is fine for the nation to set goals for its educational system, as President Bush and the nation's governors did in 1989, national goals cannot take the place of school-by-school goalsetting. . . . Only local communities and individual schools can decide exactly what and exactly how they want to teach children" (99). One might fairly argue that Gerstner cannot have it both ways, unless he assumes that what he calls the dynamism of the market will produce a national consensus. But, as in Bennett's case, contradictions and inconsistencies are easily overlooked or ignored if one is well-enough placed. In addition to being a CEO, Gerstner was the sponsor of a 1996 educational summit of state governors, supported and attended by President Clinton. IBM is also involved in financing a program known as Reinventing Education, which as of 1997 had committed $25 million to developing partnerships with school systems "that have abandoned business as usual and are radically restructuring their public school systems" (IBM 1997).

One possible resolution of this contradiction, of course, might be that these writers implicitly assume that the invisible hand of the market will generate a school system that promotes appropriate civic values. Lasch asserts that classical liberals "smuggle a certain amount of citizenship between the cracks of their free-market ideology. Friedman himself admits that a liberal society requires a 'minimum degree of literacy and knowledge,' along with, a 'widespread acceptance of some common set of values.' . . . [It] presupposes not just self-interest but enlightened self-interest" (1995, 94–95). Henig believes that many advocates of choice who are not committed to the market paradigm opportunistically and unwisely ally themselves with those who are (1994, 20). Ultimately, however, a contradiction between means and ends is not addressed by these proponents of market ideology in education.

Less inconsistent is the libertarian position taken by some advocates of choice that any attempt by the society to impose civic values through the schools is potentially totalitarian. Since we cannot know what kind of education is good for everyone, any attempt by government to impose a curriculum is necessarily a step forward on the road to serfdom. Stephen Arons (1997) calls for a constitutional amendment to guarantee school choice as a means of protecting individual freedom of conscience, which he sees as threatened by such programs as Goals 2000. John Coons and Stephen Sugarman base their argument for a voucher system on the educational goal of producing the "autonomous man": an individual "distinguished by an intellectual and moral independence. Allegiance to particular values and behavior is consistent with autonomy, but that allegiance must be the fruit of continually examined assent" (1978, 72). School choice as a method for producing such individuals "rests on the proposition that a curriculum and milieu sympathetic to the particular values preferred by the family may be especially conducive to that goal" (77). James Rinehart and David Lee believe that "if we want to isolate at least one of the causes of our dissatisfaction with public education, we need look no further than our basic human trait of operating in our own self-interest" (1991, 50). Choice, they argue, would be more compatible with that trait; thus, "ultimately each person must choose what and how to learn" (64). If autonomy is the goal and self-interest is the motivator, it follows that any attempt to impose common social goals on the schools is undesirable or utopian. Myron Lieberman attacks the idea that public schools should produce more democratic and egalitarian results. Citing an article by John R. Lott Jr., he states that "higher levels of totalitarianism are associated with increased expenditures for [public] schooling," since it can be used as a form of indoctrination. He approvingly quotes Lott's argument that "these results strongly challenge the presumed public goods relationship between schooling and democracy" (1993, 153).

Somewhat more sophisticated theoretical arguments are presented by Jerome Hanus, who specifically targets advocates of a school system oriented toward "strong democracy." "This scenario," he argues, "requires general agreement on particular values that may in fact be disputed by a substantial number of groups." To Hanus, all of this smacks of "authoritarianism," especially "if one notes its close relationship to the eighteenth-century political theorist Jean-Jacques Rousseau's vision of participatory democracy" (1996, 22). James Tooley, defending the role of markets in the educational system, attacks the idea of using the schools to improve democracy on the basis of public and social choice theory as "either logically impossible . . . or politically unlikely" (1995, 32).

It is not easy to find a common thread in these arguments. Perhaps one could give the writers the benefit of the doubt and infer that they believe there is no reason that a school system organized around the principles of the free market cannot promote democratic civic values. Whatever their criticisms of government control of schools and their curricula, these people are obviously partial to liberal democracy (if not the strong variety) as a political system, and it can be assumed that they would certainly not support a school system that weakened it. It is, however, probably more accurate to state that the more intellectually consistent advocates of choice see democratic control of the schools as an inconvenient obstruction to educational improvement and schooling for democracy as an intolerable intrusion on individual liberty. In other words, they take a position ideologically consistent with that of Chubb and Moe.

Unfortunately, opponents of school choice often choose to do battle on the turf of the program's advocates. More specifically, as Kahne points out, "discussion by mainstream analysts regarding choice have been conducted almost exclusively within utilitarian and rights frameworks. When analyzing choice proposals, both critics and choice advocates focus on the same three goals: equity, efficiency, and excellence." This is done at the expense of ignoring questions related to democratic public schools: "What is a likely impact of school choice on the formation of democratic communities? Will school choice initiatives lead educators to develop more schools that are attentive to humanistic concerns? . . . During discussions of school choice policy, many issues that matter to democratic communitarians fail to receive systematic attention" (1996, 99–100). In his description of how democratic communitarians might "reorient discussion of school choice proposals," Kahne is somewhat hard-pressed to find specific examples: "Does school choice threaten democracy? Although the term 'democracy' appears frequently in discussions of school choice, the connections between choice and democracy rarely are given systematic attention by policy analysts. Fortunately, some extensive analyses that highlight these issues have been completed. Generally speaking, however, critics do not respond to Chubb and Moe's assertion that 'there is nothing in the concept of democracy to require that schools be subject to direct [public] control'" (1996, 101). Kahne cites Henig's (1994) *Rethinking School Choice* as one of the "extensive analyses"; another is by Amy Wells (1993b), who offers a theoretical analysis of the relationship of school choice to a number of educational philosophies and purposes.

Notwithstanding Kahne's citation, Henig's comprehensive and thoughtful critique of school choice is based largely on the issue of vouchers and focuses primarily on its effect on academic achievement and the problems of implementation. Although Henig cites as "ultimately most important" the risk that the market rationale for school choice "will undermine the social and political institutions that are prerequisites to achieving genuine reform," he spends little time discussing that risk. He understands that "the economic view of interests defines as out of its range some issues central to the sustenance of democracy," but he concludes that highly regulated and controlled choice can be used "as a tool . . . not a solution" (1994, 193, 201, 203). A similar approach is used in a critical study by the Economic Policy Institute (Rasell and Rothstein 1993), which bases its arguments almost exclusively on the impact of choice on student achievement and focuses primarily on the empirical evidence provided by Chubb and Moe (1990).

To some extent, a focus on achievement makes political sense; after all, that appears to be the concern of most families with schoolchildren. But that perspective sidesteps the fundamental issues of democratic values and brings the debate back to Kahne's "equity, efficiency, and excellence." The vagueness of these terms and the limited amount of reliable evidence linking them to choice make the debate inconclusive. This situation tends to favor the advocates of choice for a number of reasons. Focusing on achievement places opponents of choice in the uncomfortable position of defending the status quo. Furthermore, if choice is simply one of a number of equally legitimate methods to achieve a common educational goal, the debate tends to become narrowly technical and empirical, and the side with the best numbers—rather than the best educational values—wins. Moreover, it is on the subject of educational values that opponents of choice potentially occupy the strongest ground; when they yield it, they lose the contest. Thus, rather than compare Iowa Test scores or analyze bell curves, the focus ought to be on the societal impact of choice. This perspective puts market ideology at a distinct disadvantage, because the track record of school choice experiments demonstrates its destructive effects.

The specific examples require careful selection. As stated earlier, there have been no large-scale experiments with school vouchers. Outright privatization of entire public school systems has been attempted only rarely, most notably in Baltimore, Maryland; Hartford, Connecticut; and Chelsea, Massachusetts. The first two efforts were terminated as a result of financial disputes between the local school boards and the contractors; the third—in which Boston University took charge of the school system—continues, but there is no consensus on the results. Privatization, as pointed out in Chapter 1, has the possibility of a golden future, but it is still in its infancy.

On the other hand, the choice programs that show the greatest potential for expansion in the short run are local means-tested vouchers, interdistrict choice, and charter schools. These plans embody the basic principles of market ideology, have support from liberals as well as conservatives, and have been implemented in a significant and diverse number of locations. They also provide the infrastructure for the ultimate privatization of the public schools. They therefore present useful case studies of the effect of the social aspects of school choice and the most dramatic illustrations of the antidemocratic effects of market-based education reform. Essentially, what these experiments show is that the theory and practice of the free market diverge in education in much the same way as they do in the economic system. The real world of school choice is substantially different from the fantasy promoted by market ideology, and that world is profoundly undemocratic.

In recent years, conservatives have perfected the technique of borrowing from liberals and the Left egalitarian euphemisms or catchwords to describe their programs. Thus, for example, the repeal of affirmative action laws becomes "civil rights legislation," the privatization of public housing becomes "empowering tenants," and depriving single mothers of welfare benefits is "encouraging personal responsibility." As Joseph Viteritti describes it, "A new model of choice has begun to emerge in state legislatures and in Congress. One might call it the 'equal opportunity model.' Its goal is to give children who could not otherwise afford it the chance to attend a high-quality private or parochial school." This, he argues, is "stacking the deck for the poor," unlike public school choice programs, which favor those "who are most articulate, most informed, and least in need of improving their lot" (1996, 10–11). He is referring specifically to the Milwaukee Parental Choice Program, begun in 1990 as the first means-tested private school voucher program in the United States, providing a state voucher of three thousand dollars to low-income students for the purpose of attending nonsectarian private schools. In 1999, Florida instituted a statewide voucher program for students at public schools that received failing grades on statewide tests. These students would be eligible for vouchers worth up to four thousand dollars to attend the private schools of their choice. Diane Ravitch, a noted educational historian and activist, describes this as the ultimate democratic approach to educational policy. Citing a speech by Secretary of Education Richard Riley entitled the "State of American Education," Ravitch notes his reference to some schools that "should never be called schools at all": "Who attends these schools? African-American and Hispanic children, probably; children from very poor families, probably. . . . Somebody's children go to those schools. Not mine. Not Secretary Riley's, not President Clinton's or Vice President [Al] Gore's. . . . During the course of his speech, Riley invoked John Dewey: 'What the best and wisest parent wants for his [and, may I say her] child, that must be [what] the community wants for all of its children. Any other ideal for our schools . . . destroys our democracy'" (1994, 5–6).

In that spirit, says Ravitch, the answer is "means-tested scholarships [that is, vouchers] to needy families, who may use them to send their children to the school of their choice." This strategy will have the effect of expanding the market, since "if the scholarships are generous enough, many schools will welcome scholarship students, and new schools will open to supply the demand for good education" (1994, 4).

Ravitch's cynical attempt to put a democratic and egalitarian veneer on school vouchers is part of a political strategy described by Terry Moe: "In the new politics of education, the conservatives have become the progressives, pushing for major change, promoting the causes of the disadvantaged, and allying themselves with the poor" (quoted in Molnar et al. 1996, 242) Molnar and colleagues cite this as an example of how "neoconservatives have very effectively blunted charges from liberals, moderates, and even more traditional conservatives that their real purpose is to construct a market-based system that will inevitably harm poor families the most" (1996, 242). That, however, is exactly the effect of means-tested vouchers, notwithstanding pretensions of equal opportunity and Deweyan democratic values. This is because resources for making choices in a free market are never equally distributed. In economic life, of course, those resources are monetary. In making educational decisions the resource is information, which is not available to all on an equal basis. School choice, whether it is universal or means-tested, and no matter how it is implemented, inevitably favors those with the time, education, experience, and assertiveness to make that selection properly.

This fact is borne out in almost every study examining how parents make educational choices when they are available:

> Parents and students rarely seek out the best or most competitive school in a systematic and well-informed fashion. Rather, several factors, including expectations, racial attitudes, sense of efficacy, and alienation and isolation from the larger society, affect the amount of information parents and students have access to and the kinds of decisions they make. . . . [These factors] are strongly influenced by the social and cultural context of the choosers. Thus, I argue that competition between schools for students . . . will quite possibly lead to greater racial and social-class segregation and stratification. (Wells 1993a, 30)

In a study of intradistrict choice in Fort Collins, Colorado, Sally Bomotti concludes that parents who participated appeared to be more highly educated or have higher incomes than nonchoosing parents:

> Is this entirely healthy for public education? . . . The answer is no. Although the parents who choose alternative schools for their children are making their decisions for the right reasons, the fact remains that the reasons are often right for a limited segment of the school population only.

> Teachers in the neighborhood schools voiced their concern that the alternative schools skim off the most involved parents and the most motivated students. . . . The tendency of two of the local alternative schools to become more "exclusive" schools also breeds suspicion about parental motives: "It's a socioeconomic thing," a neighborhood teacher said. "The alternative parents don't want their kids to go to school with kids from the trailer park." (1996, 31–32)

In Boston, which has a controlled intradistrict choice program, parents use informal networks to collect information about schools. According to the January 15, 1996, *Boston Globe,* although the School Department distributes "report cards" on the schools through its parent information centers, "the best source of data remains [the parents'] own grapevine." Those who do not have the appropriately informed social network are therefore at a disadvantage. Having reviewed the available research on parental choice, Rodney T. Ogawa and Jo Sargent Dutton conclude that it does not generally support the assumption that parents will make informed choices: "Research suggests that not all parents choose to make a choice. Better-educated parents, especially mothers, seem most likely to make choices about where to send their children to school" (1994, 282).

Such distinctions between those who choose and those who do not choose occur both among and within socioeconomic classes. According to Bruce Fuller, it is not surprising that better-educated parents participate more frequently in choice programs: "What's notable," he adds, "is that this self-selection and sorting, based on social class and family practices, occurs even among low-income and working class families" (1996, 37). In San Antonio, Texas, Valerie Martinez and colleagues (1995) found that among a low-income Latino population, participants were on a higher level in terms of mother's education, parental involvement, and educational expectations. In Milwaukee, Wisconsin, John Witte and Christopher Thorn (1996) found that participants in the Chapter 220 program of interdistrict public school choice came from families with higher socioeconomic status, and parents of low-income participants in the means-tested Parental Choice voucher program tended to have better educations and higher expectations than average public school parents.

From the perspective of market ideology, this result is both justifiable and predictable. The whole point of school choice is to provide more opportunity to those with greater motivation and facilitate upward mobility for that part of the lower class that is willing to work for it. A more critical point of view would evoke the conclusion that the social and economic odds against minority and working-class families often frustrate such efforts and that any program rewarding the "survivors" is inherently inequitable. If so, school choice arbitrarily punishes those schoolchildren who, by no fault of their own, lack the needed parental involvement and support. Whatever the case, Ravitch's pretensions of promoting Deweyan principles by supporting school vouchers are false and ultimately hypocritical. As Molnar and colleagues conclude, "The strategy of neoconservative advocates of private and religious school choice appears to be to exploit the dissatisfaction of poor, predominantly minority parents who have been left behind by our economy in order to achieve the goal of creating a publicly funded private school system free of public control and oversight" (1996, 243).

The unreality of market assumptions, and their fundamentally undemocratic effects, is also illustrated by the financial impact of public school interdistrict choice programs. They allow students to enroll in public schools of their choice outside their home district; all or some of the state funding follows the student to the school chosen. Minnesota is the pioneer in such programs, having implemented a statewide open enrollment system in 1990. Several states have followed suit—including Massachusetts in 1993, as part of its comprehensive education reform legislation, which allows local school boards to determine whether they will admit students from other districts.

As in the cases mentioned above, there is a class bias in participation in the Massachusetts program. A study by the conservative pro-choice Pioneer Institute concludes that "the families who take advantage of the program are overwhelmingly white and affluent. . . . Moreover, they tended to choose to move their children to wealthier districts" (Viadero 1997, 12). But the social and educational impact of interdistrict choice goes beyond this phenomenon, and the case of Massachusetts provides a particularly interesting illustration of the damaging effects of the market competition model when applied to the public schools.

As in almost every other state, school financing in Massachusetts relies largely on the local property tax, and, as a consequence, higher-income towns have more resources for their schools. This fact holds true despite the 1993 reform law, which set a state-funded foundation under local school per-pupil spending. The state now specifies the minimum amount each town or city must budget for the schools and adds the amount of state aid necessary to reach that level. Localities are free to spend more, but a tax limitation law known as Proposition 2½, passed by popular initiative in 1980, severely restricts their revenue-raising capabilities. If they want to increase funding for the schools, Massachusetts towns and cities are thus forced to reduce other departments' budgets or take the politically risky and difficult path of seeking an override—a public referendum allowing the local government to exceed the tax limits. In short, there is tight state control, heavy dependence on state aid in lower-income communities, and almost no local leeway to raise new revenues in the Massachusetts school finance system.

The competitive market in education set up by the interdistrict choice system thus severely penalizes urban and low-income rural schools. As students leave for better schools in neighboring towns, 75% of the state aid goes with them. Given the limits of Proposition 2½, towns and cities are unable to raise the funds to replace the state aid. This process results in a downward spiral, as poor systems get poorer and rich systems get richer; the competition becomes more uneven, and the downward spiral of the low-income schools accelerates. Springfield, Massachusetts, for example, is a city with a population of 150,000, a declining economy, a significant number of low-income and minority people, and the usual array of problems affecting urban centers. Like most such cities, it borders on several middle- and upper-middle-class suburbs. The April 16, 1997, Springfield *Union-News* reported that in 1996–97 Springfield had a net loss of 216 students and almost $1 million in state aid; Longmeadow, its affluent neighbor, gained 98 students and $419,000 in state aid; the nearby rural working-class community of Ware lost 63 students and $200,000 in state aid; and the neighboring but wealthier Quabbin school district had a net gain of 89 students and $250,000.

Communities like Springfield and Ware are thus caught in a trap. They are unable to compete without improving their schools, and they are unable to make the improvements because the money is leaving the system and— because of Proposition 2½—it cannot be replaced. Similar situations exist in other states with interdistrict choice systems, even without tax limitation laws. In Ohio, researchers found that "One of the major effects of Ohio's interdistrict open enrollment policy was to move state funds away from school districts that served relatively larger percentages of poor and minority children . . . . The most vulnerable districts under such choice policies may be small and medium sized city districts that have higher percentages of poor and minority children than their neighbors" (Fowler 1996, 24).

Analyzing the Minnesota program, Janie Funkhouser and Kelly Colopy (1994) reached mixed findings regarding the validity of supply and demand theory of educational choice. There was no uniform pattern of positive response by administrators in terms of school improvement, and in some districts, open enrollment forced actions such as staff layoffs and the cancellation of programs or services. Thus the attempt to establish a free market in education through interdistrict choice plans has a profoundly inegalitarian effect. The programs do not even live up to the pretensions of market theory and, given this impact, are inconsistent with democratic public schools.

But a far more significant and complex example of the inconsistency of market ideology and democracy is provided by charter schools. More or less unheard of before 1990, they have since multiplied across the country and attracted a diverse constituency of conservatives, minority group activists, and middle-class liberals. A charter school is "an autonomous educational entity operating under a charter, or contract, that has been negotiated between the organizers, who create and operate the school, and a sponsor, who oversees the provisions of the charter. Organizers may be teachers, parents, or others from the public or private sector; and sponsors may be local school boards, state education boards, or some other public authority" (Mulholland and Bierlein 1995, 7–8).

The schools are eligible for state and local funding, as well as federal grants, usually based on the number of students in attendance. In general, there are three types of charters: specialized spinoffs established by and under the control of local public school systems; those organized by teachers, parents, or community members; and independent schools developed by private entrepreneurs (Bastian 1996). Category two and especially category three break the ground for privatization.

In 1991, Minnesota became the first state to authorize charter schools; in 1996 twenty states had charter school legislation on the books. Only about half of these states, however, have what advocates call strong charter laws, which allow sponsors other than local school boards, open applications to any potential organizer, automatically exempt charter schools from state and local regulations, permit financial and legal autonomy from the school district, and set no limits on the number of schools. At present, Arizona, Michigan, Delaware, New Hampshire, Massachusetts, Minnesota, Texas, California, and Minnesota come closest to this model and therefore provide the greatest opportunity for the expansion of privatized charter schools. As Peter Applebome reported in his September 4, 1996, *New York Times* article entitled "New Choices for Parents Are Starting to Change U.S. Education Landscape":

> Charter schools have gone in the space of a few years from an exotic sidelight to a concept ardently endorsed by both Democrats and Republicans as well as by critics and proponents of school vouchers. The 269 charter schools enrolling 70,000 students last year figure to grow to at least 350 this year, with many more sure to follow. . . . In fact, to conservatives like [Chester] Finn [a fellow at the Hudson Institute and coauthor of its recent study of charter schools], what is happening is the beginning stages of a historic reinvention of American education, with market-oriented, innovative schools replacing the current model. . . . "The lack of school choice is the Berlin Wall of domestic social policy," said Lamar Alexander . . . "and it's all going to come down."

Indeed, if privatization has a future, charter schools are the form it most likely will take. Although perhaps lacking at this time a solid national constituency and the financial resources available to private contractors, charter schools also lack the political and public relations disadvantages of voucher programs. Unlike vouchers, charter schools hold a potential appeal for all sides of the political spectrum. In *Selling Out Our Schools,* a collection of articles otherwise critical of choice and voucher plans from a progressive perspective, a number of authors support (however cautiously) the idea of charter schools. Eric Rofes, for example, states, "It should surprise no one that educators committed to progressive values are drawn to charter school efforts" (1996, 51). Furthermore, to the extent that charter schools are voluntary, community-based institutions, they are not subject to the charge of profiteering, as might be the case with private educational contractors, such as EAI or the Edison Project. A lengthy article in *Rethinking Schools,* an activist publication, whose mission statement describes it as focusing on "equity and social justice" in education, features a highly positive approach to the idea of charter schools (Nathan 1996–97).

In fact, however, "charter schools are as much small businesses as they are educational institutions. . . . Finance, marketing, accounting, procurement, personnel management, complex logistical planning, and compliance with sundry local and state rules can cripple a school with an outstanding curriculum and terrific teaching staff" (Finn, Bierlein and Manno 1996, 20). This is especially true of charters that are not spinoffs. Joe Nathan is enthusiastic about "the entrepreneurial spirit in education" created by charter schools, comparing their establishment to the efforts of Henry Ford and to Steve Wozniak and Steve Jobs of Apple Computers (1996, 17). This attempt to link charter schools to the U.S. mythology of mom-and-pop free enterprise is disingenuous, since for-profit chains have already entered the picture. The Sabis International Schools in Springfield, Massachusetts, are an example: "Sabis's Springfield school was not created from the efforts of dissatisfied parents. It was a pure business deal struck after passage of the 1993 [Massachusetts education reform] law. Sabis, with fifteen schools in the Middle East, England and Europe, has ambitions to start a chain of charter schools in America. With its cookie-cutter curriculum and packaged testing system, Sabis can profitably surf the back-to-basics reform movement and bask in public subsidies" (Vine 1997, 16).

As with any entrepreneur in a competitive market of small-scale producers, charter schools must therefore seek financial survival by targeting a particular market—more specifically, by finding a niche in the education market that other providers are not prepared to satisfy. In that sense, these schools are in much the same position as media executives in the environment of cable television. If the public schools are, shall we say, the NBC television network, the charter schools must emulate the Family Channel. A successful privately organized charter school must appeal to a particular class of consumers who cannot find the product they want in the regular public schools. Whereas conventional public schools must offer a general education to all comers and, at least in theory, be accountable to their communities as a whole, charter schools need satisfy the educational demands of only the particular group of families that they are trying to serve. Most charter schools cannot survive simply by offering an improved version of a generic education; they must offer something different from what the public schools attempt to provide. By necessity, then, successful charter schools must be highly specialized and maintain a close organizational relationship to those groups and institutions that share their particular purpose: "Only teachers who share a school's particular approach are hired—meaning that 100 percent of the staff really wants to do what the school says it will do—and only parents who want that approach enroll their children" (Finn, Bierlein, and Manno 1996a, 18–19). These are not public schools; they are special interest group schools.

Charter schools thus intensify and profit from market segmentation within education. Public schools have often been charged with promoting race, class, and gender inequality as a result of local control, an inequitable school financing system, and academic tracking. Charter schools exacerbate this fragmentation by physically dividing children into even smaller groups in separate schools based on family affinity for a particular philosophy, style of education, or socioeconomic base.

Many charter schools attempt to salvage dropouts by removing them from the public schools and creating special programs. Whatever the positive educational benefits might be, the result—contrary to the assertions of advocates of choice—often reinforces racial and ethnic separation. Jingletown Middle School in Oakland, California, was started by Latino parents who were unhappy with the violent atmosphere of the local public schools. With corporate support for start-up costs, they required students to wear uniforms and set up a bilingual and bicultural educational program aimed especially at Spanish-speaking students (Diamond 1994). The proposed Benjamin Bannekker School in Cambridge, Massachusetts, whose public school system emphasizes diversity, has created considerable controversy with its intention to recruit African-American students exclusively. Leah Pisano describes Edutrain, in Los Angeles, as "home to 600 Hispanic and black students, nearly all of whom are gang members. All of its male students have been arrested at least once, and all of its female students have at least one child" (1994, 64). Ultimately, Edutrain was closed because of financial irregularities.

Early in the twentieth century, a successful battle was waged by educators to prevent the establishment of a national network of separate public vocational schools (Kliebard 1987, chap. 5). Charter schools are proceeding in the opposite direction. The San Carlos Elementary District Charter School is "based in the business community," and will include "joint ventures with community businesses. Plans include housing a student-run branch of the local bank in the school" (Diamond 1994, 44). The Henry Ford Academy of Manufacturing Arts and Sciences, in Dearborn, Michigan, "will offer a curriculum based on technology and industry. The Ford Motor Company will provide money to build the school on the grounds of the Henry Ford Museum . . . and will provide instructional money when the school opens" (Coles 1996, 8). Skills for Tomorrow in Rockford, Minnesota, is a vocational and technical school supported by the Teamsters Union and the Minnesota Business Partnership, which "emphasizes applied learning through internships" (Bierlein and Mulholland 1994, 37).

Academic tracking has been much criticized for its class bias in separating students into curricular groupings that may well reflect family background rather than academic ability. Charter schools have provided the opportunity for public funding of schools for the gifted, such as the Stargate School in Eastlake, Colorado, which offers programs that are "interdisciplinary, flexible, individualized, [and] competency-based. Each student has a personal learning plan." The purpose is to serve gifted students, who "frequently are at-risk from under-service in their conventional setting" (Colorado Deptarment of Education 1996, 3). At the other end of the spectrum, there are plans for the Boston University Charter School, which will be "a residential school for homeless youth and wards of the state [that] will draw its staff from a downsizing military" (Harrington-Lueker 1994, 26).

Ultimately, the charter system presents the possibility of abolishing schools by providing the services needed to organize home schooling. The Noah Webster Academy in Michigan is "an electronic education network linking instructors and students by computer and modem." Its director, however, has run into church-state legal problems by approaching parents at Christian home-schooling conferences promising them they will be able to teach creationism (Harrington-Lueker 1994, 22). The New Country School in LeSeuer, Minnesota, "has no employees as such. . . . It relies on EdVisions Cooperative, a contract group of teachers and others. . . . Each of its 85 middle- and high-school students is working at his or her own pace to complete more than two thousand competencies" (Finn, Bierlein, and Manno 1996b, 14).

There are no comprehensive studies of the socioeconomic and racial composition of charter school student bodies. Advocates of charter schools, such as Nathan (1996), take great pains to emphasize their heterogeneity and diversity. But it appears is that charter schools draw primarily from the bottom and the top—recruiting students who have been unsuccessful in the public schools and students from upper-middle-class families who are more motivated as a result of direct and intense family involvement in their schooling. Of course, the two groups will never be found in the same charter school together.

The issue here is not whether these schools are academically beneficial to their students, or whether individualized programs have merit, or even whether voluntary class, racial, and ethnic separation is desirable in and of itself. Rather, the question is whether an education that promotes democratic values and civic responsibility is consistent with choice. The social fragmentation reinforced by charter schools in pursuit of a niche in the educational market would indicate that the answer is no.

As asserted earlier, democratic citizens are made, not born. Even the most limited form of liberal democracy cannot sustain itself without the necessary democratic civic values. At a minimum, this objective requires a certain amount of formal education for all children in a common setting and based on a standard curriculum that promotes those values. It can be argued that it might also necessitate at least some of what Dewey advocated: growth through unrestricted interaction among children of all backgrounds, a constant reevaluation and reconstruction of personal experience in relation to the broader community; and avoidance of a utilitarian curriculum with fixed goals. Certainly any attempt to expand democratic participation would require all of this and more.

By virtue of their need to survive market competition, charter schools must restrict themselves to specific, targeted groups of educational consumers; thus, they cannot provide a common setting for group interaction. Rather than encourage children and their families to accept challenges to their life experience and personal values and be prepared to challenge others in democratic debate, privatized schools must avoid these issues at all cost to avoid disrupting their own niche in the educational market. Moreover, the sales strategy of privatized schools cannot offer anything but promises of occupational advancement and specific, measurable educational goals, however differently those promises might be phrased for different markets. Realistically, no charter school can survive in the competition for public funding by hoping to attract parents with a pledge that their children will become civic-minded democratic citizens. Like many other socially valuable goals, it is an essential one but not an especially profitable one to produce in a market economy. It is precisely the absence of market competition that makes such a pledge possible for a public school.

The various school choice policies now being implemented indicate that market ideology is destructive of democratic values. Chubb and Moe's assertion is therefore correct: the policy choice in education must be between the market and democracy, and if we opt for the latter, we must reject those forms of school choice that strengthen the former.

References

Arons, Stephen. 1997. *Short Route to Chaos*. Amherst: University of Massachusetts Press.

Bastian, Ann. 1996. "Charter Schools: Potentials and Pitfalls." In *Selling Out Our Schools,* ed. Robert Lowe and Barbara Miner. Milwaukee: Rethinking Schools.

Bennett, William. 1992. *The De-Valuing of America.* New York: Summit.

Bierlein, Louann, and Lori Mulholland. 1994. "The Promise of Charter Schools." *Educational Leadership,* September.

Bomotti, Sally. 1996. "Why Do Parents Choose Alternative Schools?" *Educational Leadership,* October.

Chubb, John, and Terry Moe. 1990. *Politics, Markets, and America's Schools.* Washington, DC: Brookings.

Coles, Adrienne. 1996. "Partnership Revs Up to Open Michigan Charter School." *Education Week,* 8 May.

Colorado Department of Education. 1996. *Charter Schools.* Denver.

Coons, John, and Stephen Sugarman. 1978. *Education by Choice.* Berkeley: University of California Press.

Diamond, Linda. 1994. "A Progress Report on California's Charter Schools." *Educational Leadership,* September.

Finn, Chester Jr., Louann Bierlein, and Bruno Manno. 1996a. "Finding the Right Fit." *Brookings Review,* September.

———.1996b. *Charter Schools in Action: What Have We Learned?* Indianapolis: Hudson Institute.

Fowler, Frances C. 1996. "Meaningful Competition? A Study of Student Movement under Interdistrict Open Enrollment in Ohio." Presented at the annual meeting of the American Educational Research Association, New York, N.Y.

Fuller, Bruce. 1996. "Is School Choice Working?" *Educational Leadership,* October.

Funkhouser, Janie, and Kelly Colopy. 1994. *Minnesota's Open Enrollment Option: Impacts on School Districts.* Washington D.C.: Policy Studies Associates.

Gerstner, Louis V. Jr. 1995. *Reinventing Education.* New York: Plume/Penguin.

Hanus, Jerome. 1996. "An Argument in Favor of School Vouchers." In *Choosing Schools: Vouchers and American Education,* ed. Jerome Hanus and Peter Cookson Jr. Washington D.C.: American University Press.

Harrington-Lueker, Donna. 1994. "Charter Schools." *American School Board Journal,* September.

Henig, Jeffrey. 1994. *Rethinking School Choice.* Princeton, N.J.: Princeton University Press.

IBM Corporation. 1997. "Reinventing Education." Available from http://www.ibm.com/education.

Kahne, Joseph. 1996. *Reframing Educational Policy*. New York: Teachers College Press.

Kliebard, Herbert M. 1987. *The Struggle for the American Curriculum 1893–1958*. New York: Routledge and Kegan Paul.

Lasch, Christopher. 1995. *The Revolt of the Elites*. New York: Norton.

Lieberman, Myron. 1993. *Public Education: An Autopsy*. Cambridge: Harvard University Press.

Martinez, Valerie, et. al. 1995. "The Consequences of School Choice: Who Leaves and Who Stays in the Inner City." *Social Science Quarterly* 76: 485–501.

Molnar, Alex, Walter Farrell Jr., James Johnson Jr., and Marty Sapp. 1996. "Research, Politics, and the School Choice Agenda." *Phi Delta Kappan*, November.

Mulholland, Lori, and Louann Bierlein. 1995. *Understanding Charter Schools*. Bloomington, Ind.: Phi Delta Kappa Foundation.

Nathan, Joe. 1996. *Charter Schools*. San Francisco: Jossey-Bass.

———. 1996–97. "Progressives Should Support Charter Schools." *Rethinking Schools*, Winter.

Ogawa, Rodney T., and Jo Sargent Dutton. 1994. "Parental Choice in Education." *Urban Education* 29:270–297.

Pisano, Leah. 1994. "Edutrain: A Charter School for At-Risk Kids." *Education Digest*, January.

Rasell, Edith, and Rothstein Richard. 1993. *School Choice: Examining the Evidence*. Washington, D.C.: Economic Policy Institute.

Ravitch, Diane. 1994. "Somebody's Children." *Brookings Review*, Fall.

Rinehart, James, and David Lee. 1991. *American Education and the Dynamics of Choice*. New York: Praeger.

Rofes, Eric. 1996. "Charters: Finding the Courage to Face Our Contradictions." In *Selling Out Our Schools*, ed. Robert Lowe and Barbara Miner. Milwaukee: Rethinking Schools.

Tooley, James. 1995. "Markets or Democracy for Education." *British Journal of Educational Studies* 43:21–35.

Viadero, Debra. 1997. "Massachusetts Study Supplies Ammunition to Supporters and Critics of Choice." *Education Week*, 16 April.

Vine, Phyllis. 1997. "To Market, to Market . . . " *The Nation*, 8 September.

Viteritti, Joseph. 1996. "Stacking the Deck for the Poor: The New Politics of School Choice." *Brookings Review*, Summer.

Wells, Amy. 1993. "The Sociology of School Choice." In *School Choice*, ed. Edith Rasell and Richard Rothstein. Washington, D.C.: Economic Policy Institute.

———. 1993b. *Time to Choose*. New York: Hill and Wang.

Witte, John. 1991. "Choice in American Education." *Educational Considerations* 19(Fall): 12–19.

Witte, John, and Christopher Thorn. 1996. "Who Chooses? Voucher and Interdistrict Choice Programs in Milwaukee." *American Journal of Education* 104:186–214.

5 Educational Technology

An understanding of computer technology is a necessary part of a complete education. As a means of communication, an aid to research, and a facilitator of learning, the computer has a vital function in the classroom. As an important practical skill, computer literacy deserves a place in the school curriculum. More important still, in a democracy the technological expertise that facilitates participation in decision making must become the common property of all citizens. To the extent that high technology can be employed in building communities, improving society, or even creating new worlds, it is a means of empowering those who control it. In a democratic society, that control should thus be shared collectively. If computers are to become a significant part of the education process, their use should be directed toward increasing the ability of young people to master their own future and that of their communities.

Unfortunately, these practical purposes and democratic ideals are not the motivation behind the educational system's massive financial and pedagogical investment in high technology. Rather, the driving force is a combination of technological determinism and market ideology. From this perspective, computers in the schools are there to enhance the value of human capital, increase economic productivity, and adapt students to the demands of an alleged technological revolution. These purposes are presented not as a matter of choice but as a matter of historical inevitability. Technology itself, it is argued, determines the social and economic directions to be taken by society. In its interactions with the impersonal workings of the free market, computer technology is creating an information society that will shape our daily work, restructure our leisure time, and thus change our lives. The schools and their students can either choose to go with the flow or be left in the backwash.

Insofar as the use of computers in the schools is guided by this doctrine, which I refer to as techno-ideology, technology becomes the enemy of democratic education. This chapter explores the influence of this viewpoint on the educational system and illustrates its antidemocratic implications.

> We are no longer where we stood a decade ago, dazzled by changes whose relationships to one another were unknown. Today, behind the confusion of change, there is a growing coherence of pattern: the future is taking shape. In a great historical confluence, many raging rivers of change are running together to form an oceanic Third Wave of change that is gaining momentum with every passing hour. The Third Wave of historical change represents not a straight-line extension of industrial society but a radical shift of direction, often a negation, of what went before. It adds up to nothing less than a complete transformation at least as revolutionary in our day as industrial civilization was 300 years ago. (Toffler 1980, 366)

With these words, Alvin Toffler described in 1980 what he saw as an old world—the "Second Wave" of industrial society—being torn apart by the development of computer technology. A prolific, best-selling futurist writer, he had successfully popularized technological determinism—the idea that technology is a force with a life of its own that shapes human affairs—in such books as *Future Shock*. Nonetheless, *The Third Wave* was not well received by most reviewers, who criticized it as glib, superficial, and having a propensity for coining buzzwords. One exception was Harold G. Shane, an education professor at the University of Indiana, who reviewed the book for the educational magazine *Phi Delta Kappan:*

> There undoubtedly are flaws in the book . . . but I would say to his critics that the work merits an A+ for Toffler's lucid reviews of intricate problems of the present and for the way he defends the thesis that a new era of civilization is bursting into being in our midst. . . . Despite some of the modest defects noted above, educators will find *The Third Wave* both interesting and challenging. . . . The challenge is found in attempting to infer what certain of his ideas may suggest for educational practices at all age levels, both within and beyond our classroom walls. (Shane 1980, 61–62)

Views such as Shane's have, in fact, become the conventional wisdom in educational policy. Technological determinism has found a home in the school system as the driving force behind its enthusiastic reception of computer technology. That acceptance is not particularly surprising—it is part of our historical tradition. This is especially true in the field of education:

> Americans, for a number of reasons, seem particularly susceptible to a set of related propositions: that technology is good, that it is value-free, that it should find application in many fields, disciplines, and aspects of our lives. Perhaps most troubling is the assumption that, if technology makes it possible to do something, then that thing should be done. . . . So in education, the possibility (and desirability) of creating and using technologically based systems for teaching, learning, and provision of educational services are typically seen as basically transparent questions. (Kerr 1996b, 1–2)

Until recently, the introduction of technology into the schools generally followed a cycle: exaggerated claims about its potential impact; research belying the claims; and a subsequent reality check indicating imperfections in the machines, which were used by teachers mostly as a supplement to business as usual in the classroom rather than as a means of transforming education (Tyack and Cuban 1995, 121–122). Indeed, the most important reform movements prior to the 1980s did not greatly depend on new technologies. The introduction of computer technology in the schools, however, has been different. The implementation of computers has been promoted under pressure from business interests, the media, and the government, explicitly as a means of encouraging school reform—giving it tremendous significance in the politics of education. It is critical, therefore, to examine the educational policy implications of techno-ideology, the most important of which is central to the theme of this book: the connection of techno-ideology to and its mutually reinforcing relationship with market ideology. By itself, techno-ideology could hardly have much impact on education. Even the most profound pedagogical ideas do not necessarily create concrete and lasting change in the schools by themselves. Dewey had a major effect on educational theory, yet his effect on actual practice may have been far less. The real strength and influence of techno-ideology, and its potential for transforming the school system, lie in its connection with the economic system and the market ideology on which it is based.

Techno-ideology starts with assumptions about the economy that are by now quite familiar and widely accepted: computers have led us into an economic transformation, so that information is a new and increasingly important form of capital. The amount of data is constantly increasing and has become potentially accessible to everyone as a result of computer technology. Individual economic mobility and the competitive position of corporations and nations now depend primarily on access to and use of data. Thus, in an information society, the nature of work changes, opportunities for advancement increase, and economic competition intensifies, creating an entirely new set of social and economic relationships and rendering obsolete most of our contemporary institutions, especially the educational system.

In the field of education, computer technology transforms the teaching and learning processes, breaks down the established institutions of schooling, and creates the possibility of an educational utopia. These are logical and inevitable results of technological development by and of itself, independent of individual or social choices. Our rational options are limited to different methods of individual and institutional adaptation. In the school system, correct choices will be rewarded by a new era in education; incorrect ones—especially resistance to change—will be punished by a continuation of the decay, obsolescence, and irrelevance of our Second Wave school system. The use of educational technology in the schools is therefore not a political issue but a technical one: We must solve the problem of how to adjust to the new technological imperatives. The social and economic evolution of society is out of our hands, since the future is shaping us, rather than the reverse. Democratic decision-making processes in education are thus largely irrelevant.

Techno-ideology emphasizes the role of the educational system in improving our competitive position in the world economy. As Andrew Molnar puts it, "Modern high-speed computers and telecommunications have facilitated the rapid movement of financial resources, goods, and services, and have created an interdependence among the world's economies. To benefit from these markets, nations must be competitive, and to be competitive they must have a well-educated work force" (1997, 63). In an information society, human capital is more important than ever before, and the function of schools in developing it becomes absolutely critical.

It is no longer sufficient, however, merely to educate future workers in a general way. An economy based on computer technology requires very specific mental skills: information management, problem solving, understanding complex systems, and higher order thinking—in other words, abilities similar to those of computers. This demand necessitates changes in the nature of teaching and learning.

In line with this position, Molnar sees "a major paradigm shift in education from theories of 'learning' to theories of 'cognition.' Cognitive science . . . addresses how the human, as an information processor, functions and uses information" (1997, 63). Seymour Papert, one of the founding fathers of techno-ideology, argues that teaching children how to communicate with computers enables them to learn more about thinking:

> By deliberately learning to imitate mechanical thinking, the learner becomes able to articulate what mechanical thinking is and what it is not. The exercise can lead to greater confidence about the ability to choose a cognitive style that suits the problem. Analysis of "mechanical thinking" and how it is different from other kinds and practice with problem analysis can result in a new degree of intellectual sophistication. . . . Work with the computer can make it easier to understand that there is such a thing as a "style of thinking." . . . Children would be serving their apprenticeships as epistemologists, that is to say learning to think articulately about thinking. (1980, 27)

Understanding the learning process will allow us to increase our control over it and, we hope, improve it. This is what creates the possibility of an educational utopia. One of the earliest proponents of techno-ideology, George B. Leonard, offers his vision of the future in his 1968 book, *Education and Ecstasy,* which looks to twenty-first-century technology to fulfill his dream of turning learning into an ecstatic experience. In the cultural spirit of the 1960s, Leonard is interested more in expanding human potential than in increasing human capital, but that fact makes his ideas no less relevant today. He gives a lengthy description of "visiting day, 2001 A.D." at the "Kennedy School" in Santa Fe, New Mexico, which, he says, "exists not in the blazing immediacy of the twenty-first century but in the indignation and hope of today" (140). It is a school of eight hundred children between the ages of three and ten. On his visit, he notices children "in various states of consciousness. . . . While the children are on the school grounds, they are absolutely free to go and do anything they wish that does not hurt someone else. They are free learners" (141). This situation has become a practical reality as a result of advanced technology:

> No matter how many times you visit the Basics Dome, its initial effect is literally stunning. . . . You have to surrender to the overwhelming sensory bombardment that comes from every side. There are, around us, forty learning consoles, at each of which is seated a child. . . . The child's learning display, about ten feet square, is reflected from the hologram-conversion screen that runs all the way around the inner surface of the dome. . . . When a child takes the chair to begin learning, another radio receiver senses his presence through his EID (electronic identification device) and signals the central learning computer to plug in that particular child's learning history. The child puts on his combination earphones and brain-wave sensors, so that OBA (Ongoing Brain Wave Analysis) can become an element in the dialogue. (147–148)

Once the learning dialogue begins, says Leonard, the child can draw on all the resources of the computer, which include "a full bank of the basic, commonly agreed-upon cultural knowledge," the child's brain-wave pattern, and "Communal Interconnect" (CI), "one of the very latest educational developments. . . . Through CI, the material on one learning display sometimes influences and is influenced by the material on nearby displays. This makes the learning process far more communal. It also helps tie together all forty displays into a single learning-art object" (1968, 149).

Leonard's visions are remarkably prescient in terms of technology, as well as remarkably similar to those of his colleagues almost thirty years later. His associates, however, talk more about the economy than about Esalen (one of Leonard's favorite school examples), and they are certainly more impatient and less optimistic about achieving their goals. What they all advocate and foresee is a cybernetic community of self-directed learners working individually and in groups on a huge variety of educational projects, using the massive information resources of networked computers. For example, in "The Plug-in School," David Pesanelli describes an institution that "serves as a hub for receiving learning modules 'injected' into its classrooms. . . . [It is] a facility that, in addition to its traditional roles, functions at the center of a delivery and distribution system for education 'packages'" (1993, 30). "Tomorrow's Classroom," characterized in a 1993 *Business Week* advertising supplement entitled "The Future of Technology in Education," gives an account of "Jackie and Jose," two students in Middletown High School in 1997: "Jackie and Jose report to the 'Mediated Learning Center,' where students work at networked learning stations. Each one can access instruction in a variety of formats—text, hypertext, graphics, animation, simulation, visualization, and full-motion audio and video. . . . The instructional program contains a pre-test that pinpoints the best starting point for each. . . . Each student can navigate through a topic or lesson over a number of different pathways, at his or her own pace [while] working toward specific performance goals" (Gifford 1993, 95).

Lewis Perelman's concept of "hyperlearning" goes even further. "The reality is that a new generation of technology has blown the social role of learning completely inside out," says Perelman. It has become a "transhuman process people share with increasingly powerful artificial networks and brains. . . . [It] permeates every form of social activity. . . . Learning is literally the work of the majority of U.S. jobs and will be what virtually all adults . . . will do for a living." Hyperlearning is a "universe of new technologies that both possess and enhance intelligence. The hyper in hyperlearning refers . . . to an unprecedented degree of connectedness of knowledge, experience, media, and brains. . . . What learning means in this context goes as far beyond mere education or training as the space shuttle goes beyond the dugout canoe" (1992, 22–23).

Perhaps the most authoritative version of educational utopia can be found in the 1995 Office of Technology Assessment (OTA) report *Education and Technology: Future Visions.* In his introductory article, James Bosco is mildly critical of those who take a "utopian tone" or issue "apocalyptic commentary" about the impact of technology. Yet even he can scarcely contain himself:

> Information technology is transforming the amount and nature of the informational content of civilization as well as the processes whereby this information is acquired. The modest changes in the nature and conduct of schooling in recent decades stand amidst monumental changes in how, when, where, and what learning occurs in our society. As informa-

> tion technology-based learning opportunities become increasingly ubiquitous and efficacious, schooling, teaching, and learning will take on a new character and the establishment of a new balance between school and nonschool learning will be established. (27)

In the articles that follow Bosco's, the process of schooling is described as having been replaced by a project-method curriculum that encompasses the entire world—Kilpatrick for the cybernetic age. The community has become the classroom, and the classroom is a worldwide community of learners. Thus, Bruce Goldberg and Beverly Hunter describe the Big Dig project in Boston harbor as having become, by the year 2004, the actual physical location of classes for "real world" learning in a number of disciplines (1995, 57-88). (Interestingly enough, the authors work for the engineering firm of Bolt, Beranek, and Newman, and the one question that never seems to come up in the project is why there should even be a Big Dig.) Robert Kozma and Wayne Grant move up one year to 2005 and tell how computers can build "communities of understanding," where African-American, Hispanic, South African, and Filipino students can use computer networks to solve such common problems as reducing the risk of transporting hazardous wastes (short of abolishing their production entirely, of course) and building a car for a National Cyberspace Derby (1995, 121-146). The report concludes with Larry Cuban's slightly skeptical critique of technology in education, but he is a token minority in an OTA workshop dominated by industry consultants, economists, and futurists.

The ultimate policy question is the extent to which the current educational system can accommodate these changes, if at all. The response given by techno-ideology is negative. If we want only to enhance learning with new technology, perhaps the old structures and institutions can adapt and change, but if we want to transform the educational process itself—and this is the goal most often expressed—they have to be eliminated and replaced. For the most enthusiastic advocates of techno-ideology, the future of the schools lies with individual and family choices in an educational market, free of the institutional obstacles associated with a publicly owned and controlled school system. It is at this point that techno-ideology and market ideology intersect and that the very existence of any public education system, not to mention a democratic one, is threatened.

In *The Children's Machine,* Papert distinguishes between "schoolers," who are averse to and therefore resist "megachange" in education, and "yearners," who struggle but fail to find megachange in a system that rejects it and who seek such alternatives as home schooling. Papert is on the side of the yearners. In *Mindstorms*, he declares himself in favor of "revolutionary" change, committed to removing the obstructions "that grew like algae on a stagnant pond" (1980, 186). Although they avoid his rhetoric, even the more established reformers support his position. According to the U. S. Department of Education's 1993 Office of Research report entitled *Using Techonology to Support Education Reform:*

> Prevailing opinion is that piecemeal attempts at reform get swallowed up by the multiple levels and component parts of an education system that perpetuates the status quo and that if we want drastic improvements, we will have to undertake fundamental and comprehensive change. A new willingness to consider fundamental change and innovative approaches is apparent in the current wave of reform efforts. . . . Many critics of American schools see technology as an important tool in bringing about the kind of revolutionary changes called for in these new reform efforts. . . . Thus, support for the use of technology to support fundamental school reform appears to be reaching a new high. (1)

In most such discussions, there is inevitably some reference to resistance from the schoolers. The U.S. Department of Education report asks, "Why hasn't technology made a real difference in the teaching and learning that go on in more schools?" Its answer is that "the greatest part of the explanation resides in the imperviousness of the education system to any kind of fundamental change," and it cites a researcher who claims, "It is now well understood that the challenge of integrating technology into schools and classrooms is much more human than it is technological" (1993, 83–84). The common theme of such observations is that a combination of fear of change and vested interests in the status quo prevents these future visions from becoming reality. The culprits are not always named, but since students, business, and the public are usually included as supporters of techno-ideology, that leaves the educational establishment—many and perhaps most administrators and teachers, the schools of education, and the unions—as the likely offender. The position of the educational establishment in the system has historically enabled it to co-opt innovations and use them to reinforce established practices. Says Papert, "In the end, I think computers are inherently subversive, even though they are captured by the system and tamed. But the potential is still there for them to be used in other ways" (quoted in Hill 1994, 17). The system is therefore the enemy—it must be conquered.

Techno-ideologues thus have little tolerance for dissent, since they assume that the Third Wave is a fact of life. Referring to one such conception of the future, Neil Postman says, "There is a kind of forthright determinism about the imagined world described in it. The technology is here or will be; we must use it because it is there; we will become the kind of people the technology requires us to be; and, whether we like it or not, we will remake our institutions to accommodate the technology. All of this must happen because it is good for us, but in any case, we have no choice" (1995, 38). The techno-ideological vision is presented as an objective and realistic assessment of future trends; inevitable and irresistible in its advance; and progressive, egalitarian, and empowering in its impact on education. Its impact on the schools is not a matter of choice or conscious direction by an organized public. Opposition comes only from an irrational or selfish minority standing in the way of progress and the well-being of our children and the society.

Ideologies that present themselves as objective, inevitable, and irresistible are particularly dangerous and are usually based on faith or mythology rather than on empirical evidence. Dissent is silenced by placing it beyond the pale of rational discussion, often by belittling or patronizing it. Techno-ideology falls squarely within this pattern. A typical example comes from a pair of articles in *Educational Leadership* that present, rather untypically, both sides of the argument on educational technology. A detailed and well-documented 1996 critique by Douglas Noble entitled "The Overselling of Educational Technology" elicits as a rejoinder nothing more than the party line in an article by David Dwyer entitled "We're in This Together": There is "a sense of inevitability to this revolution. . . . Technology, whether we like it or not, is changing the face of the planet. . . . We can pretend that this is not happening and hold on to the past for as long as we can. Or we can grab this opportunity to build a world of peace, prosperity, and understanding" (Dwyer 1996, 26).

The strategy of advocates of techno-ideology resembles that of the half-humanoid, half-machine Borg creatures in the *Star Trek* series as they absorb other creatures into the body: a brief resort to persuasion, followed by a warning ("Resistance is futile"), and concluded with a brutal frontal assault on those who ignore it. In the case of techno-ideology, the ultimate weapon is the destruction of the current educational system—an end to school.

Leonard writes, "The most obvious barrier between our children and the kind of education that can free their enormous potential seems to be the educational system itself: a vast, suffocating web of people, practices, and presumptions, kindly in intent, ponderous in response. Now, when true educational alternatives are at last becoming clear, we may overlook the simplest: no school" (1968, 101). "Schools as we know them today will have no place in the future," says Papert, "but it is an open question whether they will adapt by transforming themselves into something new or wither away and be replaced" (1980, 9). Howard Mehlinger, director of the Indiana University Center for Excellence in Education, believes that "the day might come when 'going to school' can be accomplished by staying at home; when textbooks are replaced by electronic sources and data; when graduating from high school can occur at any age, following satisfactory demonstration of basic competencies" (1997, A22).

The most comprehensive program for abolishing school comes from Perelman. He finds conventional proposals for school choice or vouchers far too limited, since "in a realistic technological perspective, there are no effective schools in America, or anywhere else in the world." That situation calls for a truly revolutionary alternative: "Microchoice," a combination of "microvouchers" (a government-funded debit-card account usable for any educational services), intellectual "food courts" (a kind of pedagogical shopping mall), and—in line with Mehlinger's proposal—"attendance-free accounting" (outcome-based assessment without required presence at any school). Microchoice, Perelman says, "enables government to fund learners and learning instead of schools and teaching" (1992, 210). The OTA workshop participants who put together *Education and Technology: Future Visions* cite Toffler, Leonard, and Papert approvingly but reject Perelman's proposal only because "it ignores the teacher's role . . . and other inherently valuable features of the institution of school," such as student teamwork (U.S. Congress 1995, 7).

None of this is to say that all advocates of educational technology want to abolish public education. Not many enthusiasts of educational technology actually want to close down all the schools. The problem for public education is that the cult of so-called visionaries and revolutionaries has set the tone of the discussion. Their slogans, catch phrases, and peculiar view of history dominate the everyday vocabulary of educational policy making. Their perspective ultimately forms the context in which educational technology is applied to the curriculum.

In fact, opponents of the market model have offered few ideas about how to integrate technology into the curriculum in a manner that preserves and strengthens democratic public education. This failing leaves the political playing field to the techno-ideologues. Even if their objectives are not especially practical or achievable in the short run, their influence is important in that they successfully challenge the legitimacy of public education and provide a simplistic but potentially convincing historical and scientific rationale for market alternatives in education. These accomplishments leave the field wide open for the next best option to abolishing the schools: considering the supremacy of the market in determining the direction of education in the United States.

In that regard, the involvement of chairman and CEO of IBM Louis Gerstner, in line with his self-appointed role as educational policy analyst, is significant. In his book, *Reinventing Education,* he is quite specific about how what he calls the dynamism of the market can transform education, especially in a technological era: "Schools are regulated bureaucracies, [so] they are not organized in ways that lead them to the introduction of technology. . . . Rarely do educators think about technology because they are insulated from market forces. . . . One of the reasons technology is weakly developed in the nation's elementary and secondary schools is that normal market processes that lead to technological innovation in the rest of the economy don't exist in schools" (1995, 35–39).

This point is similar to the analogy used by Papert in the concluding chapter of *The Children's Machine.* Comparing the present educational system to the Soviet economy, and education reform to Mikhail Gorbachev's efforts at perestroika, Papert looks to the market economy as a model for revolutionary change. He condemns President Bush's America 2000 as "reminiscent of the Soviet style of 'solving' problems by decree"—no doubt the first time Bush has ever been accused of Marxist-Leninist tendencies. Says Papert, "While our economic system, with all its faults, is above a threshold of functionality and theirs was below it, our education system falls on the same side of the line as the Soviet economy." As bureaucratization destroyed production in the U.S.S.R., it has destroyed education in the United States: "The situation once again evokes an analogy with the Soviet economy. . . . It proclaimed that it protected everyone. But a terrible price was paid. . . . I do not see that School can be defended in its social role." Papert proposes a system of "little schools," essentially charter schools, that orient themselves to the particular educational choices and preferences of diverse groups and cites Afrocentric schools as a useful example (1993, chap. 10).

The most comprehensive statement of an educational system in a technological utopia based on market principles comes from the editors of *Wired,* a flashy and widely read journal of techno-ideology heavily subsidized by corporate advertising. The July 1997 issue offers "a history of the future, 1980–2020": "We're facing 25 years of prosperity, freedom, and a better environment for the whole world." This is, of course, contingent on continued development of high technology in an "open society." Among the "industrial-era" institutions in need of a complete overhaul is education, which occurs as a result of the election of 2000: "By the end of the 1990's, it becomes clear that the existing public K–12 school system is simply not up to the task of preparing [workers' brains]. . . . Reinventing education becomes a central campaign issue. . . . The resulting popular mandate shifts some of the billions once earmarked for defense toward revitalizing education." The renewal will come from "the emergence of small, innovative private schools. . . . Many focus on specific learning philosophies and experiment with new teaching techniques—including the use of computer technologies." These will expand as a result of "the widespread use of vouchers," which "spurs an entrepreneurial market for education reminiscent of the can-do ethos of Silicon Valley." The public schools have no choice but to get with the program, "with private schools doing much of the initial innovating, and public schools concentrating on making sure the new educational models reach all children in society" (Schwartz and Leyden 1997, 169–170).

Techno-ideology in education thus has an intellectual dynamic that ultimately leads to a free-market educational system. Computers become the means to the end of deinstitutionalizing education, so that students can become consumers of learning, picking and choosing among the various products. In a market economy, these products are, of course, offered by those who own and control the production process—the high technology industry and corporate America in general, who are then in the position to define the goals and purposes of education. Democracy is an obvious obstacle.

If all of this were merely the speculation of theorists and policy analysts, there would be no cause for concern. But techno-ideology is reflected in the real world throughout the policy-making apparatus. In March 1996, forty governors and forty-nine corporate CEOs met in Palisades, New Jersey, at a National Education Summit under the auspices of the National Governors Association. The summit—which was inspired and led by Governor Tommy Thompson (Republican, Wisconsin), a strong advocate of school vouchers, and Louis Gerstner—was held at IBM's conference center campus, where four rooms were set aside for technology demonstrations, computer displays, and software exhibits. No representatives of any other educational groups or organizations were present (Lawton 1996).

President Clinton, in a long and rambling address to the delegates, praised "the extraordinary meeting of America's business leaders and America's governors" (the fact that "some have raised some questions about it" notwithstanding). Focusing mainly on academic standards, Clinton offered the conventional wisdom of techno-ideology as an introduction:

> This is a time of a dramatic transformation in the United States. . . . It is clear to most people that the dimensions of economic change now are the greatest that they have been since we moved from farm to factory and from rural areas to cities and towns 100 years ago. In his book *The Road From Here* Bill Gates says that the digital chip is leading us to the greatest transformation in communications in 500 years. . . . If that is true, it is obvious beyond anyone's ability to argue that the educational enterprise . . . is now more important than ever. (U.S. Office of the Federal Register, 1996, 574)

The rhetoric of techno-ideology also pervades the technology plans issued by state education departments. The Ohio plan begins by saying that "97% of all information ever known will be generated" by the time a child of today is fifty years old. It continues, "The wave of technology that is directly sweeping society is directly related to the need to revise and modernize the curriculum. As technological advances change how people live, they also change how and what people must learn in order to thrive" (Ohio State Department of Education 1992, 6). A report from the Missouri School Boards Association has a more practical economic focus: "In a marketplace dominated by foreign interests, students in Missouri and the rest of the nation lack the basic competencies to compete in an increasingly complex and technologically dependent global community. . . . The technology that once gave the United States the edge as a global competitor . . . can again give this country the edge in a different arena: the learning environment" (1990, 2). The North Carolina Department of Public Instruction is concerned that "without higher level thinking and problem solving strategies, graduates will be unable to access, sort, and digest the ocean of information that surrounds us all." Thus, the schools must be transformed: "The tools and methods used in most of the state's schools cannot prepare students to fill jobs in our changed state economy. The age of information, technology, and an international economy have changed the characteristics of North Carolina's workplace and the skills required for successful employment" (1994, 3).

What is harder to document, but is readily apparent to anyone involved with local school systems, is that in school districts across the country this is the language used in day-to-day policy discussions about computers in the classroom. The point is that its pervasiveness works against the possibilities of harnessing educational technology to promote democratic goals and values. Indeed, discussion of such prospects becomes incomprehensible and otherworldly in the face of a discourse firmly rooted in the assumptions of techno-ideology.

Abolishing public schools is, obviously, not on the official agenda of federal and state reports on the subject of educational technology—at least not yet. Most of their proposals are relatively modest and conventional, involving various subsidies, incentives, and the encouragement of public-private partnerships. And perhaps educational technology policy will go no further than this, if only because federal and state governments are reluctant to commit the necessary funds. But there are powerful ideological and political forces behind the use of educational technology to dismantle public schools in favor of boosting the supremacy of market forces in determining the future of education. Techno-ideology dominates the reform agenda. Its language and assumptions pervade discussions about the future of education under a nonideological and nonpolitical guise.

Defending democratic public schools therefore requires a clear understanding that the agenda of techno-ideology, notwithstanding its pretensions at open-ended objectivity, is indeed closely tied to the goal of a free market in education, both in terms of theory and practice. This makes for a deadly combination as far as the future of public schools is concerned. An educational system organized along the lines that Leonard, Papert, Perelman, Gerstner, and their allies in policy-making circles have in mind would place it firmly in the service of corporate America and remove it from any effective democratic control.

There is a small amount of criticism of techno-ideology in the literature. Hank Bromley, for example, asserts that the unbridled optimism of techno-ideology reinforces the status quo, because it ignores the history and sociology of technological advancement by trivializing or disregarding the conflict and struggle that accompany it (1997, 52). Eric Schickler points out that technological advancement occurs in a social and historical context: "It is clear that new technologies are neither entirely liberating nor repressive; the political implications of video camcorders, fax machines, and related technologies depend on decisions about their design, distribution, and use. In the absence of strong resistance, elites can be expected to attempt to use these technologies to reduce uncertainties and monitor dissent" (1994, 180). In contrast, techno-ideology looks exclusively to the benefits and attributes these "to the characteristics of the technology itself, [which are] presumed to be more or less the same everywhere the technology is in use. This is an ahistorical position, ignoring how the impact of a given technology varies with the specificities of different times and places, with what is transpiring where the technology is used: who is deciding how to apply the technology, and what are their objectives?" (Bromley 1997, 54).

These points indicate that technology in any field, including education, has all kinds of possibilities. Indeed, it has been a historical "mixed blessing . . . with the exact mix varying with the particular technology and with the perspectives of those affected differently by it" (Segal 1996, 45). It is therefore critical that decisions about the use of educational technology recognize and appreciate the value of the conflicts, consider the pedagogical alternatives, and come out of democratic choices—that is, they must be made politically, because "technology is political to the extent that it involves, facilitates, or limits the exercise of power over human beings" (Schickler 1994, 177).

In its utopian self-assurance, techno-ideology keeps us from asking the right questions: "We readily ask of technology, 'Can it do X?,' but rarely seem to bring ourselves to ask 'Do we really want it to do X? Why do we want it to do X?' The issues of what technology is 'good for' are often either ignored or postponed until the consideration has become a moot point" (Kerr 1996b, 4). One is reminded of a comment by Henry David Thoreau: "We are in great haste to construct a magnetic telegraph from Maine to Texas; but Maine and Texas, it may be, have nothing important to communicate. . . . [It is] as if the main object were to talk fast and not to talk sensibly" (1990, 37).

This consideration is especially critical in view of the antidemocratic forces that have socially shaped information technology, which "did not arrive from nowhere. . . . The technical history of information technology is inseparable from its social context—military, commercial, government factors—and specific social shaping" (Lyon 1988, 40). Educational technology, in particular, has its origins in military research, which, according to Noble, accounts for "the current emphasis in education on problem-solving, decision-making, and 'higher order thinking'" (1991, 171).

These issues seem so obvious to Bromley that he expresses puzzlement at the prevalence of technological determinism in the field of education: "Given that these critiques of the state of discussion have been available for some time, why have they not had much effect? Why does the debate continue as before? Why has the idea not caught on, even among critically minded writers, that technology and society are best understood not as discrete entities but as a complex unity? I wish I had a good answer to that question" (1997, 64).

The answer is political. The views of these critics are sharply at odds with those of the existing power structure and are not likely to find expression outside highly specialized and little-read sources. It is no great wonder that much of the critical work cited here was published in England. It is no accident that one of Toffler's biggest fans is Newt Gingrich. Clinton and Gerstner speak louder than ten thousand Nobles, just as ten times more of the federal budget is spent for the military than for education. Corporate support for the thought and work of Papert (not necessarily the brilliance of his ideas) keeps him in the public eye and makes him publishable by major presses. In short, the marketplace of ideas in education is about as free and competitive as the economic marketplace in the larger society.

Techno-ideology is therefore able to dominate the field by depoliticizing itself and establishing its credentials as the conventional wisdom in educational circles. This ability has profoundly antidemocratic implications for educational policy making:

> The information society concept connects politics and technology in a peculiarly modern way; it often obscures the vested interests involved in information technology, it deflects attention from some embarrassing contradictions, while at the same time giving to the coming of the information society the appearance of an entirely natural and logical social progression. . . reducing political debate to the technical means that people are denied the chance to participate freely at the level of morality and

> justice and thus also to affect outcomes by means of political action. (Lyon 1988, 147)

This situation is reflected quite specifically in the notions of labor force development advanced by techno-ideology. For example, the specific technique of imposing computer literacy as a necessary component of the curriculum has little to do with its actual academic merits:

> First, the form the campaign takes . . . persuades the population that its description of the future is the correct one. Second, the content of the instruction itself—its technical emphasis, its oversimplification of issues—eases the public into "appropriate" ways of thinking about the new technology. The third, and perhaps the most effective . . . is the rapid institutionalization of computer literacy through the premature installation of new requirements for schooling and jobs, which literally forces the population to accept a new set of dubious realities. (Noble 1985, 70–71)

This approach insulates techno-ideology from the criticism that it richly deserves since most of its assumptions about education are highly questionable at best. For example, in its emphasis on the possibilities of self-directed learning, techno-ideology presents a highly fanciful individualistic notion of human behavior. A typical vision, quoted by Neil Postman, is offered in a 1993 *Economist* article by Diane Ravitch: "In this new world of pedagogical plenty, children and adults will be able to dial up a program on their home television to learn whatever they want to know, at their own convenience. If Little Eva cannot sleep, she can learn algebra instead. At her home learning-station, she will tune in to a series of interesting problems that are presented in an interactive medium, much like video games. . . . Young John may decide that he wants to learn the history of modern Japan, which he can do by dialing up the greatest authorities and teachers on the subject" (Postman 1995, 39). Postman goes on to comment, "Little Eva can't sleep, so she decides to learn a little algebra? Where did little Eva come from, Mars? . . . How did young John come to this point? . . . Or is it that he, too, couldn't sleep and decided a little modern Japanese history was just what he needed?" (1995, 39). Postman's sarcasm is on target, but little Eva is not a

Martian—she is a creature of free-market mythology. She, along with young John, is a rational, well-informed, autonomous, self-directing individual—the ideal type of consumer in a market society. Without her, the emancipatory prophecies of techno-ideology fail. She is where market ideology and techno-ideology intersect—and, as Postman points out, she does not exist.

Techno-ideology implicitly accepts the view of society propagated by neoclassical economics—free and open competition among sellers and rational choices by informed consumers, leading to an equilibrium that adjusts in line with supply and demand, thus satisfying all sides. Translated into the educational system, producers of technology will compete to fulfill the needs and wants of educational consumers based on their individual pedagogical goals. However, this is not and cannot be the real world of education any more than it is the real world of capitalism, because of economic inequality.

According to Riley, Clinton's secretary of education, "Technology will be the great equalizer. . . . Technology can take a school in the poorest of communities and provide its students a wealth of learning opportunities that will give them the same intellectual riches that students in the wealthiest school districts have" (quoted in Sheekey 1997, 27). This may make sense in the world of market ideology, but the reality is that the "savage inequalities" of the school system (to use Jonathan Kozol's phrase) cannot be eliminated by machines, if only for the simple and obvious reason that inexplicably seems to escape Riley's awareness: not all schools can afford the machines.

School finance is perhaps the most significant and contentious issue in the politics of education. In particular, the inequities of the property tax as the primary basis for funding schools are well known, much discussed, and the subject of countless court cases. The federal share of educational spending is 5 percent; a 1994 proposal to spend $350 million for educational technology never got past a Senate committee. Yet there is no mention of any of this in the literature of techno-ideology. Plug-in schools fall out of the sky, computers spring into existence spontaneously, and sophisticated software appears as if by magic. In the real world, even the most modest technological advances involve significant cash outlays:

> Suitably equipped, even the most impoverished school or school district can gain equal access [to the Internet]. . . . [It] does require multiple telephone lines, however, and these are scarce commodities in most schools. . . . Satellite technology can address the equity gap by allowing students in rural areas and inner cities to take specialized courses. . . . But [it] also has major limitations. Although the receiving equipment is inexpensive, the costs to produce and deliver the courses are enormous—running into the thousands of dollars per hour of instruction. (McDonald, Lynch, and Kearsley 1996, 27).

Techno-ideology implicitly accepts the notion that the market will lead to the development of educational technology in the liberatory and communitarian directions they favor. But corporate America has other ideas. Arthur D. Sheekey states, "We do know that private competitive interests will dominate the development of advanced networks and services. . . . [Investments] are justified by business plans directed to growing commercial markets, rather than abstract visions of an educated or informed society." Public schools in particular have a low priority: "CEOs of telecommunications companies have a much grander vision. They foresee the evolution of numerous interconnected and interoperable digital networks that will enable commercial providers of entertainment and information services to reach all U.S. households." It is those with the greatest market clout—that is, the rich—who will have the most influence on the shape of those services, thus perpetuating inequality in educational access. "The gap between high-income and low-income families using modem-equipped computers is extremely wide. . . . Several writers identify this problem as the great digital divide or another example of savage inequalities of educational opportunities." Sheekey concludes with an understatement: "Public and private visions of electronically networked services, including educational services, may not necessarily be complementary" (1997, 27, 28).

Corporations have already taken the lead in shaping the educational market, often in the form of "donations." IBM put $25 million into ten school districts under the auspices of its Reinventing Education Foundation; the purpose, according to foundation president Stanley Litow, was to "figure out the ways you can use technology to systematically fix the flaws in the school system." Bill

Gates donated $3 million in proceeds from his best-selling book to the National Foundation for the Improvement of Education, to be used for professional development of teachers: "By giving free Windows-based software and computers to schools, Microsoft hopes to accelerate the movement away from the old Apple II's. . . . Some believe that certain Microsoft philanthropic efforts cross the line to commercialism" (Southwick 1997, A13–14).

New businesses are springing up to provide educational Internet services. The Family Education Network, based in Boston, builds educational web sites for public schools. According to an article by Robert Keough entitled "An On-Line Learning Experience" in the July 16, 1997, edition of the *Boston Globe,* it is "the first for-profit venture welcomed into schools with open arms"; its profit is derived from advertisers, such as AT&T, which sees the network as an opportunity "to gain and retain customers by being associated with a positive thing in the community."

The world of Third Wave visionaries is a market utopia: one of consumer sovereignty in making choices from an endless array of technological possibilities, provided by vendors whose prime interest is to satisfy the educational needs of its market of students, teachers, and families. The outcome is an educational paradise that frees individuals from the institutional restraints of the present school system while giving them equal opportunity to build up their own human capital to advance themselves and the society as a whole economically. In reality, their visions lead to corporate control of education in a deschooled environment that will perpetuate or exacerbate existing social inequalities and continue the trend toward vocationalization of the curriculum. Papert is an apt symbol of the true meaning of techno-ideology, promoting a libertarian philosophy under corporate sponsorship by Nintendo and Lego. A continuation of current policies in educational technology thus has profoundly antidemocratic implications.

Outlining a democratic perspective and political strategy on the issue of educational technology is a daunting task, and it is somewhat outside the purpose of this book. The way to start, however, is to strip techno-ideology of its legitimacy explicitly and publicly by exposing its inconsistency with U.S. democratic values and the falsehood of its economic assumptions. In its place, an alternative approach must be developed that emphasizes values and ideas to which ordinary Americans can relate.

The first step is to ask the questions that techno-ideology does not want to answer and therefore has ruled out of bounds. Indeed, the power of most ideologies is not necessarily in the answers they offer, but in deciding which questions may or may not be asked. Therefore, "a rethinking of educational ends and means in a progressive computer environment must frame eduational issues not in terms of technical or procedural rationality, but in terms of placing at the forefront the instructional and curricular issues that are part of a more socially responsible education" (Callister 1994, 241). Steven Kerr (1996a, 223–228) lists the most critical questions:

(1) Do we want technology in our schools?
(2) Who will pay for technology in the schools?
(3) To what end do we want to use technology in the schools?
(4) Does technology bring us wisdom, or just more information?
(5) What should the schools teach?
(6) How can the isolating effects of technology in the classroom be avoided?
(7) What does technology do to us?

Raising any of these questions, especially the third and fifth, immediately forces a different and more democratic perspective on the issue of educational technology. Asking them establishes the legitimacy of democratic community decision making on educational policy and avoids the technological mystification that can accompany discussions of computers in the schools.

If educational technology is ultimately to be used to enhance democratic education, there must be a challenge to economic utility as the primary rationale for its use. This means a rejection, along the lines of Dewey's thinking, of education as a preparation for something else or as a fulfillment of some utilitarian economic goal. As Tyack and Cuban put it, "When the purposes of education become narrowed to economic advantage, and the main measure of success is higher test scores, an easy next step is to regard schooling as a consumer good rather than a common good. Then it is logical to propose alternatives to the common school such as an open-market system of schooling" (1995, 140). Techno-ideology is designed to facilitate that process. The response must be an alternative that can "identify essential human concerns, make these the focus of the educational system, and make decisions within the framework of these concerns. In this kind of education system, the primary focus of schools, and therefore of instruction, would be on human values, not economic utility" (Kerr 1996b, 7).

Techno-ideology has followed the pattern of conservative political forces in co-opting phrases formerly used by the Left. As we discuss in the next chapter, in education the word "empowerment" is such an example and has been connected with the operation of a free-market educational system. The word must be recaptured and given its old meaning—not merely the power of a consumer to select a prepackaged product from the limited menu provided by producers but the power of a community to make collective decisions about its own future well-being. The bias of techno-ideology is revealed in its implicit condescension and even hostility toward teachers—they are most often portrayed as obstacles to reform, and a good part of the task of bringing technology into the classroom is overcoming their resistance and training them to use the machines. In other words, reform is imposed from the outside on an unwilling insiders' group.

A democratic alternative is what Tyack and Cuban call inside-out reform—that is, starting with the classroom and the teachers and working from there. In relation to technology, instead of allowing corporate interests to define the needs of schools, we should ensure that teachers, students, and the community define what they need and have the power to create a response. Technology does have the capacity to open up new learning environments and to create "wired communities." "These developments," says Sheekey, "set the stage for local authorities and the families they represent to assume a greater role in deciding what has to be learned, by whom, when, and where." Although localities are at a disadvantage in trying to influence or control national computer networks, "each and every community can decide what local public services should be made available to its local residents, families, and school children" (1997, 30–31).

Any such attempt, of course, will create significant political conflict, but the outcome at this early stage is still up for grabs. As Schickler puts it,

> Elites clearly will resist those technologies that challenge their control, and will attempt to design and to distribute new technologies in ways that reinforce their power. The question is whether democratic commitments can be used to mobilize popular opposition to such efforts and to ensure that the democratic potential of many technologies will not be stifled. The strength and insistence of citizen demands for democratization will determine whether new technologies are structured in ways that undermine rather than reinforce existing constellations of power. (1994, 199)

References

Bosco, James. 1995. "Schooling and Learning in an Information Society." In *Education and Technology: Future Visions,* ed. U.S. Congress, Office of Technology Assessment. Washington, D.C.: U.S. Government Printing Office.

Bromley, Hank. 1997. "The Social Chicken and the Technological Egg: Educational Computing and the Technology/Society Divide." *Educational Theory* 47:51–65.

Callister, Thomas. 1994. "Educational Computing's New Direction." *Educational Theory* 44:239–256.

Dwyer, David. 1996. "We're in This Together." *Educational Leadership,* November.

Gerstner, Louis Jr. 1995. *Reinventing Education.* New York: Plume/Penguin.

Gifford, Bernard, ed. 1993. "The Future of Technology in Education." Supplement to *Business Week,* 15 November.

Goldberg, Bruce, and Beverly Hunter. 1995. "Learning and Teaching in 2004: The Big Dig." In *Education and Technology: Future Visions,* ed. U.S. Congress, Office of Technology Assessment. Washington, D.C.: U.S. Government Printing Office.

Hill, David. 1994. "Focus on Technology: Professor Papert and His Learning Machine." *Teacher Magazine,* January.

Kerr, Stephen. 1996a. "Questions for Further Study." In *Technology and the Future of Schooling,* ed. Stephen Kerr. Chicago: University of Chicago Press.

———. 1996b. "Visions of Sugarplums: The Future of Technology, Education, and the Schools." In *Technology and the Future of Schooling,* ed. Stephen Kerr. Chicago: University of Chicago Press.

Kozma, Robert, and Wayne Grant. 1995. "Using Technology to Build Communities of Understanding." In *Education and Technology: Future Visions,* ed. U.S. Congress, Office of Technology Assessment. Washington, D.C.: U.S. Government Printing Office.

Lawton, Millicent. 1996. "Summit Accord Calls for Focus on Standards." *Education Week,* 3 April.

Leonard, George B. 1968. *Education and Ecstasy.* New York: Dell.

Lyon, David. 1988. *The Information Society.* Cambridge, England: Polity Press.

McDonald, Jane, William Lynch, and Greg Kearsley. 1996. "Unfilled Promises." *American School Board Journal,* July.

Mehlinger, Howard D. 1997. "The Next Step." *American School Board Journal/Electronic School,* June.

Missouri School Boards Association. 1990. *A Roadmap to School Improvement: A Strategic Plan for Educational Technology in Missouri.* Jefferson City.

Molnar, Andrew. 1997. "Computers in Education: A Brief History." *T.H.E. Journal,* June.

Noble, Douglas. 1985. "Computer Literacy and Ideology." In *The Computer in Education—A Critical Perspective,* ed. Douglas Sloan. New York: Teachers College Press.

———. 1991. *The Classroom Arsenal.* London: Falmer Press.

———. 1996. "The Overselling of Educational Technology." *Educational Leadership,* November.

North Carolina State Department of Public Instruction. 1994. *A Technology Plan for North Carolina's Public Schools.* Raleigh.

Ohio State Department of Education. 1992. *State Plan for Technology.* Columbus.

Papert, Seymour. 1980. *Mindstorms.* New York: Basic Books.

———. 1993. *The Children's Machine.* New York: Basic Books.

Perelman, Lewis, 1992. *School's Out.* New York: William Morrow.

Pesanelli, David. 1993. "The Plug-in School." *The Futurist,* September–October.

Postman, Neil. 1995. *The End of Education.* New York: Knopf.

Shickler, Eric. 1994. "Democratizing Technology: Hierarchy and Innovation in Public Life." *Polity* 27: 175–199.

Schwartz, Peter, and Peter Leyden. 1997. "The Long Boom." *Wired,* July.

Segal, Howard P. 1996. "The American Ideology of Technological Progress: Historical Perspectives." In *Technology and the Future of Schooling,* ed. Stephen Kerr. Chicago: University of Chicago Press.

Shane, Harold G. 1980. "Despite Many Flaws, Toffler's Book Earns A+ for Presaging a Social Transformation." *Phi Delta Kappan,* September.

Sheekey, Arthur D. 1997. "Public and Private Interests in Networking Educational Services." *Techtrends,* April–May.

Southwick, Karen. 1997. "Big Deal." *American School Board Journal/Electronic School,* March.

Thoreau, Henry David. 1990. *Walden*. Philadelphia: Running Press.

Toffler, Alvin. 1980. *The Third Wave*. New York: William Morrow.

Tyack, David, and Larry Cuban. 1995. *Tinkering toward Utopia*. Cambridge: Harvard University Press.

U.S. Congress, Office of Technology Assessment, ed. 1995. *Education and Technology: Future Visions*. Washington, D.C.: U.S. Government Printing Office.

U.S. Department of Education. 1993. *Using Technology to Support Education Reform*. Washington, D.C.: U.S. Government Printing Office.

U.S. Office of the Federal Register, National Archives and Records Service. 1996. *Weekly Compilation of Presidential Documents*. Washington, D.C.: U.S. Government Printing Office.

6 School Restructuring

Democratic schools require democratic systems of governance. Ostensibly, we have such a system, since communities elect school boards, which are responsible for administrative, financial, and personnel decisions. In theory, the community controls the schools through its elected officials, but the reality is quite different. Public education is, as countless observers have pointed out, mired in bureaucracy and dominated by professional administrators. Teachers and parents have some influence, at best, but no real power over the system. And, of course, students are entirely excluded. Thus, any movement for democratic schools requires at the very least a revitalization or reorganization of the existing structure, or perhaps a complete transformation. In fact, it appears that just such a trend has been underway for some time: Known most commonly as restructuring, the movement is a combination of administrative decentralization and participative management that has become the centerpiece of school reform in the 1990s. Restructuring means shifting away from centralized, bureaucratic, top-down administration toward a devolution of authority and responsibility to the individual school, and toward a higher degree of collaborative rather than adversarial involvement in decision making by the various stakeholders in the educational system.

The question, however, is whether restructuring really delivers on its democratic promise. Does it really place critical decisions in the hands of teachers, parents, and students? Do communities actually "own" their schools in any practical sense? Are administrators displaced from their accustomed role of authority and forced instead to operate in accord with a community consensus? Finding answers to these questions requires exploration of the origins, theory, and practice of restructuring in U.S. schools.

The practical model for this approach is derived from the business world, from which it originated in the 1960s. More specific applications are known as "employee involvement"; "employee participation"; "flexible work organization"; and, most notably and recently, "high performance practices" (Parks 1995, 18). These strategies have taken a variety of organizational forms, including quality circles, total quality management, employee ownership programs, team-based work structures, and worker representation on corporate boards. Despite a report by the U.S. Commission on the Future of Worker-Management Relations that they "are only partially diffused across the economy, . . . and many remain rather fragile," and less than 5 percent of the Fortune 1000 companies had combined a number of such programs into a total high-performance organizational system (Commission 1995, 38–40), such innovations have received considerable attention from economists, specialists in business administration, and the media. The idea of decentralized decision making and employee participation is still a hot topic in the business community.

Political and theoretical support for applying these methods to the public sector and to education in particular comes from several sources. On the political level, reinventing government has become the watchword for public officials within the Clinton administration. Put simply, this involves reorganizing government services along the lines of the private sector by introducing the ideas and practices of the market economy: stimulating competition among public agencies, viewing citizens as customers or consumers, debureaucratizing the public sector, and reorienting the role of government away from providing direct service and toward encouraging and facilitating community self-reliance (Gaebler and Osborne 1992). On a theoretical and academic level, the new institutionalism has become an influential approach in the politics of education. The shorthand description of this strategy is that institutions matter—that is, complex social organizations have a life and a force of their own, which guide their behavior, often in less-than-optimal directions; most important, they tend to resist change despite all efforts to alter them. As Rick Ginsberg puts it, "The new institutionalism suggests that institutions create constraints analagous to the instinctual behavior of animals in the wild, whose entire frame of reference is governed by past behavior and practices comfortable for their environment. In human terms, institutional approaches foster a faith about ways to behave" (1996, 159). This point has obvious implications for education reform in that the institution of school itself, rather than individuals within it or the social context around it, must be the focus of change, and strong resistance to such change is to be expected.

Real world experience in government and business and theoretical developments in academia have thus combined to inspire efforts across the country to change the educational system by restructuring the schools themselves. Decentralization in most places has taken the form of school- (or site-) based management (SBM). Participative, collaborative, and high-involvement management has taken a number of forms, but most commonly it is based on some or all of the precepts of the corporate restructuring program known as total quality management (TQM).

According to Jane L. David, SBM "may be the most significant reform of the decade," although "no two people agree on what it is, how to do it, or even why to do it" (1995–96, 4). Rodney Ogawa and Paula A. White offer a definition in their statement that SBM "can be viewed conceptually as a formal alteration of governance structures, as a form of decentralization that identifies the individual school as the primary unit of improvement and relies on the redistribution of decision-making authority as the primary means through which improvements might be stimulated and sustained" (1994, 56).

Such authority is usually delegated to representative decision-making councils at individual schools to make certain budgetary, personnel, and program terminations. Although the councils themselves vary widely in composition, they generally include principals, teachers, parents, community residents, and occasionally students. They also differ considerably in the extent of their formal authority and in terms of to whom and for what they are accountable. SBM was implemented as national policy in England, Australia, and New Zealand during the 1980s and began to develop in the United States as a voluntary and experimental program on the local and school district level. By 1990 one-third of all school districts had some version of SBM (David 1995–96, 5). Since then, an increasing number of states—beginning with Kentucky and spreading to Maryland, Texas, and Massachusetts, among others—have included mandatory SBM as part of statewide reform legislation.

TQM, to put it as simply as possible, is the application of principles consistent with the managerial philosophy of W. Edwards Deming (1900–1993). Since TQM is a general theory using a somewhat esoteric vocabulary, it is subject to varying interpretations (and misinterpretations) by its supporters and opponents. However, we can probably correctly begin its description with Deming's concept of Profound Knowledge as a means of evaluating and improving methods of production. Deming emphasizes the necessity of a systemic perspective, an understanding of the causes and potentially destructive effects of variation in performance, a grounding of empirical analysis in theory, and the ability to use psychological insights to understand human behavior. He recommends a reliance on statistical analysis of data on performance and quality to point the way to improvement and to get away from subjective judgments that personalize or misdirect blame for flaws in the production process. Profound Knowledge is therefore supposed to provide a basis for continuous improvement in the production process by shifting the focus toward the system as a whole rather than toward its separate parts and by holding management collectively responsible for its smooth functioning.

The emphasis of TQM—and the aspect most prominently applied in restructuring schools—is a collegial, cooperative, team approach, among all those involved in a particular organization, toward continuous improvement of quality in production. The goal is constant customer satisfaction, the level of which provides the feedback needed to adjust the system. Deming's fourteen points provide general guidelines for implementing the process, the most important of which include breaking down barriers between staff areas, maintaining unity and constancy of purpose, decreasing reliance on numbers crunching for its own sake (although reliable data is necessary to chart a path), encouraging pride of workmanship, eliminating fear as a motivating tool, and providing extensive training and education.

As a management philosophy in the private sector, TQM apparently hit its peak during the 1980s, most notably in the auto industry—Saturn was often cited as a positive example, although recently the process of collaboration in that company has broken down. The wave of downsizing in the 1990s seems to have dampened the cooperative and collegial spirit in corporate America by reintroducing fear. Nonetheless, in recent years the public sector has taken up the theme as part of reinventing government.

Applied to schools, the fourteen points call for a clear purpose expressed in a meaningful mission statement, alternatives to testing and grading as a means of measuring quality, decreased dependence on the lowest price in purchasing, leadership that encourages customer satisfaction, "joy of learning and joy in work," pride in staff accomplishments, and across-the-board commitments to strive for a continuous increase in quality (Leonard 1996, chap. 10). Resistance to these apparently desirable methods is attributed to those who have a vested interest in the existing system and those who, despite their good intentions, fear change of any kind. Partisans of TQM in the schools claim numerous benefits in their approach, but the most prominent are those that are ostensibly democratic: collective participation in decision making by all those involved in the school system and an egalitarian educational process that always seeks to satisfy the customer, both internal (the students) and external (parents, community, employers, and the like).

High-performance organizations are those that have completely redesigned themselves along decentralized and participative lines to maximize efficiency, productivity, and customer satisfaction. Few, if any, school systems have successfully taken up the entire SBM-TQM package to accomplish this. Yet the more elaborate and sophisticated models for restructuring schools aim precisely for that goal. Jerry J. and Janice L. Herman call for "combining TQM, strategic/tactical planning, effective schools, school-based and outcome-based management into a holistic Educational Quality Management change model," in order to guarantee that "change becomes truly systematic transformational change, ending in improved results and a more positive organizational culture [rather than] only a cosmetic and short-term attempt that results in visibility with no results" (1994, 139).

Examples of high-performance school experiments—"those that continually improve their level of performance and the efficiency with which they consume resources"—include Effective

Schools, James Comer's School Development Program, Henry Levin's Accelerated Schools, and Theodore Sizer's Essential Schools (Wohlstetter and Smyer 1994, 81). In line with these formulations, in this chapter school restructuring is taken to mean a systemic application of the ideas and values of SBM and TQM toward the goal of high performance.

Most restructuring programs are in their infancy, and it is not clear whether those who implement such projects on the local level are really conscious of where they are ultimately going—or where the educational consultants want to take them. But that is not the matter at hand. Rather, the issue is whether restructuring, which is being pursued to one extent or another by many—perhaps most—school districts in the United States, is consistent with democratic public schools. Although the rhetoric accompanying it is democratic and participatory, a closer examination of both the theory and practice of restructuring schools reveals the reverse, because the programs are based on the undemocratic theory and practice of the market economy.

This conclusion rests on three premises. First of all, the fact that restructuring is based on corporate organizational models precludes the achievement of a truly democratic workplace. Second, the system shares the emphasis of market ideology and corporate practice on productivity, cost-effectiveness, efficiency, and performance, all of which, if applied to the schools, displace democracy as an educational goal since restructuring cannot meet those criteria. Third, and perhaps most important, the program is almost entirely process oriented. It therefore assumes an implicit consensus over goals and values and ignores the conflicts that arise from the social context of education. This situation has the effect of imposing market values on the curriculum and corporate models on the structure of the school system. Ultimately, restructuring encourages the establishment of a competitive, nongovernmental, free-market educational system.

Certainly, any movement toward greater participation in educational decision making is positive, and SBM in particular presents at least the potential for developing a genuinely democratic decision-making structure in the school system. But in actual practice, it has not worked out that way because SBM's application has been based exclusively on corporate models, which allow administrators and bureaucrats to retain their control and impose their objectives behind a facade of democratic participation.

To begin with, an instructive contrast can be made with authentic models of workplace democracy and with older, more democratic versions of administrative reform in education. Christopher E. Gunn draws a distinction between what he calls worker self-management and worker participation in management. The former

> refers to the collective process of self-governance and democratic management within an organization that produces goods or services. It eliminates employee-employer relationships and provides an extension and reinforcement of democratic principles fundamental to modern Western thought. . . . [It] defines who is managing in this process of self-governance. . . . It locates the right to participate in the management of work in work itself, not capital ownership. It is based on the premise that all who actively contribute to production, at whatever level of skill or scope of competence, have the fundamental right to manage that production. (1984, 15–16)

For obvious reasons, therefore, "it is well known that in a predominantly capitalist economy and society, workers typically do not manage. . . . Capital conceptualizes and plans work; labor executes those plans" (Gunn 1984, 15–16). Under no circumstances would such a change be initiated by the owners of a corporation; it would have to be the outcome of a struggle by employees. Authentic workplace democracy cannot come from the top of the organizational pyramid. It is therefore perfectly understandable that a majority of SBM programs have been initiated by administrators (school boards, superintendents, state education departments) and only 4 percent by teachers or community groups (Gaul 1994, 38). Restructuring is in every sense a top-down reform, despite its bottom-up rhetoric.

Workers' participation, on the other hand, "is a truncated form of workers' self-management":

> Workers' participation generally involves spreading some management functions to a broader mix of people working in an organization. Most typically the process begins with decision-making power being granted to workers over the details of their immediate tasks. . . . The next level of involvement might include workers having greater responsibility for

> quality control, participating in the selection or dismissal of fellow employees, or determining how to meet production targets. But it is precisely the status of workers as employees that sets limitations on the issues in which they can participate. For the logic of the system to hold, those decisions that most directly affect profit must remain the province of those who work in capital's interests. (Gunn 1984, 20)

This is fundamentally different from workers' self-management, in which all decisions about production belong to all the members of the organization. This approach would require "a nonhierachical form of organization and a democratic process for management. . . . Workers' control [of the organization], then, is a necessary condition for workers' self-management" (20).

Advocates of restructuring the schools do not claim to be promoting worker control or self-management. Their emphasis is more often on the need to improve student achievement and educational effectiveness than on the principle of democratic governance (David 1995–96, 5–6). Yet, typically, the selling point is a focus on the latter as a means of achieving the former. Even if restructuring has no intention of eliminating administrators, self-direction in both teaching and learning is a major goal. Words like "empowerment," "participation," "ownership," and "involvement" are consistently used in association with restructuring programs, along with implicit promises to break up the bureaucracy and lessen administrative power. Parents and the community as a whole are to have more control over the direction of the schools, students should identify more strongly with their work, and teachers will have greater freedom to use their professional judgment. The issue is not whether restructuring is workplace democracy—clearly it is not, even if it is sometimes presented that way—but whether its democratic spirit is anything more than a veneer. It is therefore useful to contrast restructuring with more explicitly democratic models of school organization and administration.

Unfortunately, progressive educators, including Dewey, did not have much to say specifically on that subject, limiting themselves mostly to general comments about the need for teacher participation and a few case studies of school councils. Unlike restructuring today, there were no plans or blueprints providing democratic models of school organization. What is significant, however, is that progressive educators' views on all educational issues, including administration, were explicitly and exclusively related to a democratic value system. Thus, teaching and learning, the structure of the curriculum, and classroom procedure were all to be organized around the struggle to promote democracy. Ultimately, the goal of any educational administrative system was therefore to further that struggle.

This objective did not necessarily mean greater decentralization or disdain for professionalism. At the end of the 1930s, progressives were greatly concerned with the problems of school districts that were too small to function properly and with the dangers of partisan politics intruding into school policy. A certain amount of centralization and consolidation and a higher degree of professionalism in administration were therefore considered to be solutions rather than problems. But this view was apparently not considered inconsistent with a democratic school system. A 1938 report by the National Education Association's (NEA) Educational Policies Commission (EPC) advised that "formulation of school policy should be a cooperative process capitalizing the intellectual resources of the whole school staff." Such participation "should not be thought of as a favor granted by the administration but rather as a right and obligation" (67). Community involvement is equally important: "If the schools are to serve the democracy, they must be kept in close touch with the people locally. Whatever the general program that may be mandated by the state, the schools will fail of their purpose unless they reflect the interests, the ideals, and the devotion of the community which they serve. . . . Only on the basis of complete and wholehearted cooperation among the professional staff of the school system, members of the board of education, and the community at large, can education effectively serve our democracy" (71–72).

The report endorses a system of what might be called progressive federalism, with the federal and state governments providing guidance and assistance, rather than mandates, to schools that are under strong local control. In a 1940 report on civic education, the commission expanded on these themes, agreeing that "widespread democratic participation is to be sought in the formulation of educational policy. . . . Opportunity for participation in policy-making should be extended to the entire professional staff and, as far as practicable, to the lay public" (NEA 1940, 333). It offered a number of working examples of democratic school administration practices, among them regular faculty policy-making meetings in Moultrie, Georgia, and Oakland, California; a Superintendent's Round Table every Saturday morning in Lincoln, Nebraska; citywide public school councils in Philadelphia and Denver; and community participation in curriculum revision in Shaker Heights, Ohio. The report's chapter on administration concludes by saying that democratic practices result in better policies, higher school morale, and equal educational opportunity and argues that "democratic administration should admit students, as well as adults, to participation in policy-making. . . . This is not a mere generous gesture to youth. . . . Long before reaching legal adulthood, youth should begin to work with older people in shouldering the responsibilities for affairs which concern young and old alike" (376).

Superficially, this may all sound similar to current restructuring efforts. But there is a crucial distinction between the vision of progressive educators in the 1930s and the goals of restructuring in the 1990s. To begin with, the former includes all aspects of educational policy making as potentially subject to the democratic process; in theory, by statute, and in practice, the latter is generally limited to problem solving and policy implementation. Second, the progressive objective justifies itself not only or even primarily in terms of tangible improvements in teaching and learning—although its proponents argued that these would occur—but in terms of the value of the democratic process itself. Restructuring reverses these priorities: democratic processes are important but incidental to the real goal of improving student achievement for the purposes of national economic competitiveness. The restructuring plan thus has ends separate and distinct from the means; the progressive goal in true Deweyan holistic fashion, combines the two.

In other words, progressive educators wanted to reorganize the governance of the schools to produce democracy. Contemporary advocates of restructuring schools want to reorganize governance to increase student achievement and educational productivity. Progressives would actually place power in the hands of educators and teachers; restructuring does so only insofar as it accomplishes the goals and purposes desired by administrators. Thus, restructuring is in spirit, even if not in actual form, more closely related to an earlier tradition that preceded the progressive movement: what Tyack's 1974 title refers to as "the one best system" and what Raymond E. Callahan's 1962 title calls "the cult of efficiency."

In the late nineteenth century, administrative reformers worked to create a more uniform educational system out of the relatively chaotic village-based system of school control existing at the time. Their model was the business community:

> Convinced that there was one best system of education for urban populations, leading educators sought to discover it and implement it. They were impressed with the order and efficiency of the new technology and forms of organization they saw about them. The division of labor in the factory, the punctuality of the railroad, the chain of command and coordination in modern businesses—these aroused a sense of wonder and excitement in men and women seeking to systematize the schools. . . . Efficiency, rationality, continuity, precision, impartiality became watchwords of the consolidators. In short, they tried to create a more bureaucratic system. (Tyack 1974, 28–29)

The efforts of these reformers were largely successful. By the 1930s, a school system based on professional administration, centralized bureaucracy, and decreased political—that is, democratic—control was firmly in place. Ironically, this structure created by "administrative progressives" created problems for Deweyan progressives: "It was difficult indeed to express the spirit of John Dewey's version of cooperative, democratic schooling within a hierarchical bureaucracy . . . for Dewey's ideas of democratic education demanded substantial autonomy on the part of teachers and children. . . . The full expression of Dewey's ideal of democratic education required fundamental change in the hierarchical structure of schools—and that was hardly the wish of those administrative progressives and their allies who controlled urban education" (Tyack 1974, 197–198).

Within this structural context, the cult of efficiency, based on Frederick Taylor's theories of scientific management, thrived as a movement to reform school administration. Taylor's brainchild "was essentially a system for getting greater productivity from human labor. . . . According to Taylor, there was always one best method for doing any particular job and this best method could be determined only through scientific study," specifically, time and motion studies. The "best method" was rarely applied, because workers deliberately did less work than they were capable of doing and managers did not take steps to remedy this situation. Scientific management thus meant more comprehensive and detailed management control of production and, as a result, much less freedom and discretion for workers (Callahan 1962, 25–26). Taylor's approach swept the business world, and the educational system soon followed suit.

In his classic book, *Education and the Cult of Efficiency*, Callahan describes in great detail how educational administration was affected by the "strongest social forces" of the time, namely, "industrialism—the application of mechanical power to the production of goods—and along with that the economic philosophy of the free enterprise, capitalistic system under which industrialism developed in America" (1962, 1). Thus, between 1900 and 1925, the drive for "a more businesslike organization and operation of the schools was fairly well standardized. . . . It consisted of making unfavorable comparisons between the schools and business enterprise, of applying business-industrial criteria (i.e., economy and efficiency) to education, and of suggesting that business and industrial practices be adopted by educators" (6). Advanced by a vanguard of efficiency experts among school administrators, this trend spread through the schools of educational administration and found its ultimate expression in platoon schools, based on Taylor's theories of scientific management, which ultimately became a national movement. The focus was on the most efficient use of school space, and the goal was 100 percent utilization of all space at all times by moving students from room to room; thus, curriculum was organized and departmentalized not around educational principles but around the need to economize on staff and facilities. Ultimately, says Callahan, the program's most important effect may have been to transform the role of superintendent: "By 1925 the position had more of the characteristics of a managerial job in business or industry than it did of an educational one in the schools" (148). Indeed, the social efficiency movement spawned the new profession of educational administrator. Callahan calls this "an American tragedy in education. . . . The tragedy itself was fourfold:

that educational questions were subordinated to business considerations; that administrators were produced who were not, in any true sense, educators; that a scientific label was put on some very unscientific and dubious methods and practices; and that an anti-intellectual climate, already prevalent, was strengthened" (246).

It may seem contradictory to connect restructuring programs that advocate decentralization and participation with earlier reforms that promoted directly the opposite. Indeed, TQM advocates cite some of the most liberatory models of curriculum as examples of what they are trying to achieve. Maurice Holt (1993) cites the Foxfire project; Mike Schmoker and Richard B. Wilson (1993) commend Meier's (1995) Central Park East schools. This praise notwithstanding, however, for both authors the market economy and its goals of productivity and efficiency are a model for the schools. In the early twentieth century, centralization and scientific management seemed to produce the best results; at the end of that century, decentralization and participative management appeared the most promising. These changes parallel the transformations in business management ideology. Certainly, the later trend is preferable to the earlier in terms of the day-to-day operation of the schools. But the difference is in means, not ends, and neither model presents democratic education as an end.

In the case of "the one best system," antidemocratic impulses are explicit. The administrative progressives openly rejected democratic control as corrupt, inefficient, and counterproductive and were enthusiastic about professional expertise and a business perspective as the most suitable qualifications for educational decision makers. The rhetoric, and perhaps even the beliefs and intentions, of today's reformers is democratic and participatory, but their programs are not.

The old corporate models of school organization kept dissent out of the system by removing the dissenters and avoided conflict over goals and values by repressing the opposition. The new models are more subtle—and more effective. Restructuring closes off debate about educational values and goals by ignoring or avoiding the social context of conflict that surrounds them—in short, it depoliticizes education. As Gary L. Anderson and Alexandra Dixon put it, "Much of the current site-based management movement is still modeled on entrepreneurial, free enterprise ideology with its emphasis on individualism fully intact. Conflict is effectively silenced within this framework because the norms in which the decision-making occurs reject the notion of competing or contradictory group interests" (1993, 59). Lawrence Angus states that restructuring embodies a "curiously unproblematic conception of schooling . . . in which education is reduced to school management problems that are represented as being amenable to direct solutions within the school. . . . The narrow focus on schools as neutral institutions that are to deliver quality outputs . . . diverts attention from the problematic nature of education in its social context and from the social and cultural issues which education must address" (1993, 29). All of this reinforces the "antipolitics" of education referred to in Chapter 1 (Plank and Boyd 1994, 264). In a genuinely democratic educational system, policymakers must constantly examine competing educational goals and values. In that context, restructuring moves in precisely the wrong direction because it is consciously, even aggressively, process oriented.

In the corporate world, high-involvement methods bring teamwork and collaboration into every aspect of the production process except two: the decisions about what will be produced and who will profit from it. TQM in particular calls for a clear mission statement, but in any corporation that would have to be the responsibility of those who own and control it, because under capitalism it could not be otherwise. The owners' right to determine the goals of production and to appropriate and distribute the profits as they see fit is a fundamental principle of a capitalist system. TQM and similar programs therefore do not and cannot address the most basic issues of power and control in the workplace. By concentrating attention on the means of implementing the goals already decided on by management, they avoid discussion of those goals, thereby covertly imposing a preestablished and undebatable consensus that forms the context of all debate over how the workplace will be organized. A more humane workplace and improved working conditions may still result, but that is hardly democracy. Indeed, TQM is particularly objectionable because it adopts the style and rhetoric of democratic decision making but not the actuality, and the former conceals the absence of the latter.

Restructuring has the same effect in the schools and for the same reasons. In the public sector, of course, there are no private owners, no profits, and no markets. Public budgets determine capital investment, salaries, and spending on current expenses. But issues of power and control over the school system are still critical precisely because there is no consensus on what the educational system should produce. Conflict over the basic values and purposes of education is inevitable and unavoidable. If these disagreements are resolved collectively through a democratic decision-making process, constructive and socially beneficial change can result. A democratic philosophy of education recognizes this fact. Both the goals and the process for achieving them must be open to discussion, debate, and challenge. Dewey's ideas about education make this the focal point of the educational system: The schools become laboratories of democracy as they connect with the life, and therefore the problems, of the community of which they are part. Upon examining its contemporary theory and practice, it becomes evident that restructuring precludes this possibility.

A revealingly undemocratic characteristic of restructuring is its emphasis on overcoming resistance to change, particularly from teachers. Jerry and Janice Herman, for example, discuss that process even before they define what it is that might encounter such resistance: "Principals, superintendents, boards of education, change agents, and planners can take many steps that will lessen the degree of resistance to change(s). . . . Leaders should provide detailed information about what will be changed and what will remain as it always has operated. They should provide security statements to the individuals who will be expected to initiate and maintain the desired changes. Finally, they should assure the individuals involved that they will be important sources of information" (1994, 11). Of course, some advocates of restructuring still favor the old-fashioned method of eliminating the opposition. As Baltimore middle-school principal Craig E. Spilman describes it, "Too often, reform efforts have foundered because of a district's inability to place in its schools the quality of staff needed to effect radical change. It became evident that if we were to achieve our goal of school-based management, these resistant teachers needed to make room for energetic, creative professionals committed to improving conditions at the school. Consequently, we encouraged teachers who were opposed to fast-paced change to consider transferring to more traditional schools" (1995–96, 35).

The popular Comer School Development Program "promotes group collaboration, because the group as a whole is responsible for the solution. Team members are forced to move beyond their individual orientations to consider a broader view of the problem; they can't settle an issue simply by assigning blame. . . . Consensus decision-making eliminates voting, decisions made exclusively by the principal, and a general win-lose syndrome. . . . Decisions are carried out only when everyone agrees not to block or sabotage implementation, as sometimes occurs when a vote is taken" (Squires and Kranyik 1995–96, 31). All of this has a curious resemblance to Leninist democratic centralism—explicit dissenters are eliminated, and voteless decisions within the organization are binding on everyone. It is hardly surprising that, as Andrew Gitlin and Frank Margolis assert, "There is much evidence to suggest that teacher resistance [to restructuring] does indeed reflect good sense" (1995, 397).

Restructuring is not unique in its antidemocratic inclinations. All approaches to educational decision making that ignore or avoid dealing with value conflict are antidemocratic. In a totalitarian system, for example, it is the exclusive responsibility of the political elite to determine educational goals and values, as well as the process for achieving them, and it is the duty of the citizens to accept the entire package without question. A considerably more benign example is provided by radically child-centered approaches, which leave the decision about the purposes of education to each student in the faith that he or she will naturally evolve in a socially constructive or personally functional direction. The process of achieving those purposes is left up to the individual. Whatever their merits, such methods are not democratic, because they do not result from any social decision-making process and, if one uses Rousseau's ideas as a model, have an implicit and predetermined pedagogical goal based on naturalistic assumptions about human behavior. Voucher systems are undemocratic because they replace community debate over the purposes of education with a free market, which allows individual consumers to pick and choose in an educational shopping mall. Choice may be an attractive policy option if one accepts the logic of market ideology, but it is not the same as democracy.

Logically, the ultimate model of high performance schools is a competitive, individualistic, mostly privatized system, even if many advocates of restructuring do not necessarily favor it, and even if those who do rarely say so. It is no coincidence that SBM became a nationally mandated policy in Great Britain as part of Margaret Thatcher's free-market educational program (Maddaus, 1991). Richard J. Murnane and Frank Levy (1996) approvingly list SBM among a number of policy proposals "based on a single underlying theory: if schools were free to design their programs and market these programs to families, U.S. education would improve"; they add that SBM is incomplete without "the other half of reform," which by their description bears a strong resemblance to TQM. Susan A. Mohrman and Priscilla Wohlstetter discuss the need to expand on SBM to promote "radical changes in [school] service-delivery processes" such as those occurring among insurance companies and health care providers. They see it as an entering wedge to raise questions about the basic organizational design of public schools: "Are there other ways to provide the support that districts provide? Are there other ways to audit and hold schools accountable?":

> At the core of redesigning school organizations for high performance is the notion of changing fundamental assumptions and rules of operating. . . . Teacher associations for instance may need to change from a districtwide teacher collective to one focused on individual school sites. . . . Establishing school choice would be one method of inducing educators to be more innovative, since choice would provide important feedback and consequences to schools based on their ability to attract students. . . . Individual schools, within parameters set by the district or state, will begin to design their organizations in various ways, based on members' consensus around a particular mission and goals for the school. What will emerge then will be a constellation of different models of schooling. (1994a, 285)

The current movement to restructure schools is based on theories and models that are undemocratic by virtue of their connection to market ideology. Corporate versions of participative management as applied to the schools are not only inconsistent with workplace democracy; they actively discourage it. The market economy goals of productivity, efficiency, and cost-effectiveness take priority over, and ultimately eliminate, democratic practices in the school system. Consensus-based collaborative models of school management have the effect of repressing conflict and ignoring the social context of educational politics. And finally, public education itself is threatened by the fact that a free-market educational system is potentially a much better fit with current restructuring programs.

Beyond theory, research into the actual practice of restructuring offers evidence to confirm these conclusions. The tumultuous history of educational politics itself is enough to prove that any broad consensus on educational values and goals is necessarily ephemeral or superficial. It is not surprising, therefore, that a 1994 study by the Institute for Responsive Education found a gap between policymakers and parents on the goals of education reform. The study involved focus groups of policymakers, on one hand, and parents in fourteen schools in various parts of the country serving low-income populations, on the other. The researchers found that although "in most school change efforts, educators assume a consensus on goals," Senate and congressional staff members involved with education reform placed a priority on "economic dominance" and "graduates with higher skills. . . . Without exception, legislators felt reform must be a priority in order for our country to remain competitive. Discussion was short and unanimated, almost as if it were a silly question, one for which everyone knew the right answer." However, "in sharp contrast . . . parents and community members gave intense and often lengthy responses. . . . Issues related to values and students' lack of motivation were at the top of their lists." The researchers conclude, "Hearing these divergent voices helps us understand better what different groups mean when they talk about school reform: policymakers and business leaders want new skills and higher standards; parents in disadvantaged communities worry about their children's lack of hope and eroding values; teachers and principals want the central office to take their concerns seriously; students want schools to be more respectful and engaging" (Wagner 1995–96, 44).

The researchers add that "only by bringing all the groups together can we understand what must change in our schools and why" (Wagner, 1995–96, 44). But restructuring in practice limits the agenda of discussion, so that the priorities of the most important policymakers prevail by default. This is evident in the case of SBM. Jane C. Lindle notes that in Kentucky, the first state to mandate SBM as a part of education reform, decentralization can strengthen local elites: "Rituals are entwined in the culture and climate of a school and its district. In Kentucky some schools and districts remain political enclaves dominated by political parties, religious affiliations, or influential families. . . . The degree to which districts have been able to decentralize is directly related to the degree of influence these dominant groups wield over them. Thus the exclusion of various constituencies . . . severely restricts the degree of open discussion and willingness to address educational decisions" (1995–96, 21).

SBM in Kentucky, as in most states, operates within an extensive framework of state regulations, which "have been the bane of many council operations. . . . This legalism frames and directs the councils' attention away from substantive discussion. . . . [SBM] councils become bogged down in ceremonial debates about the adequacy of bylaws, modifying them again and again to fit some nuance of administrivia." (Lindle, 1995–96, 22) Also in Kentucky, Thomas Guskey and Kent Peterson find that "the true locus of power and authority remains where it always has been—with school boards, central office staffs, and state authorities. . . . School based decision making is a process that defines how decisions should be made. It does not, however, prescribe what issues should be addressed" (1995–96, 11).

On a broader theoretical level, Hans N. Weiler sees conflict management, rather than democratic conflict resolution, as a primary function of SBM: "Conflict is thus a fairly constant element in the pursuit of educational policy in most countries and tends to become particularly intense when it comes to plans for reforming the educational system in some major way. . . . In this context, decentralization becomes a potentially promising strategy for coping with highly conflictive situations. . . . It allows the state to diffuse the sources of conflict and provide additional layers of insulation between them and the rest of the system" (1993, 68).

TQM has a similar impact. It operates in the educational system as it does in the corporate world by starting with a consensus on values and goals determined by those who are in control of the program. Although TQM gives lip service to developing a mission statement for the schools, very little of the literature about it deals with the decision-making process related to its formulation. The assumption appears to be that this is the responsibility of leadership, with, at best, some community discussion. Even if that discussion occurs, the debate over the purposes of education ends there, when—for the purposes of democratic decision making— it needs to go on continually. The result is that the most important determinations about the schools—what they should teach and for whose purposes—are omitted from the agenda for discussion. This exclusion leaves the power to determine the direction of education with those who occupy the institutional positions of authority over the system, who will have a stake in maintaining a consensus that favors their continued control:

> In many ways, TQM paints a picture of an organization where rationality has won out over politics. In the TQM perspective, organizations are cast as responding clearly to customer needs and wants. . . . Within the organization, rational processes of choice, closely tied to a customer perspective, guide the conceptualization and analysis of problems, usually in the context of teams. . . . In a rational webbing such as this, politics would seem, virtually, to disappear as rational and collectivist controls outweigh individual and coalitional preferences. (Pallas and Neumann 1995, 50)

By eliminating "politics," TQM also eliminates conflict—and therefore democratic decision-making.

It might conceivably be argued that restructuring provides the empowerment necessary for stakeholders in the educational system to assert themselves, thus creating a precondition for democracy in the school system. That is, restructuring could be in itself an educational process that takes time to show its effects. The concept of power sharing is ostensibly at the heart of the restructuring process. But again the question is whether such sharing actually results in democratic change; the answer appears to be negative.

Part of the evidence for this argument is simply common sense:

> Around the world educational bureaucracies are biting the dust at an alarming rate or so it seems. It looks as if there has been a wholesale dis-

> mantling of centralized educational bureaucracies and their replacement by devolved forms of school-based management. . . . At the level of simple logic there is a problem with this move towards self-managing schools. We need to ask ourselves the question: why would the powerful educational mandarins want to blow their collective brains out in this way by seeming to give away power? . . . Educational systems are about acquiring more power, not giving it away. So, what are they up to? (Smyth 1993, 1)

Ogawa and White cite a definition of participatory management that identifies four necessary elements: the decentralization of power, information, rewards, and knowledge or skill. Existing SBM experiments, they claim, "emphasize one element of participatory management—power—over the other three elements and over the degree to which a school district is involved" (1994, 74). They are primarily concerned with the impact of SBM on student achievement and state that "evidence on the efficacy of SBM programs is not compelling" in that area (54). Drawing on their data, however, one can also conclude that SBM fails in terms of empowerment as well, because formal power is useless without the other three elements they mention. Ogawa and White find no evidence concerning an increased downward flow of information; "SBM programs generally have not focused on rewards" (67); and the decentralization of knowledge and skills "has received less attention in SBM programs than information or rewards" (69). Power without the resources to use it is purely symbolic and thus politically vacuous.

This research is consistent with an earlier study by Betty Malen and Rodney Ogawa, which indicates that even the formal power-sharing mechanism is so limited as to be ineffective: "It is not at all apparent what site participants can do that they could not do before site based management was adopted. . . . [SBM] plans tend to cast established options as new opportunities. . . . [They] tend to shift task responsibility but not delegate decision-making authority. . . . Where plans do alter the formal decision-making arrangements, the adjustments are often confined to select domains of school policy" (1992, 189–190). Because Malen and Ogawa are partial to SBM as a reform, they are reluctant to draw unfavorable conclusions, noting that "the tendency to keep these plans ambiguous is certainly understandable. It is both technically troublesome and politically risky to specify arrangements" (191). Nonetheless, they are concerned that "site councils operated more as ancillary advisors or pro-forma endorsers than as major policy-makers or potent policy actors" and conclude that "it is not at all clear that current attempts to implement site-based management frees, inspires, or equips site participants to address school problems, engage in schoolwide planning, or develop and implement major changes in the instructional components of schools" (198).

Dale T. Snauwaert draws a broader set of conclusions. He criticizes the tendency of state regulations toward the "confinement" of autonomy to certain policy areas, which ends up leaving local boards firmly in control. "This retention of power," he states, "may be designed to provide increased efficiency and implementation success without giving up managerial control. . . . Partial participation is used to instill ownership in policy in order . . . to increase the efficiency of the system, not to empower its members" (1993, 94). This, he says, "provides a democratic veneer. . . . Although school-based management appears decentralized, it retains a significant, potentially debilitating, degree of elite control" (103).

What is at issue here is not whether this process is deliberate or accidental, whether this is an administrative plot or the flawed implementation of a well-intentioned program. In fact, it is probably neither. The problem lies in the theoretical roots of restructuring in market ideology and the corporate models on which it is based. Since neither of these is democratic or "empowering," neither is restructuring. At most, restructuring can be, in the words of Anderson and Dixon, "individually" rather than "socially" empowering. By this, they mean to make "a distinction between empowerment that empowers individuals and that which empowers social groups." The focus on the former results in an unrepresentative, even if participatory, process of decision making: "Middle class parents have access to the school environment which is denied lower social class groups. Middle class parents are related to schools by language and experience, while lower class parents are not. Teachers also share this economic and political base. This difference in 'cultural capital' often leaves poor parents and their children out of the participatory process" (1993, 58). It is therefore small wonder that "preliminary results of the decision-making [by SBM councils in the United States] show remarkably similar patterns of conformity to mainstream 'norms'" and that "more stringent and control-oriented policies involving student conduct" are far more commonly implemented than "significant changes in curriculum and instruction, equity issues and fundamental restructuring of schools . . . [which] have gone untouched" (57).

It is no accident that business interests are the most active stakeholders in restructuring. They have and always have had a very clear mission for the schools—developing a suitable labor force—although their historical record of success has been mixed. This agenda has some obvious appeal to the public because parents are rightly concerned with the employability of their children. The problem is that, under restructuring, the free discussion of that agenda cannot occur. These goals are not open to challenge from those favoring more democratic and egalitarian directions as long as school restructuring focuses on means rather than ends. A democratic educational system may or may not produce policies that progressives consider desirable, but what it can produce is citizens who have a sense of community, a willingness to listen to others, and a commitment to open discussion of alternatives. A hidden agenda of preestablished goals is the antithesis of a democratic educational system.

It is interesting to note that much of the TQM literature has a cultlike tone, especially when reference is made to Deming. Indeed, one is reminded of old-fashioned Marxist references to the authority of Joseph Stalin or Mao Tse-tung, or of contemporary paeans to the rulers of Communist North Korea. Ron Warwick refers to Deming as "a prophet in our own land" (1995, 196) and expresses his gratitude, saying "Even in his last days, Dr. Deming took the time to send me a note of thanks and support. I am glad that news of this progress elevated his spirits. . . . His work will live on through those who study and implement his philosophy" (161). James F. Leonard observes, "Deming taught me that transformation must begin with the individual; all else follows" (1996, xiii). What might be called "Deming thought" is uncritically accepted and applied as the ultimate solution for all management problems, including those in education, and Deming's words are literally gospel to his adherents. "Deming wanted to take [the] modern world forward and make it better for us all," explain Lloyd Dobyns and Clare Crawford-Mason. "It sounds simplistic, even childish, but that is the aim of the revolution he started—to make life better for us all. . . . All we need to do is replace the quantity management system with Deming's quality management system that we will need in the future. It will work perfectly well—everywhere" (1994, xii, xxiv).

Ultimately, however, it is market ideology that shapes restructuring into an antidemocratic approach to school reform, although criticisms from that direction are relatively uncommon. Alfie Kohn claims to be "enthusiastic about TQM in a business context" but believes that "*a marketplace model, even correctly applied, does not belong in the classroom.* The difference between two management approaches . . . is less significant that the difference between any method for managing workers and what happens in the classroom" (1993, 58; emphasis in original). Paola Sztajn claims that TQM recycles the business metaphor and is thus an inappropriate model for the schools (1992, 35–37). Gary Alexander and Carolyn Keeler strike the same chord: "Total Quality Management's form of empowerment remains based on management themes, bureaucratic rules, and management protocols. . . . [It] promotes a metaphor based on factory organization and structure, the language of business, and corporate leadership authority to restructure education" (1995, 34–35). Alexander and Keeler also question whether the type of educational leadership envisioned by TQM is in fact the kind of moral and ethical leadership that is really needed.

Broader structural criticisms are offered by Carolyn Kelley, who argues that although market-based models "are potentially useful for addressing public sector organizational problems," they are not generally feasible in the schools, given their special circumstances. SBM in particular "assumes a high level of internal control over financial resources, inputs, and participant selection, and a high degree of agreement on organizational goals," which schools generally do not have. Moreover, "the lack of an educational 'market' means there is no mechanism for replacing extremely poor performing schools with newer, more innovative organizational forms"—unless, she adds disapprovingly, we develop full-blown markets for schools (1994, 21). Clair Brown offers a similar analysis, arguing that the economic, political, and social structure surrounding the public schools differs from that governing the private sector and that "market exchange" is an imperfect mechanism for evaluating the relationship between inputs and outputs of the school system. "The production process in education is vastly more complicated than in the private sector," says Brown, "because of the large number of intervening social, political, and economic variables that are outside the control of the schools" (1993, 224–225). Put in plainer language, "The [formal] organization metaphor does not fit the nature of school purposes, the work that schools do, the relationships needed for serving parents and students, the context for work that teachers need to be successful, or the nature of effective teaching and learning environments. . . . Schools are just too different. Their purposes are different, the people they serve are different, the work conditions needed to serve effectively are different, and the relationships needed to serve effectively are different" (Sergiovanni 1996, 13, 15).

Thus, restructuring as it is now being implemented across the country may be not only undemocratic but also irrelevant to the actual needs of the school system and therefore ultimately ineffective in creating meaningful change of any kind. This is not just because of its need for fine tuning or more careful administration but because of its theoretical foundations in the market economy. Whatever its weaknesses, restructuring can do serious damage to the school system, because so many enlightened educators have bought into its deceptive rhetoric. There is nothing more politically dangerous than a conservative program successfully disguised as a progressive reform. Unless not only the means but also the ends of restructuring are openly debated and discussed, we risk destroying the public, social, and democratic nature of our schools in the name of participation.

In the 1957 movie *The Bridge on the River Kwai,* the Japanese prison camp commandant who addresses the prisoners of war as they build the bridge (and die of disease and starvation in the process) customarily ends his speeches with the phrase "Be happy in your work." The British colonel in charge of the prisoners decides that, under the circumstances, their survival and morale depend on striving for quality in the construction of the bridge and thus collaborating toward that end with their captors, even though their work will aid the Japanese military effort. He would have taken heart from a quote by Deming: "Joy on the job comes not so much from the result, the product, but from contribution to optimization of the system in which everybody wins" (quoted in Warwick 1995, 122). In the end the bridge is destroyed by a U.S. soldier who sees the truth of the matter: Means and ends are inseparable; the freedom to determine the former is worthless without the opportunity to debate and decide on the latter. Dewey said as much in regard to the schools, and democratic educators should not forget that lesson.

References

Alexander, Gary, and Carolyn Keeler. 1995. *Total Quality Management: The Emperor's Tailor*. Boise: University of Idaho Department of Educational Administration.

Anderson, Gary L., and Alexandra Dixon. 1993. "Paradigm Shifts and Site-Based Management in the United States: Toward a Paradigm of Social Empowerment." In *A Socially Critical View of the Self-Managing School*, ed. John Smyth. London: Falmer Press.

Angus, Lawrence. 1993. "Democratic Participation or Efficient Site Management in the United States: Toward a Paradigm of Social Empowerment." In *A Socially Critical View of the Self-Managing School*, ed. John Smyth. London: Falmer Press.

Brown, Clair. 1993. "Employee Involvement in Industrial Decision-Making: Lessons for Public Schools." In *Decentralization and School Improvement*, ed. Jane Hannaway and Martin Carnoy. San Francisco: Jossey-Bass.

Callahan, Raymond E. 1962. *Education and the Cult of Efficiency*. Chicago: University of Chicago Press.

Commission on the Future of Worker-Management Relations. 1995. "Employee Participation and Labor-Management Cooperation in American Workplaces." *Challenge*, September–October.

David, Jane L. 1995–96. "The Who, What, and Why of Site-Based Management." *Educational Leadership*, December–January.

Dobyns, Lloyd, and Clare Crawford-Mason. 1994. *Thinking about Quality*. New York: Times Books.

Gaebler, Ted, and David Osborne. 1992. *Reinventing Government*. New York: Addison-Wesley.

Gaul, Thomas. 1994. "Reform at the Grass Roots." *American School Board Journal*, January.

Ginsberg, Rick. 1996. "The New Institutionalism, the New Science, Persistence and Change: The Power of Faith in Schools." In *The Politics of Education and the New Institutionalism,* ed. R. L. Crowson, W. L. Boyd, and H. B. Mawhinney. Washington, D.C.: Falmer Press.

Gitlin, Andrew, and Frank Margolis. 1995. "The Political Aspect of Reform: Teacher Resistance as Good Sense." *American Journal of Education* 103: 377–403.

Gunn, Christopher E. 1984. *Worker Self-Management in the United States.* Ithaca, N.Y.: Cornell University Press.

Guskey, Thomas, and Kent Peterson. 1995–96. "The Road to Classroom Change." *Educational Leadership.* December–January.

Herman, Jerry J., and Janice L. Herman. 1994. *Education Quality Management.* Lancaster, Pa.: Technomic.

Holt, Maurice. 1993. "The Educational Consequences of W. Edwards Deming." *Phi Delta Kappan,* January.

Kelley, Carolyn. 1994. "The Applicability of Market-Based Solutions to Public Sector Problems." Presented at the annual meeting of the Association of Public Policy Analysis and Management.

Kohn, Alfie. 1993. "Turning Learning into a Business: Concerns about Total Quality." *Educational Leadership,* September.

Leonard, James F. 1996. *The New Philosophy for K–12 Education.* Milwaukee: ASQC Quality Press.

Lindle, Jane C. 1995–96. "Lessons from Kentucky about School-Based Decision Making." *Educational Leadership,* December–January.

Maddaus, John. 1991. "Making Education Accountable to the Marketplace." Presented at the annual meeting of the New England Educational Research Organization.

Malen, Betty, and Rodney T. Owaga. 1992. "Site Based Management: Disconcerting Policy Issues, Critical Policy Choices." In *Restructuring the Schools,* ed. John J. Lane and Edgar Epps. Berkeley: McCutchan Publishing.

Meier, Deborah. 1995. "How Our Schools Could Be." *Phi Delta Kappan,* January.

Mohrman, Susan A., and Priscilla Wohlstetter. 1994. "Conclusion: New Directions for School-Based Management." In *School-Based Management: Organizing for High Performance,* ed. Susan A. Mohrman and Priscilla Wohlstetter. San Francisco: Jossey-Bass.

Murnane, Richard J., and Frank Levy. 1996. "What General Motors Can Teach U.S. Schools about the Proper Role of Markets in Education Reform." *Phi Delta Kappan,* October.

National Education Association (NEA), Educational Policies Commission. 1938. *The Structure and Administration of Education in American Democracy.* Washington, D.C.: NEA.

———. 1940. *Learning the Ways of Democracy.* Washington, D.C.: NEA.

Ogawa, Rodney T., and Paula A. White. 1994. "School-Based Management: An Overview." In *School-Based Management: Organizing for High Performance,* ed. Susan A. Mohrman and Priscilla Wohlstetter. San Francisco: Jossey-Bass.

Pallas, Aaron M., and Anna Neumann. 1995. "Lost in Translation." In *Restructuring Schools: Promising Practices and Policies,* ed. Maureen T. Hallinan. New York: Plenum Press.

Parks, Susan. 1995. "Improving Workplace Performance: Historical and Theoretical Contexts." *Monthly Labor Review,* May.

Plank, David, and William L. Boyd. 1994. "Antipolitics, Education, and Institutional Choice: The Flight from Democracy."*American Educational Research Journal* 31: 263–281.

Schmoker, Mike, and Richard B. Wilson. 1993. "Transforming Schools through Quality Education." *Phi Delta Kappan,* January.

Sergiovanni, Thomas J. 1996. *Leadership for the Schoolhouse.* San Francisco: Jossey-Bass.

Smyth, John. 1993. Introduction to *A Socially Critical View of the Self-Managing School,* ed. John Smyth. London: Falmer Press.

Snauwaert, Dale T. 1993. *Democracy, Education, and Governance.* Albany: State University of New York Press.

Spilman, Craig E. 1995–96. "Transforming an Urban School." *Educational Leadership,* December–January.

Squires, David A., and Robert Kranyik. 1995–96. "The Comer Program: Changing School Culture." *Educational Leadership,* December–January.

Sztajn, Paola. 1992. "A Matter of Metaphors." *Educational Leadership,* November.

Tyack, David B. 1974. *The One Best System.* Cambridge: Harvard University Press.

Wagner, Tony. 1995–96. "Seeking Common Ground: Goal-Setting with All Constituencies." *Educational Leadership,* December–January.

Warwick, Ron. 1995. *Beyond Piecemeal Improvements.* Bloomington, Ind.: National Education Service.

Weiler, Hans N. 1993. "Control vs. Legitimation: The Politics of Ambivalence." In *Decentralization and School Improvement,* ed. Jane Hannaway and Martin Carnoy. San Francisco: Jossey-Bass.

Wohlstetter, Priscilla, and Roxane Smyer. 1994. "Models of High Performance Schools." In *School-Based Management: Organizing for High Performance,* ed. Susan Mohrman and Priscilla Wohlstetter. San Francisco: Jossey-Bass.

7 Curriculum

What should children learn? The answers to that question have been determined by the outcome of conflicts over the direction of the school curriculum. According to Kliebard, the foremost historian of these disputes, during the first half of the twentieth century "there were no unconditional surrenders or overwhelming triumphs" among the interest groups involved (1987, xiii). He points to a "constant ebb and flow of curriculum fashions," a cyclical pattern related to changing political and social trends, as well as resistance from the organizational and administrative culture of the schools (1988, 31–32). But he also notes that the "massive entry by the federal government into curriculum matters [after 1958] . . . dramatically changed the political balance and the nature of the interplay among the protagonists in the struggle" (1987, xiii). This has been especially true in recent years; during the last fifteen years of the twentieth century, federal and state governments placed themselves solidly behind a modernized version of the ultimate expression of market ideology in curriculum development: social efficiency. The September 20, 1998, edition of the *New York Times* reports:

> While education has long been one of the voters' top five or six concerns along with crime, drugs, the economy, and foreign threats, the issue has been cited by pollsters this year as the voters' primary focus. . . . The debate over education often tracks the liberal-conservative divide. . . . Nevertheless, what is striking about the debate is that if there is not agreement on the means, there is near-universal consensus on the ends of this education campaign. "The traditionalists have won," remarked Larry Cuban, an education professor at Stanford University. "New math and whole-language reading are in retreat. Today there are more phonics, more multiplication tables, more tests. There is a consensus between the public and officials that the basic, traditional model is the one to pursue. Whatever experimentation is occurring today challenges the boundaries far less than two or three decades ago."

Cuban is not specific about the traditional model to which he is referring. But in fact, the new consensus has its intellectual roots in the social efficiency movement of the 1920s. That decade, like the 1990s, was characterized by the dominance of market values in social, political, and economic issues—when, in Calvin Coolidge's words, the business of the United States was business. That could just as well be the watchword of curriculum development today.

This direction is profoundly at odds with democratic public education and utterly in line with market ideology. Productivity becomes the sole end of education. The explicit purpose of the schools is to prepare young people for their economic roles in the future. The curriculum is organized to develop the kinds of thinking and skills that so-called experts believe to be necessary for those roles. This task involves formulating a very specific and detailed set of curriculum standards and developing elaborate measures of assessment to determine whether the schools are sufficiently productive. Since the early 1980s, this has been the path taken by the educational system throughout the nation.

The control of the schools is thereby removed from the community and placed in the hands of those who control the market economy. The development of young people as social beings and democratic citizens takes a back seat—if it has any place at all—to their development as commodities in the labor market. And the curriculum itself is fragmented into thousands of separate strands of knowledge related to specific vocational skills, each to be pursued separately and evaluated quantitatively. The result is a generation of young people who are not given the education they need to build their own futures or the future of their society. It is evident that the antidemocratic doctrine of social efficiency in education, adapted for the age of high technology and given such names as "systems management," has once again come to the fore.

The original social efficiency movement had three main components. It called for administrative organization of the schools along the lines of corporate models, as discussed in the previous chapter. It declared the purpose of education to be the preparation of young people for their future responsibilities in society, in particular for the specific occupational roles they would fill. And it emphasized the importance of standardized testing, measurement of achievement, and the need to sort students according to their apparent talents and abilities. With the partial exception of sorting, by the end of the twentieth century, some eighty years later, these principles had once again become the policy guidelines for public education.

Kliebard describes the social efficiency movement in curriculum as "a science of exact measurement and precise standards in the interests of maintaining a predictable and orderly world. . . . It became an urgent mission. That mission took the form of enjoining curriculum-makers to devise programs of study that prepared individuals specifically and directly for the role they would play as adult members of the social order. . . . Social utility became the supreme criterion against which the value of school studies was measured" (1987, 89–90). The key figures in this movement were Franklin Bobbitt (who played a major part in the administrative social efficiency movement), W. W. Charters, and David Snedden.

In his 1924 book, *How to Make a Curriculum,* Bobbitt claims, "It is helpful to begin with the simple assumption, to be accepted literally, that education is to prepare men and women for the activities of every kind which make up, or which ought to make up, well-rounded adult life; that it has no other purpose; that everything should be done with a view to this purpose; and that nothing should be included which does not serve this purpose." In sharp contrast to Dewey's position, Bobbitt argued that "education is primarily for adult life, not for child life. Its fundamental responsibility is to prepare for the fifty years of adulthood, not for the twenty years of childhood and youth" (7–8). "Education," he says, "is the process of growing up in the right way" (44). The process of curriculum design, therefore, must focus on building the curriculum around "the activities which ought to make up the lives of men and women; and along with these the abilities and personal qualities necessary for proper performance" (8).

Along those lines, Bobbitt lists ten major "objectives of education," based on "the practically unanimous judgment of some 2700 well-trained and experienced adults" (1924, 10). He breaks these down into 150 "principal subdivisions" and adds, "We have not here attempted to go into the more minute subdivisions." Thus, under "general mental efficiency," he specifies 9 principal subdivisions, one of which is the "ability effectively to perform the mental activities involved in the proper exercise of the many specific functions which one should perform." This entry has 49 minor subdivisions including everything from "delight in the experiences involved in the exercise of the ability" to "disposition to be active." He itemizes 8 different goals related to dealing with errors and faults, such as "an active dislike of things faulty when measured by proper standards." The tenth major objective is "occupational activities," of which "there are hundreds, even thousands," and for each of which "a separate list of abilities must be formulated" (11–29). Sorting these out by discipline, Bobbitt offers sets of "guiding principles and assumptions" (146 in the social studies), objectives from the lists mentioned above (17), and pupil activities and experiences (21). For the study of Latin alone, he enumerates 30 principles and 5 objectives. Among the occupational activities, he includes "unspecialized practical arts for men" (the use of tools and the like) and "practical arts of women" (cooking, sewing, and child care).

Charters sets out much the same guidelines, but in a somewhat less obsessive and orderly fashion. His method, "job analysis," is the determination of skills and traits necessary to perform certain activities, which he compares to the components of a recipe or a job description. His recommended approach is to "determine the major objectives of education by a study of the life of man in its social setting" (1923, 102) and then to divide them into "ideals," "the objective equivalents of satisfaction or dissatisfaction," and "activities," "the means through which dissatisfaction is eliminated and satisfaction is obtained" (28–29). The curriculum then "consists of both ideals and activities on the one hand and their methods of realization and performance on the other hand" (74). Thus, for an elementary school, "the activities and ideals of a society must be determined, evaluated, and selected; the best methods of performing the activities under the domination of appropriate ideals must be collected; and the material so determined must be presented at the psychological moment in the life of a child" (147). His discussions of curriculum building in specific subjects therefore involve massive data collection—especially surveys among "experts"— to establish a consensus of opinion about what kind of skills and information is needed in any particular discipline. In mathematics, for example, he cites a survey of Indiana businessmen; a questionnaire sent to 1,700 school superintendents; a review of several thousand sales checks from department stores (to find the most common mathematical errors); and a study involving a standard cookbook, the payrolls of a number of artificial flower and feather factories, mark-down sales advertisements, and a general hardware catalog to determine the relative importance of the various content elements in the course of study in arithmetic (chap. 17).

Snedden's "sociological" approach to organizing the curriculum fits well into this arrangement and was an inspiration for the practice of academic tracking. Given the obvious individual differences among young people, he argues, it hardly makes sense to provide a uniform curriculum for all of them. Therefore, he favors at least partial group differentiation by the age of twelve. Although one could not predict the ultimate educational path of each individual, "a shrewd social diagnostician, knowing the facts as to the home conditions, school standing in studies, intellectual interests, general moral behavior, and physical conditions of one hundred children at twelve years of age, could. . . . guess right as to 90 per cent of them" (1921, 46–47). Applying standards of efficiency (the typical U.S. high school being "only from 10 to 50 percent efficient" in terms of its general education offerings), the goal would be to adjust the curriculum to the sociologically determined needs of students. Thus, if "in any school, for example, it is reasonably certain that from 70 to 90 percent of the girls will eventually be homemakers . . . an elective prevocational course in the known mathematics of homemaking might well be offered." Similarly, if in a rural school "30 to 60 percent of the boys will follow the local types of farming . . . short intensive prevocational courses in mathematics adapted to the prevailing local types of farming can be devised" (130).

The objectives of education were therefore to be matched to the social background and qualities of groups of students. In the social sciences, Snedden suggests the following example:

> Let us take at random one hundred men of from thirty to forty years of age. Let us rank these hundred men in a series from lowest to highest according to the consensus of opinion of several competent judges directed to base their decisions on the extent to which each individual of the hundred is a cultivated man and a good citizen, using, as far as practicable,

> what the world holds as approved qualities of these descriptions. . . . Let us call the twenty highest, A grade men, the next thirty, B grade men, the next thirty, C grade men, and the lowest twenty, D grade men. . . . Suppose, now, that a fairly complete social survey of the character here illustrated [that is, the relative levels of knowledge in each category] could be made, to cover all our classes of adults. . . . Following such procedure, we should be able to define a very acceptable scheme of objectives, so definite they would readily suggest the means and methods by which they could be realized. (1921, 221)

In relation to civic education, for example, Snedden describes a social "Group M" consisting of low-income, middle-aged shopkeepers with large families, and a "Group N" of "prosperous business men of American ancestry." Each, he says, will have different comparative civic values; members of the former group will attach a priority to cleaning the street in front of their houses, rather than subscribing to a government war loan; the priorities will be reversed for the latter group (1921, 260).

In short, Snedden envisions an educational system in which curriculum is organized to match the social values, requirements, and abilities of specific social groups, as determined by those who are capable of making such judgments. He also sets forth a calculus of "peths," "strands," and "lotments," which are individual components of a particular curriculum for each social group. Kliebard describes the result as "a vision of a school and its curriculum [that] was almost a caricature of Taylor's vision of a factory and the manufacturing process virtually replete with the stopwatch which had become practically a symbol of industrial efficiency." And this was not some eccentric expression of ivory-tower academia, for "he was representing what amounted to the dominant curriculum ideology of his day" (1988, 112–113).

Social efficiency demanded that the school curriculum be developed on the basis of the needs of the existing system, that is, a market economy. Ascertaining those needs required a form of market research—finding out the specific skills and abilities required by the economy of the time. These would be translated into specific educational criteria, which could then be measured and tested.

Not coincidentally, the techniques of psychological testing and measurement were coming into their own as well during the

1920s. The trend began with intelligence testing for army recruits in World War I. The era of mass testing began as psychologists evaluated the results and attempted to make a science out of it. Schools jumped on the bandwagon; in 1929, the first so-called Iowa Tests were developed. Students could thus be sorted into the academic pathways that most suited their particular social group. The curriculum could now be differentiated according to their respective potentials and the nature of economic demand for a suitable workforce.

With the partial exception of the tracking, this is the exact pattern of curriculum development of the 1990s. Even if the current language of curriculum development is far more sophisticated, and even with the availability of high-technology methods of gathering data, organizing concepts, and testing and measuring, the philosophy is the same. What is more, in a strangely egalitarian twist, tracking is no longer the object of reform—rather, the goal is to restructure the entire curriculum to apply to all students.

At the time, social efficiency encountered criticism from progressive educators, in particular Bode. In his 1927 book, *Modern Educational Theories,* he offers subtle and understated yet pointed critiques of the ideas of Bobbitt, Charters, and Snedden from the point of view of an advocate of democratic public schools. All three see education as training for specific objectives, which, according to Bode, "cannot be the whole aim of education, for the reason that the purpose of this [progressive] movement is precisely to make over the social order and our present modes of living so that we may progressively substitute new objectives for old ones. Any scheme of education that fails to make provision for this element of progress is, so far forth, hostile to the democratic purpose of humanizing both education and life" (79).

Bobbitt, Charters, and Snedden more or less explicitly claim to be applying scientific method to curriculum construction. "No right-minded person can object to the scientific study of education," says Bode. "But we cannot afford to forget that the significant objectives of education must spring from a comprehensive theory of education" (1927, 92). He argues that Bobbitt's priorities are "essentially a reflection of his own personal philosophy of life. . . . My criticism is that personal bias or preference is smuggled in under the guise of an objective, impersonal determination of fact. When this happens, educational objectives become once more, as in the past, an excuse for the perpetuation of tradition and the status quo" (84–85). Bobbitt, Charters, and Snedden all develop curriculum on the basis of consensus of "expert" opinion as a substitute for theory, he says. Essentially, they start with a collection of what they consider to be relevant data and build an educational objective on it. Bode argues that this is backwards: "Our objectives determine what sort of facts are needed, and consequently how the method is to be used" (112). Their notion of curriculum building is based on approaches that "apparently reduce to methods for taking a vote, and the scientific determination of objectives evaporates into a recommendation to try a questionnaire" (13). More to the point, a curriculum by consensus of this kind ratifies the educational judgments of those with the greatest social and economic power and ends up serving their interests.

The progressives were not particularly effective in limiting the success of the social efficiency movement. That was accomplished by a far more impersonal force—the Great Depression. With the collapse of the economy, any suggestion for using education as a pathway to the job market became hollow. And the social turmoil of the time gave progressives at least an ideological advantage in their assertion that the time had come for considering major changes in the organization of the U.S. economy.

It may seem odd to revive a 1920s debate on curricular change as a means of understanding today's policy directions. Yet the questions and controversies are much the same; the differences are that the progressive voice is silent, and the partisans of social efficiency have the government, academia, and the educational bureaucracy behind them. The consensus on curriculum reform today in most respects parallels almost exactly, though in more sophisticated form, the arguments of social efficiency educators of the 1920s. The underlying philosophy of education is the same as that of Bobbitt: the purpose of the schools is to train and educate children for the world of the future, or more to the point, the world that adults have already created for them. It is more explicitly linked to techno-ideology and is thus more connected to the tenets of market ideology.

Chapter 5's discussion relates this issue to the use of technology in the schools. The empirical argument is that the world has changed, or, more accurately, the twenty-first century will see drastic changes in the form and organization of work that will require a whole new and different set of skills and abilities on the part of workers. The assumption, like that of the social efficiency theorists of the 1920s, is that we can list these skills and abilities in a way that can be applied to all areas of the curriculum and that we can develop standardized tests and methods of assessment that can determine our success.

From the standpoint of democratic values, this approach is a disaster. First of all, it links the curriculum to questionable assumptions about the future of the economy and deprives the community, especially students, of choosing their future. Second, it shatters the curriculum into thousands of separate and unrelated fragments of knowledge, rigidly organized into lists of what students must learn at a particular time. Finally, through an ever-expanding system of statewide achievement tests, it sets up arbitrary standards that completely ignore the realities of the "savage inequalities" that exist in the U.S. educational system. All of this destroys the foundations of any potential for a democratic school system.

The underlying assumption is, once again, that high technology has a liberatory effect. In the future, workers will need to master a much wider repertoire of skills because jobs will require a higher level of proficiency in an economy based on information technology. The workplace itself will demand more independent thinking and decision making, as well as the ability to assume responsibility for a wider variety of tasks. It will also demand a higher degree of flexibility and versatility, because employment security is going to vanish. In a 1994 article in *Fortune* magazine entitled "The End of the Job," William Bridges states that "the modern world is on the verge of another huge leap in creativity and productivity, but the job is not going to be part of tomorrow's economic reality. . . . In place of jobs, there are part-time and temporary work situations. . . . Today's organization is rapidly being transformed from a structure built out of jobs into a field of work needing to be done" (63).

This point of view about changes in the workplace has been strongly promoted in elite commission reports. The first of these was issued in 1990 by the National Center on Education and the Economy (NCEE), a think tank led by a group of corporate executives, public officials, and academics. Entitled *America's Choice: High Skills or Low Wages!* it argues for the need to improve worker productivity in what it calls "a third industrial revolution." The report states that the structure of work is changing from "Taylorism" to "new high performance work organizations," requiring workers to take on more responsibility. "Management layers disappear as front-line workers assume responsibility for many of the tasks—from quality control to production scheduling—that others used to do" (2). The NCEE proposes a comprehensive national school-to-work program that would set educational performance standards for all students; the standards would have to be met by age sixteen, their successful completion culminating in the award of a Certificate of Initial Mastery. At that point, the student could choose to go to work, enter a college preparatory program, or study for a Technical and Professional Certificate. A system of employment and training boards, established by federal and state governments, would organize and oversee the process (5–9).

Thus, the educational system must orient itself toward producing an appropriate labor force. The U.S. Department of Labor, Secretary's Commission on Achieving Necessary Skills (SCANS) issued a highly influential report along those lines in 1991. Entitled *What Work Requires of Schools,* it identifies five "workplace competencies" and three "foundation skills" needed for the new type of workplace. The competencies include the knowledge of how to allocate resources; interpersonal skills; the ability to acquire, process, and evaluate information; an understanding of systems; and technological expertise. The foundation skills are basic knowledge (the three Rs), thinking abilities (decision making, reasoning, and problem solving), and personal qualities (responsibility, sociability, and integrity).

SCANS issued a more detailed follow-up report in 1992. It notes that the previous report was criticized for its assumption that places of employment would grow and change to accommodate the new workers. Acknowledging this "chicken-and-egg argument," the commission responds that "it can be resolved only by recognizing that both high-performance workplaces and highly trained workers are needed. Whatever their order, each reinforces the other, and the absence of either can retard the other's development. . . . What remains true is that firms cannot organize for a truly competitive and productive future around skills they cannot find. Conversely, students contemplating work will not be motivated to develop new skills unless employers value those skills" (8–9).

This comment illustrates what is most remarkable about this perspective: for the most part, its more sophisticated advocates do not claim that the corporate world is actually undergoing a change in its work organization or that the jobs of the future will match the new kind of education they are proposing. Rather, they argue that such a change needs to occur and will be hastened by a transformation of the schools. As Lauren B. Resnick and John G. Wirt put it, "We are faced, then, with a dual problem . . . to prepare both young people and the economy at large for a new, high-performance future" (1996, 6). In short, if you build it, they will come. This view goes beyond the undemocratic idea of orienting education toward preparation of young people for the future: it prepares them for a future that might not exist.

A more precise name for this hypothesis might be "supply-side neoliberalism." (Engel 1991). Supply-side economics, the basis of Reagan administration economic policies, was so named because of its assumption that a greater amount of available capital—provided by tax breaks to business—would in and of itself promote increased investment, production, and therefore employment. Ultimately, it was argued, the tax breaks would pay for themselves as profits soared, unemployment decreased, and revenue yields increased at lower rates of taxation. In the 1990s, among curriculum planners and education reformers, this view appears to have combined with the neoliberal conviction that a more active government role is needed in planning and investment to steer private enterprise in a more internationally competitive direction. The result was a new kind of human capital theory—that an appropriately educated labor force will in and of itself promote economic development if both business and the public schools abandon their short-range perspectives and plan for the future.

In much of the writing elaborating this standpoint, there is a strong streak of optimism, similar to that which accompanied expressions of supply-side economics. The business cycle seems to disappear; there is an implicit assumption that there will be a steady demand for a flexibly skilled stream of potential employees. The weaknesses of this hypothesis, of course, are the same as those of the economic theory from which it originates: it is a form of theory that sounds hard-nosed and realistic, when in fact it is totally divorced from the real world. It is, to use C. Wright Mills's famous phrase, crackpot realism.

Supply-side thinking is reflected in the NCEE's idea that an educational change of this magnitude would stimulate businesses to take the risks involved in restructuring their work organizations in line with high-performance standards. In fact, its own surveys showed that employers were not particularly concerned about a skills shortage, and the 1992 report admits, "We found little evidence of a far-reaching desire for a more educated workforce" (26). But this is because the costs and risks of change are too uncertain for corporations, and therefore "most American companies still cling to old forms of work organization" (40). Therefore, to reduce that risk, and to enable future workers to participate in sharing the fruits of the third industrial revolution, the educational system needed to change. Whether corporate America was ready or not, effective competition in the international economy would require "a high productivity work organization," and the educational system ought to take the lead.

These perspectives are echoed in other governmental reports. Put in plain language, the argument became that even if the data did not support the idea that workplace changes were necessarily in the offing, the schools needed to change anyway. In a curious way, these reports echoed the economic determinism of the social reconstructionists of the 1930s: certain economic transformations are inevitable, so the schools should take the lead in reorganizing the economy. In a 1994 report published by the Department of Education, Anthony Carnevale and Jeffrey D. Porro concede that the labor market may not be ready for an influx of "high-performance" workers. Nonetheless, they conclude that "these more negative recent trends reflect short-term realities and do not conflict with the consistent long-term trend toward increasing skills and education requirements on the job. . . . As the recovery [from the 1991 recession] takes hold and accelerates the long-term trend in favor of more educated workers, labor will reassert itself aggressively" (33–34). Richard F. Elmore, a strong advocate of school-to-work programs, allows that "the empirical case for this view of the transformation of the American economy is, as with all economic predictions, somewhat uncertain." He deems it "implausible" to assume that firms will "arrive at a sudden recognition that they need a different kind of worker and immediately change their hiring practices, work organization, and technologies" (1996, 64–66). Paul E. Barton acknowledges that "there is, of course, a debate about the degree to which a changing economy is requiring higher levels of education and training. The facts are not as clear as one would like them to be." "There is less doubt, however," he adds, "about whether the economy and international competitiveness can benefit from a better-educated workforce. I certainly believe they can" (1996, 133).

Some members of the education community have gone so far as to lecture corporate America on its responsibility to upgrade its workplaces. Educator Clinton E. Boutwell criticizes the corporate "shell game" of blaming the schools for their own lack of competitiveness. He argues that corporations need to recognize their own failure to develop and use more highly skilled workers: "Isn't it possible for corporations to take some responsibility for the well-being of the nation? Even if only on a small scale, some American companies have already demonstrated that they can make a handsome profit while still being socially responsible. . . . A first step would be for America's major corporations to face the fact that they should be a major part of the solution, just as they are part of the problem. . . . They need to change their corporate attitude" (1997, 198–199). Boutwell believes that high technology will change the workplace and calls for "the new high school," which will "consciously and systematically educate students so that their ability to use higher-order thinking and intellectual processes is accelerated, and in which they have an opportunity to actively practice collaborative and healthy interpersonal skills" (287). But this means we must "avoid political posturing and the diatribe coming from certain business executives. . . . If we insist on job expansion from Corporate America, then together concerned parents and educators can bring about the changes needed for education in the 21st century. . . . Then everyone will be winners of the shell game" (358).

The reality of the future economy may be more in line with the description offered by Douglas Henwood: "Since most social analysis in America is powered by caricature rather than fact, the evidence for the skills argument is spotty at best. . . . Employer surveys reveal that bosses care less about their employees' candlepower than they do about 'character.' . . . Bosses want underlings who are steadfast, dependable, consistent, punctual, tactful, and who identify with their work and show sympathy for others; those who are labeled creative and independent received low marks" (1996, 2–3).

Henwood notes that Bureau of Labor Statistics projections refute the idea of "bountiful jobs of the future"; the fastest-growing occupations are primarily unskilled or semiskilled. Thus, he sees an outline for the future that "sounds pretty familiar: basic production employing ever fewer, with ever more in ill-paid service jobs" (1996, 7.) David Paris agrees, concluding that "there is not a clear and compelling skills gap, save for those individuals with few educational credentials who can no longer compete because less-skilled manufacturing jobs are disappearing" (1994, 13).

Nonetheless, supply-side neoliberalism helped create the necessary climate of opinion so that in May 1994 President Clinton signed the School to Work Opportunities Act (STWOA), which authorized $300 million in the first year to offer students on-site, work-based career training. The program, which was to be administered jointly by the Departments of Education and Labor, was different from conventional vocational education programs in that it was intended for all students, regardless of economic means, and "acknowledge[d] that preparation for earning a living is a legitimate and important role of school for all children, college and non-college bound" (Charner 1997, 2). In the 1920s, social efficiency was primarily a theory of vocational education, and to a considerable extent the movement at the time was for the establishment of separate vocational schools. It is the universality of STWOA that is particularly significant: for the first time, the curriculum is to be vocationalized for everybody. And it is in this regard that the new trend is most threatening for the idea of democratic education.

The goal of school-to-work advocates is implementing the "SCANS competencies" in all areas of the curriculum for all students. "The competencies outlined by SCANS and [the NCEE's] New Standards are generic in nature," state Resnick and Wirt. "They are not targeted to any particular job or even a group of occupations" (1996, 11). Thus, the competencies can serve as a basis for organizing the entire curriculum, that is, as a national and universal standard for all public schools. "The purpose of public schools, in this new view," says Elmore, "is not simply to provide access but also to impart a common body of knowledge, skill, and personal qualities. Their purpose is less to accommodate diverse interests and aptitudes within a structure that provides multiple opportunities for everyone than to provide a relatively strong common set of academic experiences for every student" (1996, 61). Barton calls for integrating academic and vocational education, thus ending the schism between the two that has existed since the passage of the Smith-Hughes Act in 1917 (1996, 128). It should be recalled that this law was a compromise response to the demands of industrialists for separate academic and vocational high schools—the two tracks would, instead, generally be housed within the same comprehensive institutions. The contemporary advocates of the school-to-work plan would eliminate the distinction completely. John R. Frederiksen and Allan Collins go even further in stating that for students "to acquire the necessary competencies while they are in school . . . the lines between school and workplace will have to be blurred so that students have opportunities to explore the world of work and teachers can acquire knowledge of workplace tasks and competencies" (1996, 194).

What this means for the curriculum is nothing less than an entirely different approach to learning. A useful illustration is provided in the U.S. Department of Labor's 1992 SCANS report, which provides a chart comparing the conventional classroom with the SCANS classroom. In the conventional classroom, the teacher knows the answer, plans all activities, makes all assessments, and usually teaches thirty students; students work alone, are "expected to conform to teacher's behavioral expectations," and show poor self-esteem. The curriculum is fragmented into separate disciplines, and "listening and speaking often are missing." In the

SCANS classroom, on the other hand, there is always more than one solution that is not necessarily the teacher's; educational stakeholders plan and work together; "organizing systems are complex"; disciplines are integrated, and students are to be responsible and self-managing. Most important, instead of encouraging thinking that is theoretical and academic, the SCANS classroom encourages problem solving, reasoning, and decision making.

Superficially, the SCANS classroom appears to be liberatory in comparison with the conventional classroom, but only because the latter is a caricature and the former is a facade. This is demonstrated by considering what is meant by practical problem solving. The phrase "problem-based learning" has become something of a buzzword. It involves constructing the learning process around a particular problem. Students are then to collect data, brainstorm solutions, evaluate and implement those solutions, and assess what they have produced (Seifert and Simmons 1997). It is a process of self-directed learning, assisted by a teacher in the role of facilitator, whose job is to "model higher-order thinking" by asking probing questions, while avoiding expressing an opinion or giving information to the students (Savery and Duffy 1995). This approach is intended to parallel the process of labor in the new workplace, where employees will supposedly organize themselves to perform the task assigned by managers.

Indeed, some advocates of the school-to-work plan cite Dewey as their authority: Resnick and Wirt claim that "today's high-performance workplace calls for essentially the same kind of person that Horace Mann and John Dewey sought: someone able to analyze a situation, make reasoned judgments, communicate well, engage with others and reason through differences of opinion, and intelligently employ the complex tools and technologies that can liberate or enslave according to use" (1996, 10). Lynn Olson compares the "school to work revolution" with Dewey's perspective, since he "advocated rewriting the curriculum to reflect the 'urgent realities of contemporary life.' . . . He thought the study of occupations would help students make sense of the rapidly changing industrial world. He believed that by engaging young children in projects and in manual activities that more closely reflected their daily lives they could be drawn into a study of the traditional academic disciplines" (1997, 40). This, of course, is an egregious but not untypical distortion of Dewey's views. Among other things, Olson completely misunderstands what Dewey meant by "occupations." And the problems Dewey intended to solve were those of building a democratic community. The school-to-work advocates are talking about solving the problems that are of concern to the students' future employers. The SCANS classroom is training, not education. It is a parody of Dewey: the classroom becomes a microcosm of the workplace, where the boss defines the problems to be solved by the workers, and the workers demonstrate their competence by being as productive as possible for the ultimate benefit of the boss.

An example of this can be seen in a pilot testing program developed by the New Standards Project, which was formed by the NCEE and the Learning Research and Development Center at the University of Pittsburgh; the center was directed by Resnick, a member of the SCANS commission. Robert Rothman cites the following problem, administered to eighth graders in 1992, as illustrative of its approach: "Suppose you work for a shoelace company. You receive the following assignment from your boss: We have decided to sell laces for sports shoes. We will sell different lengths for shoes with different numbers of eyelets. . . . You have to figure out what lengths to make and which lengths go with which shoes, based on the number of eyelets. . . . Write your decisions about lace length so the advertising people making the sign can understand it" (1995, 125–126).

Hannah Roditi sees in all this the development of "high schools for docile workers, [which] will give business a pivotal role in determining what young people should know and be able to do when they graduate, and how they should think about themselves and society" (1992, 340). Gerald Bracey, author of the "Bracey Report," which frequently appears in the *Phi Delta Kappan,* puts it in even plainer language: "'School-to-work transition' [is] a distressing indicator of the increasing corporate control of education. . . . The alliance between business and schools is itself an alliance made in hell. . . . [To] claim that schools ought to be teaching students to be critical thinkers is ludicrous and hypocritical. The last thing an employer wants is someone who thinks critically. Critical thinkers will challenge the idiotic rules laid down by businesses" (1996, 109–110).

In a curious convergence, the school-to-work plan has been attacked by both the Left and the Right, though for sharply different reasons. Many on the Left focus on its dubious assumptions about both education and the economy. Paris argues that there is not much clear empirical support that schools can produce "critical thinkers, individuals with certain generic skills and competencies, who can step into a job situation and develop the more specific skills required by the job" (1994, 16). Kuttner, in his challenge to market ideology entitled *Everything for Sale,* states that "the most careful research on this subject suggests that the skills gap is largely a mirage. . . . Millions of people who are literate and numerate and offer good work habits still receive dismal wages" (1997, 103). W. Norton Grubb cautions that

> changes in schools should rest in part on educational principles and not entirely on occupational imperatives—not only because occupational goals are only some of the purposes of education, but also because those imperatives cannot be precisely known. The forms of the new vocationalism that require education to be driven solely by the requirements of employers and the demands of the 21st century labor force should be particularly suspect: no one can forecast what these demands will be, and those who pretend to do so impose an overly narrow conception of education on the schools. (1996, 544)

In the current political climate, however, progressive critiques do not have much impact. In the case of the school-to-work approach, it is the radical Right that has been most effective in its opposition, which is based on resistance to federal control of the schools. Phyllis Schlafly, for example, uses pseudoprogressive rhetoric in criticizing the school-to-work system as "tracking children into specific lines of work as chosen by business-school partnerships," but her real complaint is that "its directions come from the federal government. It's an attempt to control the curriculum" (quoted in Zehr 1998, 12). The February 3, 1998, edition of the *New York Times* reports that Lynne Cheney sees the school-to-work plan as "seek[ing] to inculcate attitudes," such as requiring "that young women be encouraged to consider 'nontraditional employment'"—and notes critically that the program is indirectly associated with Hillary Clinton. Schlafly's organization, the Eagle Forum, and the Family Research Council—both of which are associated with the Christian Coalition—urge their members to oppose the school-to-work system mainly for what they see as the negative effect on family values.

The future of the program is in fact unclear at this point. Its federal funding winds down after the year 2001, and the initiative for its continuation rests with the states and localities. Only a few states have designed and implemented comprehensive school-to-work programs. Oregon is a notable example; its Educational Act for the Twenty-first Century establishes a credentialing system not unlike that proposed by the NCEE. However, in general the program has not taken deep root elsewhere. As of 1997, thirty-four states had formed over eleven hundred school-to-work partnerships, but most of these were career development programs rather than new curriculum reforms.

The real triumph of social efficiency is reflected clearly in the powerful national trend toward statewide curriculum standards, detailed frameworks imposing those standards on local districts, and state-mandated achievement testing to assess student progress in meeting the standards. By the mid-1990s, nearly all states were developing or revising such frameworks and designing statewide tests to assess performance in relation to the standards they establish. This represents the ultimate application of industrial models based on the goals of social efficiency and the needs of a market economy. It promises to have a strong, and strongly antidemocratic, impact on the direction of education in the coming years.

The connection between standards and assessment has in fact been the strategy of the more sophisticated advocates of the school-to-work plan. They support "the idea of using outcome standards as a policy instrument, as a means of steering educational institutions. . . . The new education reform movement is aiming for governance by outputs—that is, requiring education institutions to meet outcome criteria but leaving them free to devise their own procedures" (Resnick and Wirt 1996, 6). This strategy is designed to overcome the institutional inertia and resistance that has always stymied curricular reforms in the past.

In short, the school system is to function exactly like the new workplace. The market—or more accurately those who have the power in the market economy—determines the specific educational commodities to be produced by the system; state authorities decide how to produce those commodities, determine production quotas, and measure the outcomes; and local educators design methods of production. In some respects, it sounds like the worst of all possible worlds: market ideology combined with a command economy. In any case, in its destructive effect on community decision making for the schools, and on the ability of students to participate in such decisions, it bears no relation to anything resembling democratic education.

Attempts to set this program up on a national level have failed. In 1994 the Goals 2000: Educate America Act was signed into law. It established eight national education goals, and set up a National Educational Standards and Improvement Council to develop national curriculum content. State participation was to be voluntary; $400 million in grant money was to provide an incentive. It had little effect. Attempts to develop national testing programs have also failed to take hold. The states, however, have filled the gap and have acted remarkably alike in imposing social efficiency standards to the curriculum. The contrast with democratic models of school curriculum are evident.

Dewey's concept of curriculum was indeed based on "occupations," which he saw serving as a unifying mechanism. As Kliebard points out, that choice "was an unfortunate one because it could easily be identified with vocational education or with an overriding emphasis on overt activity" (1987, 69). What he meant, however, was the characteristic daily activities of all kinds in which humans engage to build their communities and societies. The point of the curriculum was to explore the different aspects of those occupations—mathematical, scientific, historical, cultural, and so forth—in the process of actually performing them. An interdisciplinary, real world democratic curriculum is the result. In the Laboratory School that he organized in Chicago in 1896, he utilized a curriculum that "traced the evolution of the basic social activities that Dewey called occupations." The point of this, in Dewey's own words, was to "reproduce, in miniature, the activities fundamental to life as a whole, and thus enable the child . . . to become gradually acquainted with the structure, materials, and modes of operation of the larger community . . . [and] to express himself through these lines of conduct, and thus attain control of his own powers" (Kliebard 1987, 71). It is precisely this control that makes Dewey's curriculum democratic—young people are not just trained in skills but learn to understand the relation of those skills to social living. This enables them to use that expertise to construct their own world, not just operate in a world constructed for them by adults.

The typical state curriculum framework is based on an entirely different concept, and the results can be summed up as a Bobbitt's Frankenstein monster, designed for the twenty-first century by E. D. Hirsch. At the end of his widely read book *Cultural Literacy* (1988), Hirsch provides a sixty-three-page list of "what every American needs to know." He follows this up with a series of fundamentals books, each titled *What Your [First, Second, Third,* and so on] *Grader Needs to Know*. Essentially, this has been the approach of the states in designing curriculum frameworks. For the most part, they are lists of educational "product" divided into separate disciplines and organized in a way that can be subjected to regular quantitative assessment. It is a social efficiency method beyond Bobbitt's wildest dreams, perfectly suited for determining educational productivity and limiting the boundaries of learning to that which has market value in an information society.

An exploration of Internet web sites for state departments of education is instructive in that regard. In Arizona, for example, the arts curriculum framework ("students know and are able to do the following") is divided into three sets of standards; each, in turn, is divided into five academic levels (readiness, foundations, essentials, proficiency, and distinction), with a half-dozen or more specific skills under each level. California's mathematics standards involve eight grade levels (K–seven), each individually broken down into number sense; algebra and functions; measurement and geometry; statistics, data analysis, and probability; and mathematical reasoning. Each of these thirty-five categories is then further divided into several skills and then into subskills. Thus, under "Grade three—Number Sense," students must "understand the place value of whole numbers" (five specific skills), "calculate and solve problems involving addition, subtraction, multiplication, and division" (eight skills), and "understand the relation between whole numbers, simple fractions, and decimals" (four skills). For grades eight through twelve, there are nine different subjects apiece, with up to twenty-five specific skill standards. The ultimate framework may well be that of history and social science in Massachusetts. One hundred and thirty pages long, it is the product of several years of contentious debate. The material is organized into six guiding principles of core knowledge and twenty learning standards categorized into four strands, each broken down into three grade levels. (Massachusetts Department of Education 1997). All that is missing is Snedden's peths and lotments.

This neurotically compulsive approach to curriculum provides a basis for rigorous quantitative assessment of student progress in relation to the frameworks. Accompanying the wave of new curriculum frameworks, therefore, has been the development of mandatory statewide achievement tests given to all students. As of 1997, every state but Wyoming had a testing system of this kind; many of them were requiring students to pass a test for high school graduation. In the words of a report by FairTest, an organization critical of standardized tests, "Most state programs still rely predominantly on traditional multiple-choice tests, and many states use them inappropriately to make high-stakes decisions." This was especially true of southern states; only Vermont's tests, which used no multiple choice questions and assessed writing with a portfolio, met Fair Test's standards of equity and accuracy (Lynn 1998, 27).

Chapter 2 discussed the impact of human-capital theory on educational policy. In line with market ideology, the theory argues that investment in public education can be justified primarily in terms of its productivity in increasing human capital and that such increases can be quantitatively assessed by analyzing economic growth rates. Standards-driven education reform, characterized by detailed curriculum frameworks linked to statewide assessment systems, is the ultimate expression of that theory applied to an age of high technology. Curriculum is designed to emphasize work-related skills, imposed uniformly on all local school systems, measured by a single standardized test, and used as a criterion to determine whether the state's financial investment in education is justified. The result is an educational system whose purposes are directly linked to the economy and detached from democratic community control. Worst of all, the students are harnessed to a machine over which they have no power and by means of which their direction in life is determined.

A democratic educational system also involves a certain level of uniformity and equality. That is, arbitrary academic distinctions based on gender, race, or ethnicity, or classifications based on spurious measurements such as IQ, are to be eliminated. The school-to-work movement, curriculum frameworks, and standardized statewide tests give this appearance—they apply to everyone uniformly. In sharp contrast, the social efficiency movement of the 1920s had no reservations about sorting out students according to ability, and it often took on an explicitly racist tone. It is no accident that Snedden was a strong believer in eugenics.

But that very uniformity results in massive inequality. Introducing a single standard into the educational system and claiming that it will empower all students to cope with a new kind of economy and society willfully ignores the fact that all students—and, most important, all schools—are not the same. For despite some movement on the state level toward school finance reform, low-income schools cannot match high-income schools in terms of meeting the criteria set by the state. Standards-driven curriculum reform is a formula for failure on the part of those who have no power in U.S. society.

In January 1997, *Education Week* issued a report card entitled "Quality Counts," on the condition of education in the fifty states. Among the topics covered was school finance. The study documented continuing educational spending differences among and within the states. Adjusted for cost differences, New Jersey was spending twice as much per pupil as Utah, and within New York, high-income districts were annually spending as much as $1,275 per pupil more than low-income districts. The report graded states on adequacy, allocation, and equity. Only five states received A grades for adequacy; Arkansas got the only F. On the equity scale—that is, how funds were distributed within a particular state—five states received A's, twenty-four received B's, sixteen received C's, and six got D's. New Jersey received an A for adequacy but a D for equity. More than one-third of these states were graded D for their methods of allocating funding. Of course, since low-income communities have a deficient tax base, the property tax-based system of educational finance, which still predominates, is largely responsible for these differences.

Massachusetts provides a useful example of the relationship between wealth and performance on achievement tests. A calculation of eighth-grade state achievement test scores from 1988 to 1994 shows most of the lowest-income communities in the bottom 5 percent and the highest-income communities in the top 5 percent (Bradbury 1998). The December 9, 1998, *Boston Globe* reports that the first Massachusetts Comprehensive Achievement System tests were administered in 1998 to fourth, eighth, and tenth graders with the same results. Although an education reform bill that shifted more state school aid to the poorer communities had been passed in 1993, it had not significantly altered the relative financial position of school systems in the state as a whole. The high-income districts could still significantly outspend the low-income districts and meet the state standards more easily.

Uniform standards in an unequal system simply provide another basis for blaming students and teachers in low-income districts for their own failures. By claiming that students are now going to learn what they need for economic advancement but failing to provide the necessary resources, standards-based reform implicitly promotes the same kind of racial and economic bias that was an explicit part of the social efficiency movement in the 1920s. Nel Noddings states, "If all high school students in a given district are required to take algebra, for example, do they thereby have an 'opportunity to learn' algebra? . . . If their teacher is not fully competent, if they are crowded into an unpleasant room, if they have to share outdated textbooks, can the requirement be regarded as an opportunity to learn?" (1997, 185). Herbert Kohl provides an answer to this question in a discussion of Hirsch's books: "Teaching the same material to all students guarantees nothing about the way they will respond. If the core reproduces the inequities that exist in society, it is simply another attempt to keep power relations from changing" (1992, 460). Linda Darling-Hammond quotes the 1992 report of the National Council on Education Standards and Testing: "If [standards] are not accompanied by measures to ensure equal opportunity to learn, national content and performance standards could help widen the achievement gap between the advantaged and disadvantaged in our society" (1994, 501).

But what is even more inequitable and, ultimately, undemocratic is the effect of the standards movement on students themselves. These same progressive educators emphasize that point as well. Kohl adds that we must "consider what should be the core content of a curriculum that promotes democratic thinking. . . . We must also examine what knowledge our students need in order to survive, persist, and even thrive. . . . Process and content must be merged into a thoughtful and critical pedagogy (1992, 461). Noddings asks, "Is the standards movement aimed at producing better citizens, more loving and effective parents, persons with greater moral sensitivities, individuals with enhanced social graces and healthy psyches? . . . If we are serious about raising standards, we have to help students understand what standards are and how they are related to the students' own purposes" (1997, 187–188) Darling-Hammond calls for standards that focus on how "to prepare students to inquire successfully into new areas of study, to find and use information so that they will be able to analyze and generate ideas for themselves, to produce ideas and products so that they will have the tools, as new needs arise, to continually educate themselves for the world they will live in" (1994, 491).

The current standards movement stunts the growth that Dewey saw as the goal of education. Notwithstanding its advocates' rhetoric about the desirability of critical thinking, it is designed to place limits on the extent of such criticism. The objectives of schooling are placed beyond the reach of democratic decision making, and students are entirely excluded from any influence over their own education. They become objects to be controlled and manipulated toward the ends dictated by a market economy.

This is not to say that there cannot or should not be a common core of school curriculum. In fact, the first step toward democratic education ought to be the determination of what all young people need to learn in order to share involvement in constructing a livable community. In that regard, Maxine Greene probably says it best:

> As we ponder educational purposes, we might take into account the possibility that the main point of education (in the context of a lived life) is to enable a human being to become increasingly mindful with regard to his or her lived situation—and its untapped possibilities. The languages and symbol systems we make available ought to provide possibilities for thematizing very diverse human experiences. . . . What I have been calling the common, then, has to be continually brought into being. . . . The focus should be one that dislodges fixities, resists one-dimensionalism, and allows multiple personal voices to become articulate in a more and more vital dialogue. (1995, 182–183)

References

Barton, Paul E. 1996. "A School-to-Work Transition System." In *Linking School and Work*, ed. Lauren B. Resnick and John G. Wirt. San Francisco: Jossey-Bass.

Bobbitt, Franklin. 1924. *How to Make a Curriculum*. Boston: Houghton Mifflin.

Bode, Boyd Henry. 1927. *Modern Educational Theories*. New York: Macmillan.

Boutwell, Clinton E. 1997. *Shell Game*. Bloomington, Ind.: Phi Delta Kappan International Foundation.

Bracey, Gerald. 1996. "Schools Should Not Prepare Students for Work." *NASSP Bulletin*, September.

Bradbury, Katharine, Karl Case, and Christopher Mayer. 1998. "Chasing Good Schools in Massachusetts." *Federal Reserve Bank of Boston Regional Review*, July–September.

Bridges, William. 1994. "The End of the Job." *Fortune*, 19 September.

Carnevale, Anthony, and Jeffrey D. Porro. 1994. *Quality Education: School Reform for the New American Economy*. Washington, D.C.: U.S. Department of Education.

Charner, Ivan. 1997. "New Bottle or New Wine: Unique Policy Features of the School-to-Work Opportunities Act." *Politics of Education Bulletin*, Winter.

Charters, W. W. 1923. *Curriculum Construction*. New York: Macmillan.

Darling-Hammond, Linda. 1994. "National Standards and Assessments: Will They Improve Education?" *American Journal of Education* 102: 478–510.

Elmore, Richard F. 1996. "Policy Choices in the Assessment of Work Readiness." In *Linking School and Work*, ed. Lauren B. Resnick and John G. Wirt. San Francisco: Jossey-Bass.

Engel, Michael. 1991. "'Supply-Side Neoliberalism' and Higher Education in Massachusetts." *Business and the Contemporary World* 4(Autumn): 59–67.

Frederiksen, John R., and Allan Collins. 1996. "Designing an Assessment System for the Future Workplace." In *Linking School and Work,* ed. Lauren B. Resnick and John G. Wirt. San Francisco: Jossey-Bass.

Greene, Maxine. 1995. *Releasing the Imagination*. San Francisco: Jossey-Bass.

Grubb, W. Norton. 1996. "The New Vocationalism: What It Is, What Could Be." *Phi Delta Kappan,* April.

Henwood, Douglas. 1996. "Work and Its Future." *Left Business Observer,* 3 April.

Hirsch, E. D. 1988. *Cultural Literacy*. New York: Vintage.

Kliebard, Herbert M. 1987. *The Struggle for the American Curriculum 1893–1958*. New York: Routledge and Kegan Paul.

———. 1988."Fads, Fashions, and Rituals: The Instability of Curriculum Change." In *Yearbook of the National Society for the Study of Education,* ed. Laurel Tanner and Kenneth Rehage. Chicago: University of Chicago Press.

Kohl, Herbert. 1992. "Rotten to the Core." *The Nation,* 6 April.

Kuttner, Robert. 1997. *Everything for Sale*. New York: Knopf.

Lynn, Leon. 1998. "States Get Failing Grade in Assessment." *Rethinking Schools,* Spring.

Massachusetts Department of Education. 1997. *History and Social Science Curriculum Frameworks*. Boston.

Noddings, Nel. 1997. "Thinking about Standards." *Phi Delta Kappan,* November.

Olson, Lynn. 1997. *The School-to-Work Revolution*. Reading, Mass.: Addison-Wesley.

National Center on Education and the Economy. 1990. *America's Choice: High Skills or Low Wages!* Rochester, N.Y.: NCEE.

Paris, David. 1994. "School, Scapegoats, and Skills." *Policy Studies Journal* 22:10–23.

Resnick, Lauren B., and John G. Wirt. 1996. "The Changing Workplace." In *Linking School and Work,* ed. Lauren B. Resnick and John G. Wirt. San Francisco: Jossey-Bass.

Roditi, Hannah Finan. 1992. "High School for Docile Workers." *The Nation,* 16 March.

Rothman, Robert. 1995. *Measuring Up: Standards, Assessment, and School Reform*. San Francisco: Jossey-Bass.

Savery, John R., and Thomas M. Duffy. 1995. "Problem-Based Learning: An Instructional Model and Its Constructivist Framework." *Educational Technology,* September–October.

Seifert, Edward H., and David Simmons. 1997. "Learning-Centered Schools Using a Problem-Based Approach." *NASSP Bulletin,* March.

Snedden, David. 1921. *Sociological Determination of Objectives in Education.* Philadelphia: J. B. Lippincott.

U.S. Department of Labor, Secretary's Commissions on Achieving Necessary Skills. 1991. *What Work Requires of Schools.* Washington D.C.: U.S. Government Printing Office.

———. 1992. *Learning a Living: A Blueprint for High Performance.* Washington, D.C.: U.S. Government Printing Office.

Zehr, Mary Ann. 1998. "School-to-Work Opponents Unable to Block Funding." *Education Week,* 28 October.

8 Civic Education

Democratic public schools require a curriculum that is based on democratic values. It would obviously serve no purpose here, if it were even possible, to review the voluminous writings on the subject of what such a curriculum might look like. In any case, reference has been made to these ideas throughout this book. This chapter focuses instead on one small but vital part of the big picture: civic education. In stark contrast to the almost complete lack of attention it now receives and its absence in any market-oriented plan for school reform, learning specifically what it takes to become a citizen in a democratic society is at the heart of a democratic education.

Surprisingly, however, there is not much in the contemporary progressive education literature on the subject of civic education. In fact, not even Dewey offers much in the way of specific guidelines concerning the overall direction of a transformative civic education. As Westbrook says, "Dewey himself, alas, had relatively little to say about the particulars of civic education, though most of what he had to say about 'democracy and education' is at least indirectly relevant" (1995, 138). But the topic has not escaped the attention of more conventional analysts. The demand for more and better civic education has gained prominence on the policy agendas of many politicians, educators, and social scientists. The need to develop the values, knowledge, and skills required for democratic citizenship, especially among young people, has taken on greater urgency and received considerable public attention.

It is not coincidental that this interest has occurred at a time when education reform has once again become a critical national issue. Indeed, both are being discussed and debated in much the same way: a crisis is perceived, a common national interest is said to be threatened, commissions are formed, the media becomes involved, and solutions—especially those with the promise of a quick fix—are offered from all sides. Thus, most of the literature on civic education adopts a practical and empirical approach. Philosophical and ideological debates are put aside in favor of searching out whatever appears to work with the dominant ideology in place. Therefore, much of the discussion about civic education assumes that we are all more or less committed to maintaining liberal democracy in a capitalist economy and that active citizenship and political participation are desirable as both means and ends. In short, the overarching belief seems to be that we are all in the same boat, rowing in the same general direction, divided only by differences in the course we wish to take.

This consensus is artificial and illusory. Civic education can take the direction of educating young people to preserve the existing system (a conservative perspective) or to transform it (a transformative perspective). Because most contemporary discussions of civic education avoid making a choice, the conservative perspective predominates by default. But if we are to construct a democratic education system, we must open up the debate, and we must explore what form a transformative civic education might take.

The meanings of concepts that are at the heart of any civic education curriculum are in fact contested themselves. Of course, much has been written about different kinds of democracy, such as strong versus weak (Barber 1984) and liberal versus participatory republican (Battistoni 1985). For the most part, however, the implications of these distinctions for civic education have not been thoroughly examined. If we are to educate strong democrats, for example, do we limit their activities to government, or do we, as Dewey urged, extend them to economics? If we want to encourage greater participation in political life, do keep it within the proper channels or give it free rein? Is democracy a set of rules to be followed in the political process, or, to cite Dewey again, should it be an all-encompassing way of life? How much democratic participation is possible within the limits of the existing system? And, for that matter, is the existing system worth preserving?

Citizenship is the most significant contested concept. Is it a set of obligations and responsibilities attached to the circumstance of having been born in a certain place, or does it mean a set of values that transcend national boundaries? Is a good citizen an individual with certain knowledge and skills, or does a good citizen think and behave in a particular way, or both? Do we practice citizenship only in public life, or do we extend the practice to private life? Does citizenship imply that there is some kind of common interest that underlies our competing political interests? If so, what are we to do with persistent dissent from that alleged commonality? If not, how do we build a cohesive society? These are questions to which conservative and transformative perspectives offer radically different answers. For the most part, however, they are unexamined in the mainstream literature on civic education—or, more to the point, the answers are assumed to be a matter of consensus. There is a need, then, to explore the alternatives.

From the relatively traditional perspective of Norman H. Nie, Jane Junn, and Kenneth Stehlik-Barry (1996), democratic citizenship involves two dimensions: political engagement and democratic enlightenment. The first is the capability of citizens to engage in self-rule by means of their ability to identify political preferences, understand politics, and pursue interests. The second is an understanding and acceptance of the democratic rules of the game. Nie, Dunn, and Stehlik-Barry demonstrate that education is strongly and positively correlated with both, even while actual political participation is decreasing. They attribute this seeming contradiction to a "fixed number of [influential] social network positions" and conclude that "equality of political access can never be fully achieved. . . . Education can change only the composition of the population that is at or near the top of the rank. In the zero-sum game of political engagement, gains in proximity to the social and political center of society by one individual or group means a necessary loss of access to another" (187–188). Education does not create this inequality, but it has become the main sorting mechanism for positional social outcomes. In short, education cannot of itself guarantee political equality, which the authors implicitly see as utopian, but it is critical for teaching and maintaining democratic values.

Popular democrats reject these limiting assumptions and therefore place even more importance on education as a tool for expanding democracy. The perspective of Nie and colleagues is what Richard Battistoni (1985) refers to somewhat critically as the liberal conception of the democratic citizen, which rejects the schools as an effective means of direct political education of future citizens as active participants, choosing instead to teach them respect for the law, limited participatory skills, tolerance, and self-reliance. Battistoni contrasts this with what he calls the participatory-republican concept, which involves a far more active role for citizens in societal decision making, and a drastically restructured civics curriculum.

No matter how citizenship is defined, we cannot assume such a role unless we receive specific training for it. As Barber puts it:

> Embedded in families, clans, communities, and nations, we must learn to be free. We may be natural consumers and born narcissists, but citizens have to be made. . . . The logic of democracy begins with public education, proceeds to informed citizenship, and comes to fruition in the securing of rights and liberties. . . . Public schools are how a public—a citizenry—is forged and how young, selfish individuals turn into conscientious, community-minded citizens. . . . Certainly there will be no liberty, no equality, no social justice without democracy, and there will be no democracy without citizens and the schools that forge civic identity and democratic responsibility. (1993, 39–46)

Civic education must be consciously and explicitly pursued as part of a school curriculum. The question, however, is what kind of civic education that should be.

The term "conservative" is meant here to define the commitment to conserve a pluralist political system, a market economy, and the existing political rules of the game. Civic education conservatives are not as concerned with the ends of political decision making as they are with the means. In relation to civic education, it is the integrity and stability of the political process that concerns them, not the policy outcomes. Thus, they aim to promote a shared obligation among citizens to value the existing political system and to become involved with it in a manner that sustains and improves it. Toward these ends, the primary goals of civic education must be to preserve civil society and build social capital.

"Why civil society? Why now?" asks Elshtain, who defines the term as "a sphere of associational life that is, yes, 'more' than families and 'less' than states . . . the many forms of community and association that dot the landscape of a democratic culture" (1998, 5). Essentially, it is the network of voluntary civic organizations that allows a pluralist liberal democracy to function. Elshtain, a leader of the civic education task force of the American Political Science Association, ultimately answers her own question by citing the crucial role of civil society in citizen and neighbor creating and in building and sustaining decent institutions. A better answer to her question, however, might be that the reason is fear. There is an insecurity among socioeconomic and political elites that an angry and alienated populace may, in a time of crisis, reach what Kevin Phillips (1993) calls the "boiling point." As Susan Tolchin puts it, "'Anger' has become the political watchword of the 1990s: Leaders from both parties worry about the absence of civility, the decline of intelligent dialogue, and the rising decibels of hate in political discourse. . . . A political form of bipolar disorder has emerged that is a symptom as well as a cause of anger. At peace for the first time in almost a century, Americans question the legitimacy of their own democracy. They are 'mad as hell,' and political leaders constantly ask why" (1996, 3).

Civic education conservatives share an overriding concern with political instability. That explains why "analyzing and absorbing the end of a civil society has become one of Washington's most popular academic pursuits," resulting in the proliferation of elite study commissions with impeccably centrist and mainstream credentials. Among them are the Council on Civil Society—whose members include Senators Dan Coats (R-Indiana) and Joseph Lieberman (D-Connecticut), Francis Fukuyama, Cornel West, and twenty others—and the National Commission on Civic Renewal, which the June 25, 1998, edition of the *Boston Globe* described as "a high-powered panel of academics, business executives, and Washington insiders" chaired by William Bennett and Sam Nunn. Both have issued reports bemoaning the state of civil society and urging Americans to become more involved in public life, especially by joining civic groups and neighborhood organizations. The Center for Civic Education, financed in part by the Pew Charitable Trusts and supported by the U.S. Department of Education, has become the primary research organization in that area.

A stronger civil society is seen to benefit the system at least in part by building up the supply of social capital, defined by Robert D. Putnam as the "features of social life—networks, norms, and trust—that enable participants to act together more effectively to pursue shared objectives" that benefit the society (1995, 664–665). Putnam's clever use of a homely "bowling alone" metaphor (that is, the decline of league bowling) and his placement of the blame on television widely publicized his contention that social capital is in decline. It was a sure-fire formula for media attention, and it fit well with the conservative concern about the deterioration of civil society.

As a result of approval by mainstream political and intellectual elites, financial support, and media attention, the conservative perspective has become the politically correct context for defining the problems and developing their solutions across all ideological boundaries. From the political right, William A. Schambra sees a "new strategy for American conservatism" in the call for a "new citizenship . . . which would empower families to take back their schools and neighborhoods . . . rolling back the incursions of the therapeutic state into the everyday lives of Americans." This is a crucial goal since "the central project of the modern progressive liberal state is to eradicate civil society" (1995, 101-102). From the perspective of free-market enthusiasts, Douglas Henton, John Melville, and Kimberly Walesh see the civic entrepreneur as a "new type of leader [who] combines two important American traditions: entrepreneurship—the spirit of enterprise—and civic virtue—the spirit of community." These individuals are busy rebuilding civil society from the grassroots by constructing collaborative networks to promote economic change, enabling capitalism and democracy to move ahead together (1997, 149–150).

Firmly in the middle of the road is former senator Bill Bradley, who sees "deterioration of our civil society and the need to revitalize our democratic process" as "America's central problems." He defines civil society as "a space in which the bonds of community can flourish" and sees its "crucible" as the American family. To strengthen civil society, he argues that "we must recouple sex and parental responsibility . . . in part by holding men equally accountable for out of wedlock births." He proposes to accomplish this in some measure by warning young men, "If you have sex with someone and she becomes pregnant, be prepared to have 15 percent of your wages for 18 years go to support the mother and child."

Perhaps more effectively, he calls for more "civic space" in the public schools, a more "civic-minded" entertainment media, campaign finance reform, and a lessening of "rights talk" in the civic culture (1995, 97, 98).

Even some strong democrats, who probably see themselves as progressives, use much the same language. According to Barber, civil society is the victim of corporate expansion as well as of government, whose response to corporate expansion "inadvertently encroached on and crushed civil society from the opposite direction." Civil society thus vanished "sometime between the two Roosevelts," and "its denizens were compelled either to find sanctuary under the feudal tutelage of big government or to join the private sector." Barber cites Bennett's *Book of Virtues,* noting that "the virtues it celebrates are the product of neither government nor markets, but of families and citizens acting in the free space of civil society" (1995, 114–118).

The conservative perspective on civic education has thus managed to forge a strong, well-financed, and highly prominent coalition drawing on the Right, Center, and Left in U.S. political life to promote an agenda based on strengthening civil society. From this standpoint, what civic education must teach is civility in personal behavior, a willingness to subordinate one's self-interest for the common good, and a working knowledge and appreciation of the pluralist virtues of the U.S. political system. Obviously, such an approach precludes any uncivil challenges to the dominant ideology.

"Civility," which has become the watchword of civic education conservatives, is generally used to mean self-control and common courtesy in social situations. Barber, giving the concept a participatory democratic emphasis, sees this as a critical pedagogical need:

> At the most elementary level, what our children suffer from most, whether they're hurling racial epithets from fraternity porches or shooting one another down in schoolyards, is the absence of civility. . . . Civility is a work of the imagination, for it is through the imagination that we render others sufficiently like ourselves for them to become subjects of tolerance and respect, if not always affection. . . . Education creates a ruling aristocracy constrained by temperance and wisdom; when that education is public and universal, it is an aristrocracy to which all can belong. (1993, 44)

Related to this concept is the ability to put our own selfish interests behind us for the good of the community as a whole. In that context, John I. Goodlad, like most other civic education conservatives, attacks what he sees as "identity politics":

> The current problem of the American democracy is that of coping with a virtual explosion of individuals and collectives seeking to define their identity for themselves in the face of the realization that those in power over the years have been defining it for them. This drive . . . has been accompanied also by a narcissistic obsession with self that has both hurt just causes and strained community. With the public interest being constantly redefined to accommodate diversity, the core of common vision shrinks. . . . For education to undergird the renewal of both political and social democracy, it must transcend the divisions in philosophical and religious persuasion that exist in a diverse population and reach for some higher and more universal meaning of human existence. (1995, 92)

Similarly, Jerry M. Chance sees the "ideal behaviors of democratic citizens" as including a "voluntary restraint on their self-interests . . . informed resistance to demagoguery and perversions of power and office . . . [and constructive participation] in the society with a judicious combination of positive action and forbearances." In this light, he is particularly critical of demands for "equality of result," the "societal fragmentation" that came out of the 1960s, and, of course, multicultural education (1993, 159–160).

Finally, civic education must teach a willingness to negotiate, bargain, and compromise in politics and must show how the U.S. political system can work to accommodate demands for change if the rules of the game are followed. Secretary of Education Riley praises as a "highly acclaimed" example the framework in *National Standards for Civic Education,* developed by the Center for Civic Education (1994, 6). The section on standards for high school students presents an elaborately detailed list of what students need to know about U.S. politics and government. It includes an understanding of the importance of civil society for maintaining limited government, the distinction between public and private life, and the significance of civic virtue and the common good in republican government. Students must learn that the U.S. political system is characterized by a value consensus on social equality, with the "notable exceptions" of slavery, the treatment of Native Americans, and discrimination against "various groups." The political system is also characterized by a low intensity of political conflict, with "notable exceptions such as the Civil War, nineteenth century labor unrest, the 1950s and 1960s civil rights struggles, and the opposition to the war in Vietnam" (1994, 70, 89). It would seem, however, that a U.S. history course consistent with this framework would be both brief and boring with the "notable exceptions" removed.

Judging from these observations, civic education conservatives must indeed be an anxiety-ridden group. They evidently perceive the U.S. political system as threatened by a growing mob of ill-informed, uncivil, hot-headed folk, who need only some kind of political catalyst to set them off. Thus, civic education must be a protective Great Wall of mainstream historical understanding, and good manners must guard the system against barbarian incursions. The prevalence and high profile of the conservative point of view would seem to settle the matter once and for all, and perhaps in a political sense it has done just that. But in the context of an intellectually honest social scientific analysis, the issue is still wide open because the intellectual building blocks of civic education conservatism contain serious conceptual flaws.

Some critics point out that conservatives, in their unstinting praise of civil society, have forgotten what James Madison wrote in the Federalist No. 10 about what he called "the mischiefs of faction." Sheri Berman argues that "civil society activity often serves to fragment, rather than unite a society, accentuating and deepening already existing cleavages." The "neo-Tocquevillians" avoid this issue by "prais[ing] the groups they favor and denigrat[ing] those they do not" (1997, 565–566). She cites Putnam's work on Italy as an example. James Schmidt believes that "the meaning of 'civil society' tends to be rather elusive. . . . Opponents of authoritarian regimes employ the term to denote something like the rights and liberties long associated with liberal democracies. Radical democrats use it to denote the ideal of an engaged, active citizenry, directly involved in public deliberation. For libertarians, it designates a market society, free from political coercion. For communitarians, it evokes the network of voluntary associations and the civic virtues they engender" (1998, 414).

Michael Foley and Bob Edwards similarly criticize the "lack of clarity" in most discussions of civil society and see the notion of social capital as "generally undertheorized and overgeneralized." Their argument follows Berman's, and they cite *The Federalist Papers* to the effect that the proliferation of voluntary associations can have positive and negative effects on political stability. Finally, they see a wish for an "escape from politics" in much of the popular usage and in some scholarly accounts of civil society, which "tend to suppress [its] conflictive character, seeking in society itself and in its inner workings the resolution of conflicts that politics and the political system in other understandings are charged with settling or suppressing" (1997, 551).

The concept of social capital has come under similar attack. Popular democrats Lappe and DuBois argue that "in much of the conversation about social capital, we sense a longing to go backwards. . . . So we would like not only to broaden and strengthen the popular meaning of social capital, grounding it firmly in the concept of agency. We would like to widen the discussion of social capital, stretching it to include all aspects of our common problem-solving capacities. We would like to enlarge it far beyond any narrow association with civil society" (1997, 126).

Defining the meaning of the terms "social capital" and "civil society" should therefore not be conceded to the conservatives. David Kallick notes that one of the early analysts of the nature of civil society was Antonio Gramsci, who "was keenly sensitive to the power of cultural and nongovernmental forms of political work, and sought ways to mobilize that power to lead Italians to reject fascism." He notes that the phrase is now "being put forward [by Robert Putnam, among others] not as a revolutionary force, but as a stabilizing force. . . . Suddenly, foundations, corporations, and even conservatives such as Newt Gingrich and Francis Fukuyama started talking about the need to restore civil society in America." He suggests, therefore, that we be wary of "the connection between civil society advocates and status quo politics" (1996, 2). S. M. Miller agrees: "Civil society has become the leading political mantra of the day because the singers of its praise hear so many different chords in it. . . . The broader challenge is the image of civil society that will prevail. Will the developing civil society promote democracy, empower participation, foster social values, widen perspectives, decrease inequalities, produce a kinder, gentler society? Or will the American civil society become more self-centered, more nasty to the poor, more commercialized?" (1996, 6).

The conservative perspective on civic education therefore demonstrates several implicit ideological biases: (1) Civil society consists of associations and groups *that are committed to liberal democratic values, the existing constitutional framework, and a capitalist market economy;* (2) the purpose of strengthening civil society is to *promote political stability by encouraging negotiation, bargaining, compromise, and incremental change;* and (3) social capital is a set of attitudes and values that are *consistent with and supportive of the existing political and economic system.* Civic education conservatives take for granted that there is a nearly universal societal consensus supporting these ideas and therefore advocate making them the centerpiece of any school curriculum designed to promote good citizenship.

But to those who see a need for a transformative approach to civic education, agreement may not be so obvious. Perhaps the problem is a dysfunctional system rather than dysfunctional citizens. Perhaps nonparticipation, incivility, and even a little rage may be legitimate and appropriate responses to an illegitimate political process. And perhaps the version of history and politics favored by civic education conservatives is inaccurate—the "notable exceptions" may in fact be the rule.

Any serious program of civic education needs to be based on an explicit statement of societal goals. If we value the existing system and feel that all it needs is reform and stronger public awareness and involvement to make it work better, then the conservative program for civic education makes perfect sense. If, on the other hand, we see the problems of the existing system as symptoms of a deeper ailment requiring the cure of total reconstruction, civic education must take a different, transformative path.

A transformative perspective is characterized by a specific commitment to a Deweyan concept of democracy as an all-encompassing way of life, a more egalitarian social and economic system, and what might be called the richness of difference in gender, race, and ethnicity. Civic education must therefore be explicitly oriented toward teaching students how to search for a better way—that is, for alternatives to the present political and economic system, which has failed to achieve these goals. There may or may not be some kind of common interest or value consensus that unites us, but it can be determined only through an ongoing and unending democratic debate.

The ultimate justification for any program of civic education is, of course, the fulfillment of the needs of young people. Chapter 1 refers to the destructive effects of an educational system based on market ideology, arguing that schools that treat students as objects to be directed, trained, and sorted for a future over which they have no control increase the students' detachment and alienation. A program of civic education that seeks to adjust youth to predetermined social norms is perfectly consistent with this. If, on the other hand, we want young people to grow up with the sense that they actually have some rights and responsibilities in regard to creating their own futures, a transformative approach becomes indispensable.

The specifics of a transformative perspective can be developed from two sources that complement each other in interesting ways: (1) the idea of social reconstruction in progressive education and (2) contemporary feminist theory. Dewey's educational philosophy was the inspiration for the social reconstructionists, an intellectually influential faction of the progressive education movement. Their ideas had little effect on the schools themselves, partly because of their academic rather than activist orientation and partly because World War II and postwar anti-Communist politics shut down the progressive education movement as a whole. The issues they raised, however, were widely discussed among educators at the time and are still highly relevant to any discussion of civic education.

Dewey himself was part of this movement at the outset, but the actual leadership came from the lesser lights of progressive education: George S. Counts, Boyd Bode, Harold Rugg, Jesse H. Newlon, Theodore Brameld, and others. Using Dewey's ideas about education and democracy as their starting point, they adopted a neo-Marxist historical determinism in their vision of the future. According to the editors of the October 1934 premier issue of their monthly magazine, the *Social Frontier*, "*The Social Frontier* assumes that the age of individualism in economy is closing and the age marked by close integration of social life and by collective planning and control is opening. For weal or woe it accepts as irrevocable this deliverance of the historical process. It intends to move forward to meet the new age and to proceed as rationally as possible to the realization of all possibilities for the enrichment and refinement of human life" (4). Dewey agreed, arguing that the educational system had to make a choice:

> I do not think . . . that the schools can in any literal sense be the builders of a new social order. But the schools will surely, as a matter of fact and not of ideal, share in the building of the social order of the future according as they ally themselves with this or that movement of existing social forces. This fact is inevitable. The schools of America have furthered the present social drift and chaos by their emphasis upon an economic form of success which is intrinsically pecuniary and egotistic. They will of necessity take an active part in determining the social order—or disorder—of the future. (1934, 11–12)

Neutrality was therefore out of the question. In January 1935, the editors published a lengthy statement of their position, which included the following:

> *The Social Frontier* finds [untenable] the view that the school should confine itself to a purely objective description and analysis of social life and to the equipment of the individual with the tools and methods of thought. The school in order to function in some social setting must have some social orientation—even though it be toward the past, some values—even though they represent the interests of a narrow class, some conception of human welfare—even though it be unenlightened and partial. These things are implicit in the nature of education, when conceived in organic fullness. (30)

This statement, however, is not logically contingent on the claim that a collectivist future is inevitable—or, for that matter, on the similar and currently fashionable claim made for capitalism. Whether a particular society is the end of history or not, a conscious choice of historical perspective and political allegiance has to be made. The editors' choice was to take an explicit stand in favor of social reconstruction toward a democratic and egalitarian future. This entailed some ambitious objectives. In 1932 Counts had started the debate with a pamphlet entitled "Dare the Schools Build a New Social Order?", and in 1939 he published *The Schools Can Teach Democracy*:

> The central part of any program in defense of democracy, therefore, must be an honest and vigorous effort to apply [democratic] ideas, values, and outlooks to our life and institutions—to bring economic power under popular control, to release the energies of technology, to root out every kind of special privilege and corruption, to promote toleration, understanding, and brotherhood among races, peoples, and religions, to conduct an unrelenting war on poverty and human misery, to guard civil rights and liberties as a priceless heritage, to prosecute the free and untrammeled search for knowledge in all fields, and to engage positively in the creation of a civilization of justice, beauty, humanity, and grandeur. . . . In the achievement of [this program], the school, and particularly the public school, must play an important role. (13–14)

Ambitious—some might say utopian—expressions of this kind were the source of a debate that went on throughout the short life of the movement and that was at the core of a long-running conversation in the *Social Frontier*. If civic education is to have the explicit purpose of social reconstruction, "does this mean all education must be some form of indoctrination? Is any attempt to influence, direct, impose, guide, or direct the educated about some point of view about the nature of the good life . . . an instance of manipulation? Does this present a conflict between the methods we use and the ends we seek? Is the idea of democratic education inherently biased?" (Giarelli 1995, 33). The positions taken were not clear-cut, either-or choices; they were much more complex and nuanced and occasionally self-contradictory. Bode, for example, insisted that the schools' silence on the subject of social reconstruction was "equivalent, under the circumstances, to giving aid and comfort to the forces of tradition." However, "the whole business of [reconstructing beliefs and attitudes] becomes hypocrisy if it is decided in advance which conclusions are to be reached." He asserted that the point of progressive education is "not to prescribe beliefs, but to specify the areas in which a reconstruction or reinterpretation is needed" and provide "the conditions for sincere and careful thinking" (1935, 18–22). Newlon, on the other hand, had fewer reservations: "All education involves moulding of the individual. Education seeks to change the individual, to modify his behavior in important respects. . . . Indoctrination . . . is avoided when the whole process is lifted to the level of consciousness and understanding on the part of the teacher and increasingly on the part of the learner" (1939, 102).

What is significant and useful about this debate is that it raised precisely the right questions on the subject of civic education. In some respects, one can step back and see that the discussions themselves offer the answer that civic education toward a common social purpose need not close off dissent and disagreement; indeed, it can stimulate them. But civic education also requires a commitment to intellectual openness and honesty that may be hard to maintain. As the movement died, so did the debate. If we are to formulate a coherent strategy for civic education, especially if the goal is to improve or change society, discussion must be reopened.

What the social reconstructionists left out of the debate was a consideration of the place of conflict and struggle in the educational process. Their conviction that we were moving inevitably toward a new age and their rather rigid and exclusive class analysis of society blinded them to that reality. And although they gave lip service to tolerance, insofar as they were white, middle-class males at a time when issues of race, gender, and ethnicity were below the horizon even for most progressive educators, any discussion of the implications of these social and cultural differences was highly unlikely. More than half a century later, it is clear that an egalitarian and collectivist era is, to say the least, not on the short-term political agenda and that any discussion of social change involves more than economics.

Dewey himself had problems with issues of diversity and conflict. Walter Feinberg quotes Westbrook, Dewey's biographer, to that effect: "He wanted no atonal music in the repertoire of his cultural orchestra. . . . Dewey insisted that there were core ideals in American nationalism which stood apart from the particular values of the country's composite cultures, had priority over them, and ought to shape the lives of all the groups in society" (1993, 200). Feinberg further points out that Dewey's concept of democracy tended toward the view that "democracy could be made neat and tidy." He also failed to recognize that "democracy should allow incommensurable views to be expressed while protecting less powerful voices. . . . [It] must allow people to reject, at least for themselves, even what is desirable." Thus, "the work that remains is to examine critically Dewey's philosophy in order to seek a more adequate conception of democracy and its application to the modern age" (210, 215). This is being done primarily by contemporary feminist political theorists.

Feminist theory's discussions on the meaning of citizenship, which is of course the prime subject matter of civic education, fill in the blanks left by the social reconstructionists. Most civic education conservatives give no definition at all, apparently because to them the meaning seems self-evident. They would probably agree with the definition offered by the Center for Civic Education: citizenship is "legally recognized membership in a self-governing community; confers full membership in a self-governing community; no degrees of citizenship or legally recognized states of inferior citizenship are tolerated; confers equal rights under the law; is not dependent on inherited, involuntary groupings such as race, ethnicity, or ancestral religion; [and] confers certain rights and privileges, e.g., the right to vote, to hold public office, to serve on juries" (1994, 127).

A mainstream approach to the particular qualities of democratic citizenship is, again, offered by Nie, Junn, and Stehlik-Barry, who see it as "enlightened political engagement": "the capability of identifying and acting on political interests and the recognition of democratic principles and the rights of all citizens to express interests." This involves the ability to understand and retain concrete political facts, political attentiveness, participation in difficult [that is, time-consuming] political activities, regular voting, and tolerance (1996, 20–31). They concede that their model is open to challenge from those who view citizenship "within the context of race and ethnicity and racism in America," and from those "who question the legitimacy of the more conventional understanding of political and public, as well as challenge the notion of universal citizenship" (1996, 19).

One might expect some additional explanation from strong democrats, but most do not offer much more. Barber frames his discussion of "participatory citizenship" almost entirely in the context of his proposal for mandatory community service but never quite pinpoints what he means by the phrase (1992, chap. 7). In their edited volume *Education for Citizenship* (1997), Grant Reeher and Joseph Cammarano describe a wide variety of programs for that purpose, but none of the contributing authors go any further than defining it as active participation in civic life.

In regard to the meaning of "citizenship," conservatism in civic education actually has two wings, which Walter C. Parker accurately refers to as "traditionalist" and "progressive": "Traditionalists concentrate on knowledge of the republican system, progressives on this plus deliberation on public issues, problem solving/community action that brings together people of various identities, and other forms of direct and deliberate participation in state matters as well as in the middle sector or 'civil society'" (1996, 112). Their collective purpose, however, is the same—maintenance of the existing political system. It is a difference in means, not ends.

Also evident in much of this literature is the idea that citizenship implies a commonality and a unity of purpose—a set of values and interests that we all share and that, in the process of democratic deliberation and active civic participation, we can use to resolve our differences and move the nation ahead toward our common goals. In general, civic education conservatives are, at the very least, edgy and, at most, indignant about the assertion of racial, gender, ethnic, and social class identities, which they see as an obstacle to commonality. Although Goodlad attempts to cloak it in the context of ironic humor, his point of view is clear:

> Diversity places great demands on tolerance, another democratic virtue. Just when I have become comfortable with the classical, I am confronted with modernism and postmodernism. Just as I am becoming accepting of the lifestyle next door to me, the two men propose marriage and the adoption of a child. The church and synagogue exist quite comfortably side by side in the community, but the mosque now rising toward the heavens is creating dissonance. . . . Enough already. The freedom democracy seeks to cultivate and protect appears to be running ahead of the community that must nurture it. (1997, 40–41)

Not all civic education conservatives apply their personal thresholds of comfort with diversity as a measure of what constitutes the values of good citizenship. Others are certainly more open to difference, but they too fall short in important ways when considering the meaning of citizenship. Parker criticizes what he calls the progressive wing for "minimizing social and cultural heterogeneity. . . . The two wings share the narrow conception of unity and difference. This conception has only one viable approach to the unity/difference tension, only one tool at its disposal, and that is assimilation. Assimilation is thus built into the common sense of citizenship education as one of its bearing walls" (1996, 113).

Rogers Smith's definitive book on the meaning of citizenship in the United States makes the same point in relation to the assumption that liberal democratic values constitute its basis: "U.S. citizenship laws have always expressed illiberal, undemocratic ascriptive myths of U.S. civic identity, along with various types of liberal and republican ones, in logically inconsistent but politically effective combinations. . . . The history of U.S. citizenship policies demonstrates incontrovertibly that the legal prerogatives of the majority of the domestic population through most of the nation's past have officially been defined in conformity with those ascriptive doctrines, at least as much as purely liberal and republican ones" (1997, 505).

For a view of citizenship that is at the root of a transformative perspective, we may thus look to feminist theory. "Citizenship has been one of the most contested categories of political analysis," says Kathleen Jones, noting that it is conventionally defined "as a particular type of action performed by people of a common political identity in a specific locale." That definition is seen by feminists as a "gendered" version that establishes a "masculinized" norm of citizenship. "If women's discourses, practices, and rituals of 'belonging to' were taken as paradigmatic," says Jones, "citizenship might be founded differently, and understood to be practiced in different locales" (1997, 1–2). Susan Douglas Franzosa argues that the masculinized concept of citizenship has "signified women's exclusion and invisibility" by relying on "encoded models for citizens based on generalizations about male experience and behavior" (1988, 275).

It is usually at this point that conservatives dismiss the feminist argument and shut off debate with accusations of political correctness; divisiveness; or, on a more sophisticated level, essentialism in relation to male-female differences—accusations that are simplistic and ideologically self-serving. The core of the feminist argument is that citizenship is a form of community-oriented moral and ethical behavior that transcends all kinds of boundaries, including those among nation-states. Democratic citizenship is an interactive and evolving human relationship that involves feelings of connectedness and caring; it is not just a static legal condition, a body of historical knowledge, or civil behavior in social situations. It is therefore broadly inclusive, but this does not mean that differences are suppressed in the name of some vague commonality. Rather, democratic citizenship must explicitly take into account and place a positive value on the different experiences, histories, and perspectives of a wide variety of people. This is a feminist definition because women's experiences—not their biological endowment—enable them, at least potentially, to perceive what most men cannot or will not: the importance of such qualities as caring, listening, empathy, connectedness, and emotional commitment in human relationships, including citizenship. These are characteristics that men have denigrated as female-coded and therefore irrelevant to political life, but they are critical components of feminist definitions of citizenship (Mansbridge 1996).

David T. Sehr credits feminist theory with "three central, related themes . . . that should be integrated into any valid understanding of the essential components of a public democratic society: (1) the natural social connectedness and interdependence of individuals, and the need for an ethic of care and responsibility that corresponds to that interdependence; (2) reconceptualizing the relationship between the private sphere and the public sphere; and (3) equality for all in terms of economic, social, and political rights" (1997, 66). Each theme needs to be examined in some detail for a full understanding of feminist notions of citizenship.

Citizenship necessarily involves such political relationships as authority and power. Mainstream—that is, masculinized—definitions generally stress impersonality, coercion, conflict, and position. These are obviously not irrelevant, but feminists argue that they exclude other possibilities—such as those cited by Sehr—that are based on the experience of women. Jones offers a feminist idea of "compassionate" authority, connected to an ideal of justice and based on an "imaginative taking up of the position of the other":

"Moving in the world 'as if' through other people's minds, hearts, and bodies, and seeing the world from others' perspectives, as much as that is possible, suggests that there are necessary connections between compassionate authority and concepts of justice. . . . The 'rational' modes of speech taken to be constitutive of authority exclude certain critical human dimensions" (1996, 86, 90). This does not fit the male stereotype of feminine softness based on losing oneself in pity for a victim; rather, compassionate authority is other-directed without erasing the distinction between one's own needs and perspectives and those of someone else. Compassion has the potential for humanizing authority, says Jones; authority without compassion, based on conventional definitions of the term, is inhuman.

Politics, too, feminists argue, needs to be seen from a perspective other than the conventional ones of power and conflict. Wendy Sarvasy uses the ideas and practices of female social service workers in the early part of the twentieth century as useful examples "for rethinking how the language of citizenship and democracy could be used to elaborate a vision of politics as centrally concerned with the nurturing of human life" (1997, 55). Mansbridge reconceptualizes power in a democracy as "democratic persuasion": "The goal of democracies ought to be . . . to make the processes of persuasion as genuine as possible by reducing the degree to which they are influenced by force and the threat of sanction, and to make the processes of exercising power as derivative as possible from agreed procedures and as equal as possible among the members. Feminist insights into connection and domination must inform the use of both persuasion and power" (1996, 118–119).

Although civic education conservatives make distinctions between public and private life, they are never very clear about where that line is to be drawn, perhaps again because they assume there is a consensus on the subject. Even before the early feminist slogan "The personal is political," Mills wrote about the distinction between "personal troubles" and "public issues." A trouble is "a private matter [when] values cherished by an individual are felt by him to be threatened"; issues "transcend these local environments. . . . They have to do with the organization of many such milieus into the institutions of historical society as a whole." Among these institutions he includes unemployment, war, urban development, and marriage. "Insofar as the family as an institution turns women into darling little slaves and men into their chief providers and unweaned dependents," he says, "the problem of a satisfactory marriage remains incapable of purely private solution" (1959, 10). Feminist notions of citizenship similarly rely on a broad definition of what constitutes a public issue, to a considerable extent based on women's experiences in relation to the family. As Sarvasy puts it, "From the vantage point of the early feminist notion of social citizenship, it does not make sense to contract the spaces for women's citizenship or to ignore the ways in which women's public lives require the intermeshing of the family, the administrative state, the neighborhood, the workplace, and the representative institutions" (1997, 65).

Above all, feminists argue, what conventional concepts of citizenship lack is a recognition of the real world of gender, racial, and economic inequality. A truly inclusive and participatory democracy must neither over- nor undervalue the expression of any particular group. The current social and economic structure does not allow for this, to say the least. As Nancy Fraser puts it, "Cultural differences can only be freely elaborated and democratically mediated on the basis of social equality" (1997, 107).

An egalitarian society based on deliberative democracy in which no one's position is privileged because of gender, race, or class will necessarily generate intense conflict. Commonality cannot be taken for granted, and no group should be arbitrarily told to restrain itself toward that end. Civic education conservatives either reject this model for that reason or, if they favor greater participation, avoid the issue. Parker states, "By distancing matters of race, gender, and ethnicity from the central concerns of governmental and direct democracy, the progressives, like the traditionalists, are limited in their ability to advance contemporary thinking about the unity/difference tension" (1996, 113). Feminists, on the other hand, confront them directly and creatively.

The basic feminist argument is that the unity/difference debate has been caricatured and oversimplified by conservatives into an either/or choice—either we have a citizenry united by a common interest (with due respect to and tolerance for cultural differences) or we have divisive identity politics. Feminists respond that dissent and difference are positive and potentially constructive democratic values. Holloway Sparks defends the "dissenting practices" of activist women as examples of "an expanded conception of democratic citizenship that incorporates dissent, recognizes courage as central to democratic action, and reclaims and revalues the courageous dissident practices of women activists." This means that citizenship "involves more than deliberation"; it includes "oppositional democratic practices that augment or replace institutionalized channels of democratic opposition when those channels are inadequate or unavailable" (1997, 75).

How, then, do we forge a coherent and workable democratic society? Feminists argue that democratic citizens must learn to step outside of themselves without losing themselves. We have to begin to see the point of view of the other, not just in a detached, objective, academic (that is, masculine) way but in a personal, emotional, and empathetic way, without losing sight of who we are and what we stand for.

Mills is again relevant here. Describing what he calls "the sociological imagination," he sees it as enabling its possessor "to understand the larger historical scene in terms of its meaning for the inner life and the external career of individuals. . . . The first fruit of this imagination—and the first lesson of social science that embodies it—is the idea that the individual can understand his own experience and gauge his own fate only by locating himself within his period, that he can know his own chances in life only by becoming aware of those of all individuals in his circumstances." This requires the intellectual equivalent of an out-of-body experience, and Mills means this beyond a merely academic exercise: "In many ways it is a terrible lesson; in many ways a magnificent one" (1959, 5).

From a different vantage point and with different social priorities, feminists make a similar argument. The key to balancing diversity and unity lies in recognizing that our social and political identities are indeed critical to defining who we are and where we belong but at the same time understanding that they are historical constructs that are constantly evolving as conditions change and as we come into contact with others. Identities are not demarcated by iron curtains that permanently separate us but by boundaries that are constantly shifting. They are real but not impermeable or immutable. Giving credit to "feminist discourse" for their insights, Richard Guarasci and Grant H. Cornwell state that "what is needed is a wholly different ideal of the democratic community in which both difference and connection can be held together yet understood to be at times necessarily separate, paradoxical, and in contradiction to one another" (1997, 3).

Thus, Susan Bickford contends that "the language of 'identity' need not be regarded as inimical to democratic politics, as it is by many contemporary critics of identity politics." The concept of citizenship must not be used to erase differences; thus, we need to find a concept that "would not automatically privilege certain commitments." The key, Bickford says, is to seek possible answers to the questions "In a context of inequality and oppression, how are multiple 'we's' to be democratically part of the same thing? What can make possible democratic communication with differentially placed others?" Part of the answer lies in a recognition that

> identity is a personal and political force open to active re-creation through our words and actions. . . . In this forging of identity, we connect with others and engage in collective work. I contend that this is an understanding of what democratic citizenship is, and needs to be, in an inegalitarian or egalitarian context. The kinds of actors—conditioned and creative, situated but not static—are citizens. And these activities should be understood not simply as "feminist work" or "coalition politics" but as the practice, the performance of citizenship. (1997, 117, 124–125)

As Ruth Lister describes it, this is a "dialectical" perspective on the subject of citizenship: "Our goal should be a universalism that stands in creative tension to diversity and difference and that challenges the divisions and exclusionary inequalities which can stem from diversity" (1997, 13). Our behavior as citizens might then be, as Jodi Dean (1997) describes it in a feminist context, a form of what she calls reflective solidarity—that is, knowing who we are but recognizing that this is constantly changing as we connect with and relate to others.

A transformative perspective on civic education, then, is based on two components: (1) an education system that is oriented toward developing egalitarian and participatory democracy and expanding human rights in all areas of social, political, and economic life; and (2) a notion of citizenship as membership in a community built on interdependent human relationships, an ethic of caring for and about others, and the placement of a positive value on difference, diversity, and dissent.

A choice between a conservative and a transformative perspective, it has been argued, is critical for choosing the kind of civic education we want. If our goal is conservative, and we wish to teach young people civility, self-restraint, and the existing political rules of the game, our emphasis will have to be on knowledge and experience *that confirms the values and goals of the U.S. political and economic system as it is now constituted.* This does not necessarily imply that students are to be taught that change is undesirable; rather, the orientation ought to be toward change within the limits of what the current system allows and change that improves the functioning of the system. If our goal is transformative, the emphasis will have to be on knowledge and experience *that encourages a critical frame of mind toward the existing system and develops a readiness and ability to consider and actively work for alternatives.* This does not necessarily mean we should train revolutionaries, even if we could. It means explicitly broadening the options available for students to include the consideration of major social and economic changes. Although there are areas that overlap, this implies two very different directions for a civic education curriculum.

In 1991 the Center for Civic Education published *Civitas: A Framework for Civic Education.* The Framework Development Committee included Benjamin Barber, R. Freeman Butts, John Patrick, and sixteen other scholars and educators. It was Butts, a prestigious mainstream educational historian, who "made a greater contribution to *Civitas* than any other contributor" (viii). The foreword, written by Ernest Boyer, focuses specifically on the economic challenges facing the United States that require a solid civic education. The result is the ultimate curriculum framework: a 650-page text listing in extensive and excruciating detail everything anyone ever wanted to know about civics. It starts with a discussion of civic virtue, offers rules for "competent and responsible participation," and continues with 300 pages on what students should learn about the nature of politics and government. The text goes on to describe the "fundamental values and principles" of U.S. government and politics: the public good, individual rights, justice, equality, diversity, truth, and patriotism. It offers a rather rigidly institutional curriculum on U.S. political institutions and concludes with a rights- and obligations-based concept of the "role of the citizen." The center's 1994 set of national standards, which is consistent with this approach, breaks down in a somewhat more readable and concise fashion the specific civic knowledge to be expected at each level of elementary and secondary education. On the basis of these texts, one might conclude that the ultimate goal of civic education conservatives is to wear students down with information about civic life until they no longer have the energy to make any major changes in the system.

But most civic educators also recommend participation as part of the curriculum, and it is community service that arouses the greatest enthusiasm among the conservatives. Indeed, most community service projects do not lead in politically dangerous directions; otherwise they would not be so widely used in the criminal justice system. That said, community service is by no means an inherently conservative pedagogical tool. The particular kind of service educators have in mind is of the essence, and lines between conservative and transformative examples cannot be neatly drawn. As Battistoni puts it, "Service alone does not automatically lead to engaged citizenship; only if we consciously construct our programs with the education of democratic citizens—in the broadest sense—in mind can service learning be the vehicle by which we educate for citizenship" (1997, 151). Context is everything, and projects need to be judged in relation to the content of the courses of which they are part.

Thus, Goodlad's proposal for "internships" involving participation "in the local, state, or national infrastructure through planned, guided immersion in essential elements" of service provision is consistent with his traditionalist point of view (1997, 80). The more progressive programs of community service are usually freer and more challenging but are often not clearly related to any political goal and therefore seem to be based on a faith that somehow they will stimulate civic participation by osmosis. Barber asserts, "When sited in a learning environment, the service idea promotes an understanding of how self and community, private interest and public good, are necessarily linked" (1992, 249). However, he offers no details. According to Craig Rimmerman, service proponents hope "that students who participate in service activities will begin to ask why tragedies such as illiteracy, hunger, and homelessness even exist . . . and begin to develop a social consciousness" (1997, 21). There is an apparent unwillingness, even among self-styled progressives, to commit to a particular political direction.

Thus, civic education conservatives in general propose a thorough grounding in basic knowledge of what they believe to be the values of the political system (with perhaps some critical, but not too critical, analysis) and, as a supplement, an array of service activities that will, it is hoped, stimulate further civic participation and greater awareness of social problems. If anything comes out of this kind of curriculum, it will most likely be a stronger acceptance of conditions as they stand, perhaps combined with a readiness to involve oneself in mainstream political activities, interest groups, or community organizations. Ultimately, this can serve the purpose of shoring up system stability.

It is therefore useful to look at Dewey's educational practices—which are the basis for contemporary reformers' ideas about democratic education—in combination with the ideas of feminist theorists. A genuinely transformative civic education curriculum would combine schools that are themselves democratic with a pedagogy that encourages values and behaviors consistent with feminist notions of democratic citizenship. Sehr lists five "public democratic school practices": encouraging students to explore their interdependence with others and with nature; study social justice issues; discuss, debate, and act on public issues; critically evaluate their social reality; and develop participatory skills (1997, 89). These practices are possible only in schools that are themselves democratic and intimately connected to and involved with their communities, which is exactly what Dewey proposed. Recall that Dewey did not want schools to be a "place set apart in which to learn lessons" but a "genuine form of active community life . . . a miniature community, an embryonic society" (1943, 14, 18). The schools were to draw on the child's experience in the community and develop his or her abilities to understand that experience and use that new learning to enrich the society. The point, therefore, is to develop a curriculum that inspires students to analyze, evaluate, and ultimately improve their social experience. The classroom becomes a place where students can connect their own immediate environment to the world at large, within the framework of conventional academic disciplines. In that regard, the school should provide a model for democracy, and the experience of the students should serve as the organizing principle for the curriculum. This philosophy has served as the basis for a number of well-known experimental educational programs today, including, among many others, Eliot Wigginton's Foxfire project in Georgia, Deborah Meier's work in East Harlem, and George Wood's efforts in the Appalachian region of Ohio.

There must also be an explicit value basis to this approach, and this is where the insights of feminist theory are useful. The democratic curriculum should be structured around what Noddings calls "an ethic of caring arising out of both ancient notions of agapism and contemporary feminism." There are many calls for teaching morality in the schools today, but Noddings argues that we need "a more appropriate conception of morality. . . . Our forebears were right in establishing the education of a moral people as the primary aim of schooling, but they were often shortsighted and arrogant in their description of what it means to be moral" (1994, 173). This is directly connected to dealing with difference. Guarasci and Cornwell again credit feminism "for helping many of [their] students with breaking down the 'self-other' duality" and promoting "a wholly different ideal of the democratic community"—a "multicentric democracy in which the concept and experience of self and others are as connected as they are distinct and singular" (1997, 2–3).

A useful but now largely forgotten example of this approach can be found in the publications of the Educational Policies Commission. In the 1930s and early 1940s, the EPC issued a series of reports and books on the scope and methods of education for democracy. A specific curriculum case book, entitled *Learning the Ways of Democracy*, appeared in 1940. Its prescriptions and examples present a model of transformative civic education that has lost none of its relevance these many years later—indeed, it seems far more modern, fresh, and appropriate to the needs of the twenty-first century United States than the tedious and tiresome conventionality of *Civitas. Learning the Ways of Democracy* offers a curriculum that fits four important criteria of transformative civic education: (1) an explicit connection between democracy and social justice; (2) a pedagogical approach that is interdisciplinary, comparative, and based on asking open-ended questions on highly controversial subjects; (3) an emphasis on cooperative student planning and participation; and (4) a service orientation that is directly connected to the needs of the community and, most important, is not afraid to be political by confronting difficult issues.

Social justice goals are the "hallmarks of democratic education," according to the EPC report. These include "the welfare of people outside [students'] face-to-face groups, and particularly for people less fortunate than themselves or less able to act in their own behalf," equal educational opportunity, civil liberties, "the right to share in determining the purposes and policies of education," and democratic methods in all areas of the educational process. The publication specifically states that "to speak of liberties without reference to the economic necessities of life, to speak of democracy without reference to political institutions, is, as Charles A. Beard has said, 'to speak of shadows without substance'" (NEA 1940, 35–36). Democracy, it is argued, must not be narrowly and exclusively defined in terms of political institutions; rather, "the better practices extend the democratic concept beyond the political into every phase of our social existence" (58).

The disciplinary boundaries of a democratic civic education thus also require extension—or elimination. Civic education should not be obstructed by arbitrary limitations on the intellectual directions taken. Perhaps the most refreshingly subversive aspect of the EPC curriculum is its reliance on questions rather than answers. Like the frameworks cited in the previous chapter, the *Civitas* standards all begin with "Students are to know . . ." followed by a list of apparently undisputed facts. The EPC curriculum favors such courses as What Is the American Tradition? whose outline is based on such questions as "Is it democratic?" "Is it individualistic or cooperative?" "Is it tolerant?" and "Is it progressive?" Comparative approaches are favored in that context, such as the modern problems course, Democracy and Its Competitors, at Roosevelt

High School in Des Moines, Iowa, which compared democracy, Nazism, fascism, and "sovietism," and then examined "obstacles and threats to democracy" such as war, corruption in government, unemployment, crime, race prejudice, inadequate health services, maldistribution of wealth, waste of natural resources, and poor housing (NEA 1940, 55). Disciplinary boundaries are to be crossed: "It would seem appropriate for schools sincerely concerned about civic education to make a general and coordinated approach to the study of democracy and democratic citizenship on the entire curriculum front" (119). Thus, a class in Shaker Heights, Ohio, combined English and social studies in a course entitled The American Scene. Ultimately, the students planned and organized a unit on U.S. drama "to broaden our understanding of the American way of life" (155–156). In the same school, a geometry class learned "to think logically" by discussing a proposed child labor amendment to the Constitution (164).

Transformative civic education requires a willingness to confront controversial issues in relation to events in the community itself. Thus, an Omaha high school discussed a locally distributed leaflet that took the Soviet point of view in the 1940 Russo-Finnish War; based on a local press report about the Communist infiltration of a peace organization, a social studies class in Newton, Massachusetts, discussed the free speech rights of radicals; and a citywide student symposium in Des Moines was set up to debate the question "Is there anything we students can do to keep the United States out of the war?" (NEA 1940, 172, 290). A particularly interesting example is that of a Moultrie, Georgia, high school class that studied "the race problem" in relation to "the South as the Nation's Number One Economic Problem." Although "the need for race tolerance was not a 'felt need' on the part of some students," the outcome was that some of the most "prejudiced" students were "convinced . . . that Negroes could make progress if given a chance" (115). For Georgia in 1938, this was not a trivial accomplishment. In a less cautious mode, students at New York City's Benjamin Franklin High School, in what was then an interracial East Harlem neighborhood, did a direct study of race obviously inspired by the threat of Nazism. Again, it operated with a syllabus that posed questions rather than listing answers: Is there a pure race? Are some groups more advanced and intelligent than others? Why does a nation consider itself superior? (163).

Most of these courses and projects involved direct student participation and planning in a cooperative context. In sharp contrast to the way that class trips are usually planned in schools today, even at the college level, a number of field trips are described in which the students themselves decided on the educational objectives and itinerary. A striking example of student involvement is described in a Sacramento, California, high school, where "a third-year social problems class invited the principal of a school to talk with them about a proposal, initiated by students, to include an elective course in sex education in the school curriculum." Although it is not clear what decision was ultimately made, the transcript of the discussion indicates remarkable receptivity from the principal (NEA 1940, 178).

Finally, the EPC report is filled with examples of students collectively taking direct action to solve community problems. Community service in a transformative context does not consist of a lone student going off for a few weeks to a social service agency to feel good about him- or herself or perhaps by accident to find a social conscience. The point is rather to learn how to organize to effect change. The EPC report lists thus among others, the following projects: a student housing survey and discussions with landlords about improving East Harlem housing conditions; pressure on local government to provide more and better playgrounds in Radford, Virginia; the promotion of public health measures by Radford ninth graders, as an outgrowth of a study of venereal diseases; a survey of living standards in Framingham, Massachusetts; a student-run and -organized community center in a rural school in Ypsilanti, Michigan; the eradication of malaria mosquitoes in Georgia; and a Holtville, Alabama, high school's objective "to improve the living conditions—economic, social, and recreational—in this rural community" (NEA 1940, 322).

The EPC report concludes that there are two particular types of community service that fulfill the criteria for democratic civic education: (1) activities that school youth help to plan and execute, sharing responsibility with adults and (2) those that students initiate, plan, and take responsibility for carrying out themselves with adult assistance. These undertakings tie in with the EPC's criteria for such projects in general: the problems directly affect the students involved, the participants are able to do something about the problems, the participants are guided by democratic values in making their decisions, and there are demonstrable social benefits resulting from the action taken (NEA 1940, 326–327). In other words, students are educated to learn how to create—not just observe—social change.

The report admits that the examples it presents are uncommon, but they are probably even less common today. Still, some do exist. Morris Eisenstein (1977) cites the following example in the curriculum of the Children's Learning Center in Brooklyn, New York:

> When one of [the children's] classmates was burned out of her home, their concern, initiated by them, led to a visit to the local welfare office to inquire about the delay in getting help to the family. Concerned senior citizens accompanied them, as did staff. Though invited by the head of the local office to come talk to him, upon their arrival he changed his mind. As they left, in very orderly fashion, one of the youngsters, all of four years old, was heard to remark, "I think he's afraid of us. That's why he won't talk to us." . . . [The children] have picketed local political clubs in favor of day care, picketed together with senior citizens for maintaining services to them, and have petitioned for keeping open library services in the community.

This is a somewhat more contemporary example of what the EPC recommended in 1940: Teach students as early as possible that politics exists to solve the problems they face every day in their own communities, and let them plan cooperatively and democratically how to use politics to deal with them. That is the heart of a transformative civic education.

A transformative civic education curriculum presents certain dangers, as some of the social reconstructionists have pointed out, and there is certainly a basis for the fears of civic education conservatives. People are indeed alienated, impatient, and angry about the political and economic system, and there is a potential for a destructive and antidemocratic political response to a future crisis. However, that says more about the quality of our system than about the quality of our citizens. What is more, the political history of the United States indicates that, if anything, it is average citizens who usually exert pressure for greater democracy over the stiff resistance of the societal elites. Antidemocratic movements in the United States, whatever their ultimate popularity among the mass public, generally have had their origins in the ruling circles of society; McCarthyism is a notable example. If we are to have a democratic future, we must rely on and further develop the democratic instincts of average citizens rather than relying on the cautious, defensive, and ultimately self-serving civic education programs of those who consider themselves to be our political and intellectual leaders. A useful credo for a transformative civic education program can be found in a statement by Rogers Smith:

> Citizens need to be truer liberal democrats than most Americans have ever hoped to be. They must strive to be skeptical of flattering civic myths advanced by aspiring leaders. They must try to look unblinkingly at the reality of their history and their present, with all their deficiencies as well as their great achievements on view. And they must retain an awareness both that their regime may well merit their loyalty and sacrifices despite its flaws, and that, even if their nation is in many respects worthy of their loyalty, there may be times when its interests are not justified in light of their broader membership in the community of humanity. . . . Americans should in fact accept that a time may come when the United States itself, like preceding human political creations, is less rather than more useful as a way of constituting a political community that can engage people's loyalties and serve their finest aspirations. But they should give support and guidance to their country so long as it seems the best hope available to them for leading free and meaningful lives, and for allowing others to do so as well. (1997, 505–506)

References

Barber, Benjamin. 1984. *Strong Democracy*. Berkeley: University of California Press.

———. 1992. *An Aristocracy of Everyone*. New York: Ballantine.

———. 1993. "America Skips School." *Harper's Magazine*, November.

———. 1995. "Searching for Civil Society." *National Civil Review* 84:114–118.

Battistoni, Richard M. 1985. *Public Schooling and the Education of Democratic Citizens*. Jackson: University Press of Mississippi.

———. 1997. "Service Learning and Democratic Citizenship." *Theory into Practice* 36: 150–157.

Berman, Sheri. 1997. "Civil Society and Political Institutionalization." *American Behavioral Scientist* 40: 562–574.

Bickford, Susan. 1997. "Anti-Anti-Identity Politics: Feminism, Democracy, and the Complexities of Citizenship." *Hypatia* 12(Fall): 111–131.

Bode, Boyd Henry. 1935. "Education and Social Reconstruction." *Social Frontier,* January.

Bradley, Bill. 1995. "America's Challenge: Revitalizing Our National Community." *National Civic Review* 84: 94–100.

Center for Civic Education. 1991. *Civitas: A Framework for Civic Education.* Calabasas, Calif.: Center for Civic Education.

———. 1994. *National Standards for Civics and Government.* Calabasas, Calif.: Center for Civic Education.

Chance, Jerry M. 1993. "On the Development of Democratic Citizens." *Social Studies,* July–August.

Counts, George S. 1939. *The Schools Can Teach Democracy.* New York: John Day.

Dean, Jodi. 1997. "The Reflective Solidarity of Democratic Feminism." In *Feminism and the New Democracy,* ed. Jodi Dean. Thousand Oaks, Calif.: Sage Publications.

Dewey, John. 1934. "Can Education Share in Social Reconstruction?" *Social Frontier,* October.

———. 1943. *The School and Society.* Chicago: University of Chicago Press.

Editors. 1934. "Orientation." *Social Frontier,* October.

———. 1935. "The Position of the Social Frontier." *Social Frontier,* January.

Eisenstein, Morris. 1977. "A Philosophy and Curriculum for the Children's Learning Center." United Community Centers, Brooklyn, N.Y. Photocopy.

Elshtain, Jean Bethke. 1998. "Civil Society." *Liberal Education,* Winter.

Feinberg, Walter. 1993. "Dewey and Democracy at the Dawn of the Twenty-First Century." *Educational Theory* 43: 195–216.

Foley, Michael, and Bob Edwards. 1997. "Editor's Introduction." *American Behavioral Scientist* 40: 550–561.

Franzosa, Susan Douglas. 1988. "Schooling Women in Citizenship." *Theory into Practice* 27: 275–281.

Fraser, Nancy. 1997. "Equality, Difference, and Democracy: Recent Feminist Debates in the United States." In *Feminism and the New Democracy,* ed. Jodi Dean. Thousand Oaks, Calif.: Sage Publications.

Giarelli, James M. 1995. "The Social Frontier 1934–1943." In *Social Reconstruction through Education,* ed. Michael James. Norwood, N.J.: Ablex.

Goodlad, John I. 1995. "Democracy, Education, and Community." In *Democracy, Education, and the Schools,* ed. Roger Soder. San Francisco: Jossey-Bass.

———. 1997. *In Praise of Education.* New York: Teachers College Press.

Guarasci, Richard, and Grant H. Cornwell. 1997. "Democracy and Difference." In *Democratic Education in an Age of Difference,* ed. Richard Guarasci and Grant H. Cornwell. San Francisco: Jossey-Bass.

Henton, Douglas, John Melville, and Kimberly Walesh. 1997. "The Age of the Civic Entrepreneur: Restoring Civil Society and Building Economic Community." *National Civic Review* 86:149–156.

Jones, Kathleen B. 1996. "What Is Authority's Gender?" In *Revisioning the Political,* ed. Nancy J. Hirschmann and Christine DiStefano. Boulder, Colo.: Westview Press.

———. 1997. "Introduction." *Hypatia* 12(Fall): 1–5.

Kallick, David. 1996. "Why Civil Society?" *Social Policy,* Summer.

Lappe, Frances Moore, and Paul Martin DuBois. 1997. "Building Social Capital without Looking Backward." *National Civic Review* 86:119–128.

Lister, Ruth. 1997. "Dialectics of Citizenship." *Hypatia* 12(Fall): 6–26.

Mansbridge, Jane. 1995. "Reconstructing Democracy." In *Revisioning the Political,* ed. Nancy J. Hirschmann and Christine DeStefano. Boulder, Colo.: Westview Press.

Miller, S. M. 1996. "Building a Progressive Civil Society." *Social Policy,* Winter.

Mills, C. Wright. 1959. *The Sociological Imagination.* New York: Oxford University Press.

National Education Association (NEA), Educational Policies Commission. 1940. *Learning the Ways of Democracy.* Washington, D.C.: NEA.

Newlon, Jesse H. 1939. *Education for Democracy in Our Time.* New York: McGraw-Hill.

Nie, Norman H., Jane Junn, and Kenneth Stehlik-Barry. 1996. *Education and Democratic Citizenship in America.* Chicago: University of Chicago Press.

Noddings, Nel. 1994. "An Ethic of Caring and Its Implications for Instructional Arrangements." In *The Education Feminism Reader,* ed. Lynda Stone. New York: Routledge and Kegan Paul.

Parker, Walter C. 1996. "'Advanced' Ideas about Democracy: Toward a Pluralist Conception of Citizen Education." *Teachers College Record* 98:104–125.

Phillips, Kevin. 1993. *Boiling Point.* New York: Harper.

Putnam, Robert D. 1995. "Tuning In, Tuning Out: The Strange Disappearance of Social Capital in America." *PS: Political Science and Politics* 28: 664–682.

Reeher, Grant, and Joseph Cammarano. 1997. *Education for Citizenship.* New York: Rowman and Littlefield.

Riley, Richard. 1997. "The Importance of Civic Education." *Teaching K–8,* February.

Rimmerman, Craig. 1997. *The New Citizenship: Unconventional Politics, Activism, and Service.* Boulder, Colo.: Westview Press.

Sarvasy, Wendy. 1997. "Social Citizenship from a Feminist Perspective." *Hypatia* 12(Fall):54–73.

Schmidt, James. 1998. "Civility, Enlightenment, and Society." *American Political Science Review* 92:419–427

Sehr, David T. 1997. *Education for Public Democracy*. Albany: State University of New York Press.

Smith, Rogers M. 1997. *Civic Ideals*. New Haven, Conn.: Yale University Press.

Sparks, Holloway. 1997. "Dissident Citizenship: Democratic Theory, Political Courage, and Activist Women." *Hypatia* 12(Fall): 74–110.

Tolchin, Susan. 1996. *The Angry American*. Boulder, Colo.: Westview Press.

Westbrook, Robert B. 1995. "Public Schooling and American Democracy." In *Democratic Citizenship and the Schools,* ed. Roger Soder. San Francisco: Jossey-Bass.

9 Conclusion

> There are 31 million teenagers in the United States . . . Nearly one in seven of these teenagers—13 percent—have their own credit cards, and another 13 percent have credit cards in their parents' names. . . . As a result, said Michael Wood, director of Teenage Research Unlimited, a survey firm in Northbrook, Ill., "There's more attention to the teen market than ever before. Everybody's waking up and taking notice that this group is growing for the first time." More teenagers have part-time jobs now than ever before. They belong to the first computer-literate generation. They feel empowered and entitled. More have parents who are affluent than do not. And so, Wood noted, "Everyone is trying to figure out a way to harness their buying potential."
>
> *Boston Globe*, 29 December 1998

Rhetoric to the contrary notwithstanding, the social worth of young people in both the economic system and the educational system is now measured almost exclusively by their market value. Although in some ways this is a relatively new phenomenon, it actually represents a return to the past. At the turn of the twentieth century, children were kept out of school to become a low-cost factory workforce; today they are kept in school to become a low-cost factory workforce of the future. All that has really changed is the language used to make excuses for shortchanging their education for the good of the market economy; if anything, that language may have been more honest in the year 1900 than in the year 2000.

And "shortchanging" is certainly the appropriate term. School choice deprives students, their parents, and their teachers of the right to work as a community to control their schools. Techno-ideology preaches cybernetic liberation for the new generations to come, but its application actually stunts their intellectual growth and restricts their professional options. Corporate methods of managing schools impose administrative manipulation in the guise of self-determination. And, perhaps worst of all, the productivity-based approach to academic standards creates an intellectually impoverished curriculum. The application of market ideology to the public schools profits just about everyone but the children. For a generation of young people who find themselves increasingly cut off from and left out of a society that makes decisions for them in the economic interests of their wealthier elders, this is an educational disaster.

Market ideology constitutes a social and political disaster as well. Democracy now faces the most serious internal threat since the McCarthy era. The political system no longer possesses much legitimacy among the U.S. people. Anger, cynicism, and alienation are their understandable reactions to a government that is out of their control. All that may be holding the nation together is that most Americans seem to be reasonably content with their private lives, that is, their personal economic circumstances. But that is a fragile support for a stable society; if it gives way, there is little to prevent Americans from turning to antidemocratic and authoritarian alternatives. And there is at this time little or no effective political organization to oppose such a choice. The public schools, which might provide another line of defense against authoritarianism, do little or nothing in the way of civic education to strengthen democratic commitments among young people.

Under these circumstances, such radical options as a democratic educational system, which may appear to be utopian in the current political climate, warrant serious consideration. It is evident that progressive ideas in education, as in the society as a whole, are distinctly unfashionable at this time. The real political correctness is market ideology and all that goes with it. Challenges to its hegemony are said to have died with the Soviet Union. The best we can do, it is argued, is to make the current system work more efficiently and perhaps more humanely. In the educational system, the consensus supporting the market-oriented policies criticized in this book is nearly unanimous; the few voices in opposition are marginalized and fragmented. Promoting pedagogical alternatives that last surfaced in 1940, even if updated to accommodate a more contemporary political consciousness, may thus seem naively anachronistic. And even if the ideas make sense, the political will and popular organization needed to challenge the current direction in education is nowhere visible. There is little point in outlining alternatives if they are not achievable. We must therefore consider the question of whether a democratic educational system is politically feasible and, if so, what steps can be taken toward its accomplishment.

I would argue that even given all the negatives, there are realistic possibilities for democratic public schools as a practical political program. But this requires a strategic focus away from such conventional targets of progressive activists as the presidency, Congress, and the state governments. It also requires direct participation in activities with which many progressives are uncomfortable and unfamiliar—contesting local elections and becoming involved with labor organizations.

In *Who Will Tell the People?* (1992), Greider argues that although ordinary citizens are excluded from the major institutions of U.S. government, which are firmly in the hands of special interests and politicians who have contempt for their constituents, there is still a great deal of political vitality and citizen participation on the local community level. He calls it "the politics of rude and crude" (161), and it is in this arena that a struggle for popular control of political decision making is still possible. In many policy areas, of course, control at this level has no effect. Changes in foreign policy, for example, are not going to result from a city council election won by peace activists. Similarly, it would be difficult to effect reforms in such domestic policy areas as health care and welfare without leverage on the state and federal levels. Still, certain policies—community economic development being a prime example—do lend themselves to effective organizing on the local level. And although the window of opportunity is rapidly closing as state governments take greater control of the system, education has the same potential for effective local participation. In fact, there may be no other area of public policy in the United States that is more amenable to direct political action on the community level.

It is precisely the still largely decentralized structure of the educational system that provides a political foothold for those who would choose to work for change. Unlike the health care system, for example, U.S. public schools are owned and controlled by the people; specifically, they are governed mostly by popularly elected school boards, which is why advocates of school choice are so eager to dismantle them. At the local school level, individuals interested in democratic schools can fight for their ideas with a relatively small investment of time and money.

The fifteen thousand school boards, and the one hundred thousand people who serve on them, are the neglected stepchildren of the political system. If Americans are aware of them at all, they generally view them as uninteresting or irrelevant. Yet school boards are "among the most venerable of U.S. public institutions, embodying many of our most cherished political and cultural tenets." And although "the governance system for public schools is complex, incorporating multiple players and decision makers, including federal and state courts, the U.S. Congress, state governors and legislatures, and so on," they have potentially significant policymaking responsibilities (Danzberger 1994, 367–368), including budget formulation, personnel decisions, and curriculum development. Of course, these administrative tasks are subject to a growing amount of statutory and political restriction: "The board's discretion is squeezed from the top by increasing numbers of regulations from the legislative, administrative, and judicial arms of the federal and state governments . . . [and] squeezed from the bottom by such forces as the growth of local collective bargaining contracts, reinforced by national teacher organizations" (Kirst 1994, 381). Even within these limits, however, school boards have the potential to make a difference.

Unfortunately, most boards do not live up to their potential. They do not provide regular educational leadership, they spend much of their time micromanaging, they cater to special interest group influence, and they have difficulty developing reasonable working relationships with school administrators (Danzberger, 1994, 369). Especially in smaller districts, the boards often become captives of the administration or become obsessed with bureaucratic and public relations trivia. They are generally unsuccessful in establishing political links with other local government institutions. Few boards seem to be able to act assertively and positively as representatives of the community in guaranteeing educational accountability.

But this results not so much from flaws in the governance structure as from the inadequacies and idiosyncrasies of school board members, who generally run for office as individuals or representatives of special interests rather than as members of a political party or even a nonpartisan slate of candidates. As such, they are rarely able to come together as a coherent majority committed to a particular educational program, much less follow it through. It can be argued that a group of people with a common vision, running together and working together once elected, could energize a school board and set a direction for the schools within its jurisdiction.

Especially aware of this potential, the radical Right began to focus on school boards as electoral targets in the early 1990s. "Why target school boards? In part, these local offices serve as boot camps for fledgling political aspirants. And they offer substantial clout: Members of local school boards often control personnel decisions—as well as the purse strings—and they often set the philosophy (the 'vision') under which a school district functions." For Pat Robertson's Christian Coalition, the goal was to create an "army of politically trained Christians that will recapture lost territory for righteousness [such as] city councils, school boards, and legislatures all over this country." According to one estimate, the Christian Right had won over three thousand seats on school boards by 1993 (Jones 1993, 22–23).

The momentum of this drive seems to have slowed since that time, and it is not clear how much difference the victories have made. But the point remains that it is precisely these undistinguished and underappreciated local boards that provide an avenue for citizen influence. It is no accident that market ideologues see school boards as an obstruction to privatization. Finn, a Reagan administration official, has called for the abolition of school boards as "'a legacy of our agrarian past' and no longer an appropriate governing tool for the 'high-tech' future. . . . [He sees] this 'middle management' as 'superfluous' and 'dysfunctional'" (Wong 1995, 572). As governor of Massachusetts, William Weld made a similar proposal.

Educational activists who want to pursue a democratic agenda for the schools therefore need to consider active participation in school board elections. Indeed, they should adopt the strategy of the radical Right: organizing slates of candidates on a common platform to achieve majority control of the boards. Doing so will put them in a position to resist the kind of market-oriented programs described in this book and to develop democratic alternatives at least on a small scale.

The presence of two powerful and fairly democratic teachers' unions, which possess considerable potential for educational activism, is another unique attribute of the educational system that provides a political advantage for progressives working on the local level. One million teachers belong to the American Federation of Teachers (AFT); 2.5 million belong to the National Education Association (NEA). Until the last decades of the twentieth century, both were primarily bread-and-butter organizations, fighting mainly for better working conditions and wages and generally avoiding involvement in educational issues. In the 1980s, AFT president Albert Shanker began to push his union to become concerned with improving teacher quality and later with developing national standards. By the time of his death in 1997, he had achieved relatively limited success. That same year, however, NEA president Robert Chase called for a new unionism that would directly involve his organization in issues of school reform. It is clear that both unions have recognized the political necessity of their involvement, even if they have not yet followed through in any serious way. In 1998 the proposed merger of the two unions was rejected by the NEA membership, but the issue remains on the agenda.

It is therefore conceivable that in the coming years we will see a single teachers union with over three million members taking a more active role in influencing the direction of education. That possibility opens up an arena of activism for those concerned with democratic directions. Both unions, but especially the NEA, have a relatively decentralized and nominally democratic structure, and any merger would be likely to lean more toward the NEA organizational model. This would permit a considerable degree of input from local activists, who would have the chance to become directly involved in union activities related to the control of education reform. It would also facilitate cooperation between like-minded local union activists and school board members on the subject of curriculum development, even if not necessarily on such collective bargaining issues as wages and working conditions.

Ultimately, such activism must be directed at creating public awareness of and support for democratic education. This is not an easy task. Public opinion polls generally show that academic standards, school discipline, and teacher quality are among the top parental concerns about public education. Again, it is market ideologues who have been most successful at exploiting these concerns to build support for their programs. This success can be partly attributed to the ability to communicate their ideas in a populist language that elicits a positive response from average citizens.

In precisely this regard liberals and progressives have failed. Indeed, the radical Right has eagerly appropriated most of the slogans and organizing strategies first developed by the Left. On the academic level, postmodern jargon all too often dominates the progressive discourse. On the grassroots political level, progressives have focused almost exclusively on multicultural education and school finance, winning victories in both areas. But multiculturalism is threatened by the increasingly successful campaigns against affirmative action and bilingualism, and equity in school finance has been largely dependent on state judicial decisions. In other words, progressives have not built the community-based political infrastructure needed to sustain the momentum. The radical Right has the money, the fundamentalist Christian churches, and organized local activists using ballot initiatives to achieve its goals. The Left has none of these. And it has not really connected with the mass public in any meaningful way in terms of the issues most vital to that group.

In that respect, democratic education presents an opportunity to make this connection. Progressives must broaden their list of educational concerns to include the fight for democratic schools. This will provide an opportunity to connect with a wider constituency by addressing the issues of discipline, standards, and quality of teaching. For example, is school discipline achievable only with authoritarian "Principal Joe Clark" tactics? Does zero tolerance actually work to reduce substance abuse in the schools? In short, is our only choice to repress kids in order to make them behave in class? Democratic educators argue otherwise. They say that developing a sense of collective responsibility and personal involvement in the life of the school and connecting their education to the real world of the community give students a sense of ownership that can seriously reduce discipline problems. In fact, it is the alienating imposition of arbitrary standards, the depersonalizing effects of high-technology schooling, and the destruction of community cohesiveness through school choice that will create even more disempowered and embittered young people.

If anything, democratic education is far more demanding than the ludicrous state curriculum frameworks. It surely demands more of teachers; teaching to the test is always easier, and certainly duller, than responding creatively to student needs. It demands more of administrators, who are forced to put the rule book aside in favor of increased classroom creativity and to take risks in allowing potentially controversial elements in the curriculum. And above all, it is more demanding for students, who cannot rely on the tried-and-true methods of pleasing the teacher, following formulas, and doing exactly what has always been expected of them. A democratic education insists on active and creative imagination; it rewards difference rather than conformity; it requires students to challenge rather than accept. All of this demands higher-order thinking and problem-solving capability far beyond what the techno-ideologues and school-to-work advocates have in mind.

Teachers in a democratic education system would have to be generalists, not specialists. It would become evident that the narrow approach of most college-level schools of education is inadequate, and they would have to begin a process of change. Teachers would have to develop the connection with the community that democratic education requires. In short, on-the-job training in a democratic education system would have a highly salutary effect on the quality of teachers. Those who do not really care about learning, or have contempt for those whom they consider unteachable, or are unwilling to work cooperatively and on an equal level with people in their communities could not survive—they would have better luck finding jobs in the market economy, where such traits are often amply rewarded.

Finally, "democracy" is a term that resonates with average people far better than "world-class education," "economic competitiveness," "collaborative management," or even "choice." However high the level of political alienation in the United States today, most people still want the feeling of controlling their own lives and having a say in the lives of their children. Progressives need to communicate that this control is being taken away from them by the imposition of corporate models of education. In plainer language, the promise of freedom offered by market ideologues is a fraud—in education, as in the society as a whole, the market offers freedom only to those who can afford it or who have the power to take it. Democratic egalitarianism of this kind is deeply ingrained in and native to U.S. tradition. Progressives need to cite political role models no more radical than Jefferson, Mann, and Dewey. Their ideas can be expressed in a language that average people can identify with. And if a program of democratic education is combined with an assertion of the positive educational value of racial, ethnic, and gender diversity and a demand for nationwide equity in school finance, it is not only politically realistic—it could ultimately be a winner.

References

Danzberger, Jacqueline. 1994. "Governing the Nation's Schools." *Phi Delta Kappan*, January.

Greider, William. 1992. *Who Will Tell the People?* New York: Simon and Schuster.

Jones, Janet L. 1993. "Targets of the Right." *American School Board Journal*, April.

Kirst, Michael W. 1994. "A Changing Context Means School Board Reform." *Phi Delta Kappan*, January.

Wong, Kenneth. 1995. "Toward Redesigning School Board Governance." *Teachers College Record* 96: 569–576.

Index

Aronowitz, Stanley, 37, 39, 40

Barber, Benjamin, 47, 179, 182–183, 191–192, 200–201
Battistoni, Richard, 178–179, 200
Bennett, William, 71–72
Beyer, Landon, 40–41
Bickford, Susan, 198
Bobbitt, Franklin, 150–151
Bode, Boyd Henry: on democratic education, 58, 189; learning theory of, 56–57; on social efficiency, 154–155
Bromley, Hank, 108–109, 110
Boutwell, Clinton, 160–161
Bradley, Bill, 181–182
Brown, Clair, 143–144

Callahan, Raymond, 131–132
Center for Civic Education, 199–200
Charter schools, 83–89
Charters, W. W., 151–152
Christian Right, 165–166, 215
Chubb, John, 6–7, 71, 89
Citizenship: definitions of, 177–179, 191–193; in feminist theory, 193–195, 197–199
Civic education: commissions, 180; conservative perspective on, 179–186, 199–201; curriculum for, 183–184, 199–207; transformative perspective on, 186–190, 198–199, 202–207
Civil society, 179–182, 184–186
Clinton, William, 106–107
Comer School Development Program, 135
Community service, 200–201, 205–206
Computer technology: and democratic education, 114–117; and politics of education, 13–14; in schools, 93, 95, 112–114
Counts, George S., 188–189
Cremin, Lawrence, 10–11
Cuban, Larry, 1, 32, 115–116, 148–149
Curriculum: frameworks for, 167–170; historical development of, 148–150; and labor force, 155–161; as political issue, 14–15; standards for, 171–173

Darling-Hammond, Linda, 171, 172
DeLuca, Tom, 47
Deming, W. Edwards, 123–124, 142–143, 145
Democracy: concepts of, 44–45, 47–48, 58; decline of, 45–48, 212; and feminist theory, 48–49, 202
Democratic education, 2, 62–65, 88–89, 217–219
Democratic values: and history of public education, 1, 7–8, 49–50; and human behavior, 53–55
Dewey, John: concept of human development, 52–55; and curriculum development, 167–168; definition of democracy, 58, 190–191; educational philosophy of, 1, 55, 57–62, 201; and school-to-work, 163–164; and social reconstructionists, 187–188

Educational Alternatives, Inc., 3–4
Educational change: goals, 31–32, 137–138; in 1960s, 35–37; in 1980s, 27–30; and political activism, 213–218; politics of, 9–10; and technology, 95, 98–102; and youth, 2–3, 32–35, 41, 211–212

Educational maintenance organizations, 3–4
Educational Policies Commission (NEA), 128–129, 202–206
EduVentures, 4
Elementary and Secondary Education Act of 1965, 25–26
Elshtain, Jean Bethke, 45, 179–180

Family Education Network, 114
Feminist theory, and political concepts, 48, 195. *See also* Citizenship
Free schools, 36
Friedman, Milton, 19–21, 73
Friedman, Rose, 19–21, 73

Gerstner, Louis, 72–73, 104–105
Giroux, Henry, 37, 38, 39, 40
Goals 2000, 28, 167
Goodlad, John, 183, 192, 200
Greene, Maxine, 2, 173
Greider, William, 18, 46, 213
Gunn, Christopher, 126–127

Henig, Jeffrey, 68, 73, 76
Henwood, Douglas, 161
Highlander Folk School, 64–65
High performance organizations, 120–121, 124
Hirsch, E. D., 168
Holistic perspective, 51–52
Holt, John, 36
Horton, Myles, 64–65
Hudson, William, 46–47
Human capital theory, 24–27, 30

Ideology, 7–9

Jefferson, Thomas, 1, 49, 71
Jones, Kathleen, 48, 193, 194–195
Junn, Jane, 178, 191

Kahne, Joseph, 11, 75–76
Kelley, Carolyn, 143
Kilpatrick, William Heard, 60–61
Kliebard, Herbert, 24, 148, 150, 153
Kohl, Herbert, 171

Lasch, Christopher, 45–46, 73
Liston, Daniel, 40–41
Leonard, George, 97–98, 103

Mann, Horace, 1, 49
Mansbridge, Jane, 48, 194, 195
Market ideology: assumptions of, 19–20; and democratic values, 6–7, 22–23; and educational policy, 3, 6–7, 12–16, 41, 58–59; and politics of education, 9; and provision of education, 20–22; and responsibility of government, 19–20
Meier, Deborah, 2, 13
Milken, Michael, 4–5
Mills, C. Wright, 195–196, 197
Moe, Terry, 6–7, 71, 79, 89
Molnar, Andrew, 96–97

National Center on Education and the Economy, 157, 159
National Commission for Excellence in Education, 27–28
National Defense Education Act of 1958, 23–24
New institutionalism, 121–122
New Standards Project, 164–165
Nie, Norman, 178, 191
Noddings, Nel, 171, 172, 202

Papert, Seymour, 97, 101, 105, 114
Perelman, Lewis, 99, 103–104
Pioneer Institute, 4
Postman, Neil, 2, 102, 111–112
Postmodernism, 37–41
Privatization of schools, 3–5, 77
Problem-based learning, 163
Progressive education movement, 10–11, 23; and civic education, 50–51, 176, 202–207; and school governance, 127–128
Project method, 60–61
Putnam, Robert, 180–181

Ravitch, Diane, 78, 81, 111

Reinventing government, 121
Rose, Mike, 63–64

Sabis International Schools, 85
Sarvasy, Wendy, 195, 196
SCANS (Secretary's Commission on Achieving Necessary Skills), 157–158, 162–164
Schickler, Eric, 108, 109, 117
School boards, 214–216
School choice: critique of, 75–77; and democratic values, 13, 69–76; in Fort Collins, Colorado, 79–80; in Massachusetts, 80, 81–83; in Milwaukee, Wisconsin, 78, 80; in Minnesota, 83; and parental decision-making, 79–81; programs, 68–69
School finance, 170–171; and technology, 112–113
School governance, 120, 165, 213–214; and cult of efficiency, 130–132; and progressive education movement, 127–129
School restructuring: and corporate interests, 142; critique of, 134–137, 139–140, 144–145; defined, 120; and democratic schools, 125; goals, 127, 129; initiation of, 126; and resistance to change, 134–135
School to Work Opportunities Act, 161
School to work programs, 162–166
School vouchers, 77–79
Scientific management, 130–131
Sehr, David, 194, 201
Site-based school management, 14, 122–123, 136, 140–142; in Kentucky, 138
Smith, Rogers, 193, 207
Snedden, David, 152–153
Social capital, 180–181, 185
Social efficiency movement, 149–155
Social Frontier, 188–190
Social reconstructionists, 11–12, 187–190
Stehlik-Barry, Kenneth, 178, 191
Supply-side neoliberalism, 158–161

Taylor, Frederick, 130–131
Teachers' unions, 216–217
Techno-ideology: critique of, 108–115; defined, 93–94, 95–97; and educational change, 102–103; and educational system, 100–106; and learning, 97–100; and social efficiency, 155–156; in state technology plans, 107–108
Testing, 153–154, 169; in Massachusetts, 171
Toffler, Alvin, 94
Total Quality Management, 122–124, 132–133, 138–139, 142–143
Tyack, David, 1, 8, 32, 115–116, 130

Wired, 105
Wood, George, 64–65
Worker self-management, 126–127

Youth, attitudes toward, 32–34, 65